Scriptures for a Generation

What We Were Reading in the '60s

Scriptures for a Generation

PHILIP D. BEIDLER

The University of Georgia Press *Athens & London*

© 1994 by the

University of Georgia Press

Athens, Georgia 30602

All rights reserved

Designed by Richard Hendel

Set in Granjon & Gill types by

Tseng Information Systems, Inc.

Printed and bound by Maple-Vail Book

Manufacturing Group, Inc.

Printed in the United States of America

98   97   96   95   94   c   5   4   3   2   1

Library of Congress Cataloging in Publication Data

Beidler, Philip D.

Scriptures for a generation : what we were reading

in the '60s / Philip D. Beidler.

p.   cm.

Includes bibliographical references and index.

ISBN 0-8203-1641-5 (alk. paper).

1. American literature—20th century—

Bibliography.   2. Books and reading—United States

—History—20th century.   3. United States—History

—1961–1969—Sources—Bibliography.   I. Title.

Z2013.3.B45   1994

[PS225]

016.8108'0054—dc20   94-4172

British Library Cataloging in Publication Data available

Contents

Acknowledgments, vii

CHAPTER 1 **Mythologizing the '60s**, 1

CHAPTER 2 **'60s Readers and '60s Texts**, 14

CHAPTER 3 **'60s Texts and '60s Writers**, 31

CHAPTER 4 **Postscripts and Summations**, 206

Notes, 213

Bibliography, 235

Index, 245

Acknowledgments

My deepest gratitude goes to Linda Watson, inspired research assistant and ace bibliographer. Thanks also to a lot of good students in graduate seminars; to colleagues who contributed to my efforts with advice and dog-eared classics from their '60s bookshelves; to the interlibrary loan staff at the University of Alabama Library; and to editor Kim Cretors at the University of Georgia Press.

The University gives me good time to write. Ellen Eddins Beidler gives me loving encouragement. Our daughter, Katherine, gives us constant joy. This book is dedicated to her and the new generation.

Scriptures for a Generation

Mythologizing the '60s

Robin Williams is credited with saying that if you can remember the '60s, you weren't there. It is a good line and a memorable one. As with many good American lines, however, the fun begins in the exaggeration. Most people who went through the '60s as members of the Generation of Youth were not stoned amnesiacs then, and neither are they now.

Moreover, as a convergence of epoch and event, the '60s surely *happened,* and they happened in ways that are uncommonly rememberable and datable. From the outset, as Todd Gitlin has noted, "history rarely follows the decimal system as neatly as it did in 1960" (81). The decade began with a cluster of extraordinary events. Chief among these were the inauguration of a youth-president, John F. Kennedy, and his shocking assassination a bare two and a half years later. Apace came the perilous, bloody campaigns of black Americans for political justice in the Freedom Rides of 1961, the March on Washington of 1963, and, early in the Johnson presidency which followed, the passage of the landmark Civil Rights Act of 1964. Shortly, however, the nation also found itself engulfed in the military and geopolitical tragedy of Vietnam. At home, events were compounded by urban riots and, from mid decade onward, the emergence of an adversarial youth-culture, increasingly complex in its political organization and gaudily visible in the public eye through concerts, protests, demonstrations, marches, boycotts, and shutdowns, not to mention through the newly styled rituals of Acid Tests, Happenings, Sit-Ins, Love-Ins, Be-Ins, and a host of other celebrations and disruptions.[1]

The '60s may also be said to have had a distinct culmination of crisis. In 1968 occurred: the Tet Offensive;

the issuance of the Kerner Commission Report; the decision of Lyndon Johnson not to seek a second term; the assassinations of Robert Kennedy and Martin Luther King Jr.; riots in Washington, D.C., Chicago, Baltimore, and more than a hundred other cities; the Poor People's March on the U.S. Capitol; the counterculture siege of the Chicago Democratic Convention; and the election of Richard Nixon as president.

Likewise, the decade may be assigned a rather precise moment of political conclusion. In February 1970, the Chicago Seven—Abbie Hoffman, Jerry Rubin, Tom Hayden, Rennie Davis, David Dellinger, Lee Weiner, and John Froines—after a circus trial in the courtroom of Judge Julius Hoffman—were convicted of crossing state lines to instigate a riot at the 1968 Democratic Convention. In March, three young radicals were killed in the explosion of a Greenwich Village townhouse where they had been manufacturing bombs. In late April and early May 1970, the invasion of Cambodia by U.S. and South Vietnamese troops failed to destroy North Vietnamese Army and Viet Cong command centers and solidified domestic sentiment for abandonment of the war effort. At home, campus riots resulted in four student deaths at Kent State University in Ohio, three at Jackson State University in Mississippi, and an antiwar shutdown of virtually every major college and university in the nation. Chronologically *and* politically, the '60s were over.

What might be called the myth of the '60s, on the other hand, yields no corresponding sense of narrative or symbolic structure. Indeed, in a pronounced reversal of familiar categories of experience and explanation, the closer one gets to any idea of a myth of the '60s, the more that idea seems to spin off into some bizarre postmodern fable of its own indeterminacies. There, Williams is dead on, to the point even of casting his line in obverse: If you can remember a myth of the '60s, *it* probably wasn't there.

This is surely true of any cultural memory we might attempt to conjure up out of something called '60s reading and writing in America. On the other hand, as to the youth-culture of the era, I am going to suggest that here, at least, we may identify one dominant feature of mythic consciousness: a belief that acts of imagination, inspired modes of thinking *and* doing, might truly change the world.[2] I am also going to suggest that such a belief was often transacted exactly through the communitarian experience of printed texts. It was an experience, I propose to show, largely without cultural precedent in the history of print literacy, print production, and print consumption—a proliferation of particular texts bought, read or read about, borrowed and loaned, discussed, and often acted upon as instruments of self and social awareness and identification. Further, among a substantial population of young Americans—educated, energized, and economically enabled—it also proved to be a distinct culmination of that history, the end of the last great reading culture perhaps *in* that history. After '6os reading and writing, reading and writing themselves began to vanish as dominant forms of literate communication. To put this another way, the '6os text, given especially the larger communications revolution of which it became a part, made book history in a moment that concurrently made books themselves history. In sum, '6os reading and writing in America would mark the apotheosis of the word.[3]

At the same time it will be noted that I have not said '6os *literature* and with good reason. With few major exceptions, the body of texts I wish to specify was never nearly as literary, the commonplaces of criticism notwithstanding, as we are inclined to think it was. It will also be noted that neither have I said '6os *popular culture*. For, again with few major exceptions, according to publishing demographics then or now, the youth-texts of the '6os were not nearly as important a mass-market phenomenon as we may often assume.

I have said, rather, '6os reading and writing, and I have done so for a certain taxonomic accuracy; but I have also done so to stress exactly the ideas of textual constituency *and* cultural participation described above. That is, I am trying to describe an *experience* of language across a range of printed texts whereby a community of the word found it possible to construct itself politically and historically as a fact of consciousness and to do so in ways that have now become part and fabric of our lives. It was the experience of the word that comprised the community of relationship in much the same way that Henry Thoreau, in the section entitled "Reading" from his own counterculture classic *Walden,* could speak of "Plato, my townsman." And, as will be seen, like Thoreau's, some '6os texts achieved their status as youth-classics decades or centuries too late—and thus often just in time. Moreover, it is in this same sense of textual community that many other works produced in the wake of the decade continue to live for us as '6os scriptures in ways that ensuing years have done little to diminish.

To be sure, we can talk about certain '6os classics that conflated the categories of the literary and the popular: Sylvia Plath's *The Bell Jar,* Ken Kesey's *One Flew Over the Cuckoo's Nest,* Joseph Heller's *Catch-22, The Autobiography of Malcolm X,* Tom Wolfe's *The Electric Kool-Aid Acid Test,* Eldridge Cleaver's *Soul on Ice,* Kurt Vonnegut's *Slaughterhouse Five,* and Robert Pirsig's *Zen and the Art of Motorcycle Maintenance.*

Yet each of these, through its own textual history, reveals the strange play of influences, literary *and* popular, likely to be involved in any given case. To choose just three, consider the examples of Plath, Heller, and Pirsig.

Despite its links with '60s feminism, *The Bell Jar,* by chronology and cultural milieu, is distinctly a '50s book, with the world of its sensitive, intelligent, youthful protagonist, Esther Greenwood, much in the same provenance as Salinger's *The Catcher in the Rye,* which Plath's novel often greatly resembles. It was initially published in England in 1963 by its American author under the pseudonym Victoria Lucas. (Plath herself was by then known as a young poet of major promise for her 1961 collection *Colossus,* and concurrently, as no one then or now has seemed able to forget, as the wife of English poet Ted Hughes.) Shortly after the English publication of *The Bell Jar,* Plath committed suicide. On the basis of such compounded tragic circumstance, the novel became something of a cult book on both sides of the Atlantic. Next, at mid decade came publication in England and the United States of the posthumous collection *Ariel,* with which the myth of Sylvia Plath as literary youth-icon was permanently cemented. Then, and largely as a consequence, only in 1971 did *The Bell Jar* find American publication. By this time had also begun to appear major new texts of the American women's revolution—with works of the late '60s and early '70s ranging from *Sexual Politics* and *Sisterhood Is Powerful* to *The Female Eunuch* and *Our Bodies, Ourselves.* Accordingly, Plath's autobiographical novel found new contexts of celebration as a feminist classic; and it now continues to serve, along with a handful of sensational poems such as "Daddy" and "Lady Lazarus," as the basis of the Plath legend.[4]

Heller's novel, published in 1961, seemed initially to fall into a lineage of big military books from the generation of World War II: Norman Mailer's *The Naked and the Dead,* Irwin Shaw's *The Young Lions,* James Jones's *From Here to Eternity,* Herman Wouk's *The Caine Mutiny,* and Leon Uris's *Battle Cry.* And while *Catch-22* achieved substantial sales among a general audience, its early reputation was mainly literary, the result of widespread admiration for its complex subversions and experimentalisms. One admiring critic, Norman Brustein, pronounced it without reservation "one of the most bitterly funny works in the language" (11). Norman Mailer, a rival novelist, described it as a book that utterly "cheats evaluation": a work of genius from which, nonetheless, "one could take out a hundred pages anywhere from the middle . . . and not even the author could be certain they were gone" (Cannibals 117). On the basis of such intellectual attention, the novel started to appear on college and university literature syllabuses. Not accidentally, as the '60s progressed, students in turn made their own version of the discovery outlined by Alfred Kazin: that *Catch-22* was not really so much about World War II as about those wonderful people who brought us World War II; that it was not so much about war itself as about the war-breeding system; that if, in fact, it was about any war, it was not about the last war but about the next one (92–93). The next one, of course, was Vietnam, and somehow Heller seemed already to have written the book on it. Meanwhile, not unlike the Vietnam of the six o'clock news, *Catch-22* by the end of the decade had assumed new status as a major media event as well: a Mike Nichols film with Alan Arkin as everybody's Yossarian. New paperback issues resulted in a curricular staple that remains quite likely the most frequently assigned of all '60s texts, "a monumental artifact of contemporary American literature," as John W. Aldredge puts it, "almost as assured of longevity as the statues on Easter Island" (379).

Pirsig's work, in contrast to both of the preceding, made its appearance only in 1974, having been previously rejected, according to the author's count, by 120 publishers. In paperback, however, it caught on quickly not only with the young but also with their slightly older counterparts still searching for a reconciliation of alternative consciousness with traditional Western philosophy that might bring some sense of spiritual closure. Pirsig's text filled the bill, skyrocketing to critical and curricular celebrity, the latest in a long tradition of great American hodgepodges, in the vein of *Walden, Moby-Dick,* or the roughly contemporary *Last Whole Earth Catalog:* an attempt to speak of Buddha that is also, despite the author's disclaimer, not uninformative on small-engine mechanics either. On the other hand, even as the era embraced *Zen and the Art of Motorcycle Maintenance,* its author was busy rejecting the era. Indeed, in a tenth anniversary reissue, Pirsig would pronounce it an indictment of both straight *and* hip definitions of successful living, distinguished if at all by the conservatism of its revolutionariness, a quite utilitarian metaphysics of Quality mainly giving, he concluded, "a positive goal to work toward that does not confine" (377).

Here, then, by broad acclamation, are three authentic '60s scriptures, having virtually nothing in common save one thing: a desire, in post–World War II America, to posit newly imagined notions of personhood as alternatives to an increasingly immense and totally rationalized technology of cultural depersonalization. "The Happy Consciousness," Herbert Marcuse called the new regime, "the belief that the real is rational and that the system delivers the goods" or "the new conformism which is a facet of technological rationality translated into social behavior" (84).

And so across the expanse of '60s reading and writing came myriad forms of characteristic response. To borrow a phrase from Hermann Hesse's *Steppenwolf,* itself a major favorite of the era, the '60s text became a kind of Magic Theater—not for everyone. Yet in its inexpensiveness and availability, its widespread dissemination especially among the young, the '60s text also became an available opening to nearly anyone willing to enter some new space of personal and cultural discovery.

Moreover, the apprisals of such textual openings could themselves come in equally myriad ways. At times, promotion to scriptural status might begin with the literary establishment or the liberal academy; at others, it might arise out of the mass market and particularly the exploding paperback industry. Sometimes the process could be traced to trends in scholarship—the increasing research interest of '60s academics, for instance, in complex literary experimentalisms, as well as metaliterary questions of phenomenology, semiotics, hermeneutics, or philosophies of history or language. Sometimes it could be traced to curricular development, most often beginning at the college or university level but shortly filtering down into the public education system as well: the use of introductory anthologies, for instance, that juxtaposed canonical discourse with new selections of contemporary relevance; increased offerings in modern and contemporary literature; special topics courses combining the adventures of literary and political subversion; and the rise of multidisciplinary programs in the humanities or in such fields as American studies, black studies, and women's studies—"fields" of discourse and knowledge, that is, like '60s reading and writing itself, often drawing their materials and their intellectual purviews from both the scholarly and the mass-cultural.

Simultaneously, and often within those same academic precincts, new textual promotions were also quickly becoming the work of the youth-culture itself. Nurtured by a postsecondary educational system growing exponentially—and providing, particularly for its male constituency, exemption for most of the decade from military draft—it now assembled on campuses across the nation. Further, it did so as an intellectual and political community that for the first time in our history truly cut across lines of gender, class, and race. Accordingly, as the decade wore on, the youth-culture could only become a community firmly united against a war in Asia that increasingly came to dwarf all other issues as the era's focal point of moral and ideological crisis (Johnson 641–42). The shock of youth-recognition, to update Melville's pregnant phrase, reverberated everywhere: in classrooms, lecture halls, dormitories, apartments, cafeterias, and snack bars; on the quad, the library steps, the union plaza, out on the street, and along the student strip in every college town; in the doorways of bookstores, bars, record co-ops, coffeehouses, and head shops; and in progressive or radicalized curricula, new colleges and open universities, and revolutionary student unions and discussion circles. Here was the constituency for a new discourse called '60s reading and writing, scriptures for a generation: a nation within the nation, still looking for the Word; indeed, looking for the Word as the old dream of history and still imagining it could be made to be.[5]

Especially within the burgeoning educational system then, the youth-culture properly became *polis* and *kultur* in the largest sense of both terms: ideologically, a whole imagined "other America"[6] and thereby socially and semiotically, a true, communal laboratory of cultural experiment. Meanwhile, in the outside world, the youth-net was widened. The experiment was commemorated through concerts, festivals, demonstrations, happenings, and various other forms of public celebration. Its key images and rituals were enthusiastically disseminated by the newly ubiquitous mass media—radio, television, movies, music, journalism, advertising, and entertainment. Finally, the full apparatus of cultural communication found itself enlisted. As a ground of '60s cultural debate, the youth-culture itself had become both forum and arena.

Yet for '60s reading and writing, here too would lie the great irony of the '60s text: as a last, revolutionary achievement in print culture, it would reach its apotheosis exactly as it became swept up in the new, non-print communications revolution that would render it obsolete. To put this another way, '60s reading and writing in America became *exactly that* with a crucial finality. For it comprised not only a particular kind of communitarian experience of printed language but also, we may see now in retrospect, a last great flowering of print-literacy culture itself. It was truly the last great moment of reading and writing in the West by an identifiable mass-cultural constituency, a moment of print apocalypse, so to speak: materially, a true culmination of print production and distribution intersected with unprecedented consumer affluence and appetite; and spiritually, a last great moment of America's own faith in the Word as its basic article of political and educational reliance. Sixties reading and writing thus attempted to write the final chapter in the great Western romance of the printed word that had often found many of its fullest meanings in American culture. Out of a poetics and politics of the printed text rooted in our deepest mythological imaginings, it sought to devise a new cultural curriculum to be enacted by the Republic's latest bright and comely inheritors.

Retrospectively, then, it might not be too much to call the discourse-phenomenon described here a final American fulfillment of the one that had set it all in motion in the first place: the great discourse-event comprised initially in the West, that is, by the twinned pressures of Renaissance and Reformation. Here, finally, in the new American republic, the possibility of common literacy had first flowered as a truly popular medium of cultural invention; and here likewise, through unprecedented advances in educational opportunity and access to mass communications, a true people's hermeneutic had survived to become a basic assumption of cultural faith. Now had come the fulfillment of the modern revolution, the humanist dream of secular culture perfected in a civic religion of late-stage capitalist democracy; and now in turn had also come the last chance for that religion of progress to make good on its promises to those to whom it had promised the most—its children. The result, for perhaps one last time in our history, was a functioning revolutionary politics of discourse, a breaking of the signs in the name of genuine cultural revision. At all levels, such became the agenda and the project: wearing the national flag as clothing; spelling the name of the country "Amerika"; replacing pious euphemism with words previously unspeakable and unprintable; writing up a new set of documents of government, declarations, statements, manifestos; and founding a culture on a new canon of youth-scriptures, written by those not previously accorded voices, in subversions of traditional genre and mode.

Not surprisingly, the project, despite its affiliations with a long Western politics of the text, often assumed its own, distinctly cottage industry figurations. At times—in such works as Jerry Rubin's *Do It!* or Baba Ram Dass's *Be Here Now, Remember*—the style seemed largely that of cultural mischief, somewhere between manic disruptiveness and loony beatitude. At others—in highly innovative works such as Eldridge Cleaver's *Soul on Ice* or Robin Morgan's *Sisterhood Is Powerful;* the novels of Kurt Vonnegut or the mystical narratives of Carlos Castaneda—it came more closely to resemble the style we have now also come to call postmodern: modes of cultural critique predicated on revolutionary discourse theory and radical modes of social analysis; new formulations of political relationship unwriting older hierarchies of race, class, and gender, and older structural assumptions of power, authority, and genealogy; and new subversive ideologies of textual construction and interpretation.[7]

At the same time, two features especially of '60s thought, both relatively unique to the national experience, also served to distinguish it vitally from the historical Western tradition of philosophical critique. The first was a strain of non-Western spirituality, a peculiarly American orientalism, imparted earliest by contact with native peoples and more fully developed through the extensive national experience with Asia and the Pacific. The second was more nearly homegrown, although in its way comparably unique to the national character: a deeply interiorized conception of spiritual selfhood, likewise born of the earliest experiences of New World individualism and further evolved over a long republican history.

From the outset American orientalism must be distinguished crucially from its English and European counterparts. Indeed, it is the kind of "Western" orientalism that quite likely only an American could conceive—and with a pure American disdain, one might add, for both geography and etymology. For it always was, to use the strangely evolved phrasing of diplomatic parlance that has largely been a result of it, a Far Eastern "orientalism"—an orientalism of China, Japan, Korea, and the Pacific Rim—as opposed to the Near Eastern orientalism of the eastern Mediterranean, Asia Minor, and the Indian subcontinent, which as Edward Said has brilliantly shown, has traditionally constructed the idea of the oriental "other" in Anglo-European thought.[8] Above all, it envisioned itself as a special American geography both of historical expansion and of spiritual connection, at once a final extension of the idea of the West and a bringing of that idea into union with a vision of the East made possible only by the peculiar experience of the crossing of cultural and discursive space that was America itself. Or, to put it in terms more purely philosophical, it was a spiritual looking east—a voyaging into the non-Western, nonrational, nonintellective, and nonscientific—that could only come through a peculiar relationship, both of deep connection *and* willed dissociation, with the post-Renaissance Western vision: the tradition, that is, of Reason, Science, and Objective Knowledge out of which such voyaging began. Here, truly, was a yearning toward the ancient Asian origin wherein the West might fulfill the great myth of the eternal return. It is what Thoreau meant, of course, by the mingling of Walden and Ganges; or Whitman by his call to "eclairicize" the myths Asiatic.[9]

The second tradition of spiritual selfhood—deeply interiorized, meditative, "Orphic," we might call it, using Emerson's great word—represents a kind of folk counterpart to such Western dreaminess. It is a vision of self at once idealized, intuitive, even mystic, yet in the same moment resolutely hardheaded and pragmatic: at once immovably principled yet stubbornly practical. Beginning in the nonconformist spirit of a large portion of the nation's earliest religious colonists, it could trace itself through a variety of ensuing forms: the Christian mysticisms of Edward Taylor, Jonathan Edwards, and John Woolman; the deistic freethinking of Enlightenment figures such as Benjamin Franklin, Thomas Jefferson, and Thomas Paine; the combination of romantic individualisms and speculative adventurings evident in a host of nineteenth-century illuminati ranging from Poe and Emerson through Whitman, Hawthorne, Thoreau, Melville, and Dickinson; the tradition of radical dissent begun by figures such as Anne Hutchinson or Roger Williams and adapted by successors such as Thoreau, Frederick Douglass, and Martin Luther King Jr.; the visionary construction of nature extending from early figures such as William Bartram, St. John de Crèvecoeur, and, again, Thoreau through John Burroughs, John Muir, Aldo Leopold, and Edward Abbey; and a host of other highly individuated, if not downright eccentric forms of nontraditional "plain living and high thinking" (as David Shi has phrased it) that have so often distinguished the solitary American quest for the integral life.

In our own century especially, the two traditions, both with their tendencies toward the epiphanic and oracular, have often been spectacularly conjoined: first, in the hieratic modernisms of Ezra Pound, Gertrude Stein, T. S. Eliot, Wallace Stevens, and William Carlos Williams; and later, in the more proximate textual era under discussion, through the Zen popularizations of D. T. Suzuki, Alan Watts, and J. D. Salinger, such Beat figures as Allen Ginsberg, Jack Kerouac, Gary Snyder, and succeeding exponents such as Robert Pirsig; or through the more local visionary inheritance—itself deeply indebted to nineteenth-century popularizations of the Vedic [10]—of Emerson, Whitman, and Thoreau, and newly realized in figures ranging from Norman O. Brown and Kurt Vonnegut to Richard Brautigan and Annie Dillard. In all, it has turned out to be a synthesizing passion proving at once adaptable and decidedly opportunistic; in good democratic fashion, to use Theodore Roszak's apt phrasing, it has been the stuff of an "easy-do syncretism"; something like a dive into "an occult Jungian stew" with various currents of the nonrational and spiritualistic flowing in and out of each other at will (144–45). It came easily to accommodate, for instance, the drug mysticisms of Aldous Huxley, Timothy Leary, Richard Alpert, and Carlos Castaneda; the neo-Freudian exaltations of a wise, self-contemplative, holy madness in Paul Goodman, Norman O. Brown, and R. D. Laing; and the neo-Marxian utopianisms of C. Wright Mills and Herbert Marcuse. It could also accommodate the various '60s occult fascinations with astrology, tarot reading, the Kabbala, the I Ching, and The Tibetan Book of the Dead; with obscure, recondite oracles such as Gurdjieff, Blavatsky, Ouspenska, Thomas Merton, and Jacob Boehme; with the indigenous orientalisms of Native American myth, ritual, and magic; and with the new enterprises of such figures as Baba Ram Dass, the Maharaj Ji, or the Maharishi Mahesh Yogi—a seemingly endless train of self-promoting swamis, gurus, spiritual masters, and assorted other purveyors of transcendental consciousness.[11]

The result was a true people's priesthood, a whole consumer-cult of young believers, mixing their sacred texts high and low into a total myth of consciousness. Here, as well as in science fiction, fantasy, and a host of other styles of semiotic experimentation, they tried to recast the word itself as a kind of wiggy, Day Glo shamanism, the ultimate magic and light show. Prankish kids in costumes, their heads full of crackbrained oracles such as Hesse, Tolkien, Vonnegut, and Castaneda, they fixed the nation's attention one last time on the idea that words could still be holy and that their newest emanations into the world could still create America as the beacon of History.

Here, then, was the site of the textual action, quite literally serving as platform and agenda for the youth-culture across a vast array of political constituencies: the student movement, the antiwar movement, the black power movement, the environmental movement, and the women's movement. And these were to name only the most visible. Everywhere they waited, looking for the Word. Everywhere they rushed to embrace the latest sacred texts, scriptures for a generation. To be sure, as with virtually anything else in America, this year's fashions often became last year's fads. Yet even today, one still catches the feel of it, the enormous energy of desire—somehow funnelled into one big cultural synthesizer programmed to accommodate it all and churn it back out into print: from the Port Huron Statement to the "S.C.U.M. Manifesto," from *Eros and Civilization* to *Sex and the Single Girl*, from *The Autobiography of Malcolm X* to *The Greening of America*, from *Catch-22* to *Revolution for the Hell of It*.

For all this, one must repeat that the myth of a '60s youth-flowering in American letters as will shortly be documented remains to date hard to trace out either as a literary or as a popular phenomenon. On the other hand, to invoke even a handful of titles is still to sense its power. Further, as American myths especially are prone to do, this one also now seems to have acquired the power of its own millennial self-reification. Here, for instance, are titles typical of '60s "retrospectives": *Esquire*'s anthology of '60s writing is called *Smiling Through the Apocalypse;* Milton Viorst's documentary history, *Fire in the Streets;* James Miller's political analysis, *"Democracy is in the Streets": From Port Huron to the Siege of Chicago;* and Todd Gitlin's recent memoir, *The Sixties: Years of Hope, Days of Rage.*

Gerald Howard's anthology *The Sixties* subtitles itself "The Art, Attitudes, Politics, and Media of Our Most Explosive Decade." Peter Joseph's oral history of the era is called, simply, *Good Times.* With customary prescience, Leslie Fiedler would call an early '60s collection of essays *Waiting for the End.* His look back on the era would be correspondingly entitled: *What Was Literature? Class Culture and Mass Society.* Here, repeatedly, we see the '60s resolutely linked to a peculiar kind of cultural end-consciousness, what a religious philosopher would call an eschatology. To be sure, it is an engrained American habit, this rhetorical projection of millennial faith, as old as John Winthrop and as recent as George Bush or Bill Clinton. Yet here, for a moment, among American youth it truly had become something like a people's discourse. The City on a Hill had become the Ultimate Woodstock.

At present, across a range of philosophies and political projects, American intellectualism is still trying to write some grand synthesis of the history of consciousness that made the '60s possible. This book attempts to contribute to that history through a survey of what might be considered a generation's sacred texts. Moreover, such texts themselves, I will propose, make a large claim. They make a claim not simply to image the '60s in America but in many ways to have created '60s America in the peculiar style of the postmodern that continues to distinguish it—as the ultimate Happening, so to speak, an enactment of the cosmic East-West connection that History in the West had been envisioning for itself all along. Similarly, if in certain ways the '60s fulfilled the old dream of the conquest of time, it also brought us back into touch with the myth of the eternal return. As a consequence, while the century ends with Western intellectualism having crossed over into what was supposed to be a new landscape of the postmodern, a world somewhere beyond even the old hegemony of dialectic, in America the odd orientalism-mysticism of many '60s fascinations seems less and less farfetched. Indeed, here perhaps we have outlived our modernism—the faith in Reason, Science, Objective Knowledge, of the idea of something called civilization as a sustaining force in people's lives—by both going beyond it and by recovering a chastened, holy sense of its origins. To put this another way, perhaps we have found ourselves to be at once postmodern and yet also medieval in many of the ways we have always been. A going ahead has also been a going back. In our post-Renaissance certainties, we have often grown fond of referring to our cultural moments in tropes of rupture, disjunction, or—if one is eschatologically inclined—apocalypse. The American '60s, on the other hand, may have shown us that much of our capacity to deal with the purported end of the modern era will depend on our recognition that in many ways we also still continue to live here in the late Middle Ages. Do you believe in magic? That is what a quintessential '60s song-title asked; in the last years of the American century, it still seems a good question and much in tune with the times.

'60s Readers and '60s Texts

PEOPLE OF THE WORD

We have always been, in America, a people of the word. This is true especially of Anglo-Europeans, who largely create themselves as New World people through the dual humanistic and hermeneutic faiths of the Renaissance and the Reformation; and who thereby invent a philosophy of culture not so much logocentric, as has been routinely claimed, as perhaps more accurately called logosophic. On the other hand, the history of minority peoples in America—Asian, African, Hispanic, native—is also filled with texts documenting with intense awareness the peculiar, almost magical relationship in this culture between literacy and political empowerment.

Never indeed has a culture placed such faith in its own capacity to create and then recreate itself endlessly by linguistic fiat. Puritans and other early Protestant millennialists staked their enterprises on a belief in their own enactment of the Logos as chosen New World participants in God's vast salvific plan of creation. The eventual new nation, born of corresponding Enlightenment faith in the word, was quite literally created through its political documents as an attempt to reify itself into existential fact. Our basic discourses of government became, to use Garry Wills's brilliant phrasing, the act of Inventing America, a *polis* of the word in every sense of the term.

Then there is also the concurrent matter of print itself and the emergence in the West of mass-print literacy as a general cultural phenomenon.[1] In this aspect of public discourse, we too have been truly a people of the word—in our very formation, as Neil Postman has observed, "perhaps the most print-oriented culture ever to have existed" (26). Through language, Americans persistently invent a self and a world. American autobiographies from Jonathan Edwards and Benjamin Franklin through Frederick Douglass, Henry Thoreau, Henry Adams, and Gertrude Stein are supremely self-conscious *rhetorical* acts of *political* self-invention and vice versa. American domestic fictions, often the work of women, in both theme and form posit reading and writing as crucial activities of cultural empowerment, as deeply political modes of education and critiques of existing structures of authority. American literary fictions likewise—from Irving, Poe, and Hawthorne through Melville, Twain, and James and onward into works of this century as diverse as those of Faulkner, Hurston, Cather, Ellison, and Vonnegut— repeatedly contrive to be *about,* among other things, their own authorization and often their own genealogy. Similarly, who but an American poet would write an epic called "Song of Myself"? Where else would another contrive *Notes Toward a Supreme Fiction*? What failed divine save Emerson would try to pack into one slim monograph a whole grammar of creation, at once an ethic, an aesthetic, and a metaphysic, and call it *Nature*? What charlatan-aesthete of epiphanies save Poe could write a scientific rhapsody called *Eureka,* subtitle it "An Essay on the Material and Spiritual Universes," and then insist that it be read as a poem? What chronicler of the modern self save Gertrude Stein could name a puzzling literary experiment[2] *The Making of Americans* and then supply a gloss, entitled "The Gradual Making of the Making of Americans," that reads as follows:

I then began again to think about the bottom nature in people, I began to get enormously interested in hearing how everybody said the same thing over and over again with infinite variations but over and over again until finally if you listened with great intensity you could hear it rise and fall and tell all that there was inside them, not so much by the actual words they said or the thoughts they had but the movement of their thoughts and words endlessly the same and endlessly different. (138)

Indeed, out of our political and literary history, one could fashion a dazzling anthology of word-zingers that would comprise something like a guide to American logosophy, theoretical *and* applied. John Winthrop's biblical City on a Hill, for instance, is among the most taken for granted of our verbal figures. We also understand its visualizations, however, in L'Enfant's map of Washington, D.C., or in the famous daguerreotype of a capitol rising out of the Anacostia flats in the midst of the Civil War. So Jefferson, the architect of so much of our democracy, makes clear his own larger purposes as a language- and nation-builder: "The new circumstances of American life demand new words," he declares, "new phrases and the transfer of old words to new objects."

"Words are signs of natural facts. Natural facts are signs of spiritual facts. Nature is the symbol of spirit." In a fast and loose syllogism, Emerson in turn legitimates the project of American consciousness as a semiotics *and* a politics of national identity, a discourse of incarnation at once Logos and *kosmos,* the self that is the world.[3] Thoreau, keeping it down to earth, cultivates the bean field, he says, "to know beans" mainly "for the sake of tropes and expressions, to serve a parable maker some day" (112). Whitman, more expansively, proclaims "Endless unfolding of the words of ages!

> and mine a word of the modern, the word En-Masse." (51)
> Through me the afflatus surging and surging, through me the
>   current and index.
>
> I speak the pass-word primeval, I give the sign of democracy,
> By God! I will accept nothing which all cannot have their
>   counterpart of on the same terms. (52)[4]

Two quotations from the era to be studied here keep faith with all these possibilities. The first is from John Kennedy:

> Let the word go forth from this time and place, to friend and foe alike, that the torch has been passed to a new generation of Americans—born in this century, tempered by war, disciplined by a hard and bitter peace, proud of our ancient heritage—and unwilling to witness or permit the slow undoing of those human rights to which this nation has always been committed, and to which we are committed today at home and around the world. (Sann 34)

The second is from Jack Kerouac:

> I pictured myself in a Denver bar that night, with all the gang, and in their eyes I would be strange and ragged and like the Prophet who has walked across the land to bring the dark Word, and the only Word I had was "Wow!" (37)

Both of these continue the project of the great American logosophy. The first, as a discourse of the word, tells us much about how we got to the '60s in the first place; the second, in an analogous visionary spirit, suggests why many of us are still struggling to come out. For Kennedy and for Kerouac, the problem was imagining a future that was already, like Gatsby's, somewhere behind us. The New Frontier was at once shibboleth and impossible neologism, words in the wind and the ungraspable language of grace. So Kerouac's narrator finally seems to acknowledge: "We were on the roof of America, and all we could do was yell, I guess—across the night, eastward over the Plains, where somewhere an old man with white hair was probably walking toward us with the Word, and would arrive any minute and make us silent" (55).

Leslie Fiedler has also defined a discourse of the word in America as a conscious act of cultural imagination, something that actually made the New World possible in the West. "We have always been aware," he writes, "that ours is a country which has had to be invented as well as discovered: invented even before its discovery (as Atlantis, Ultima Thule, a Western World beyond the waves), and re-invented again and again both by the European imagination—from, say, Chateaubriand to D. H. Lawrence or Graham Greene—and by the deep fantasy of its own people, once these existed in fact" (478). What needs to be emphasized further is the degree to which such an imaginative enterprise was rooted in new technologies of language itself, in language printed and read, that is, as the medium of such cultural self-reification.

To put it simply, the invention of America took place largely through printed language. As people of the word, we are also quite specifically the people of the text, the word made modern in every sense. And so are we now—or so at least we continue to think of ourselves—even as the text itself, at least as we have known it, seeks out its own new techno-historical evolutions.

Sixties reading and writing in America, I will propose, marked a distinctive culmination in the process. It was at once the ideological and the technological apotheosis of the text as it had been known in the West: the last flowering of an idea of the word and the triumph of print literacy in unprecedentedly widespread forms of production, distribution, and consumption. Yet in the same moment, precisely in the information revolution it helped to inspire, it also marked a rapid, radical, and irreversible turning away from printed language as the dominant medium of cultural communication. Henceforth, word of the world would be electronic, visual, aural, cybernetic. Its dominant imagings and figurations would increasingly be those of radio, television, computers, movies, records, audio casettes, compact discs, and videos. News, entertainment, advertising, information: the world would now come mainly to exist in some new, vast, nonprint continuum. Even as this is written in RAM (random-access memory), all information including this seeks the new destination of ROM (read-only memory). Books themselves would literally begin to look like scribal relics.

Such developments have only begun to be written about. To be sure, they are something of what Marshall McLuhan was addressing, albeit with a rather benign futurism, in the '60s in such groundbreaking works as *Understanding Media* and *The Gutenberg Galaxy*. But only in recent years have we begun to locate their consequences specifically within the historical demise of print: "the gradual end," as George Steiner has called it, "of the classical age of reading" (44). Here truly, Steiner laments, may have been one last "oasis of quality in which very great literature, very great nonfiction, did reach a mass audience"; a "unique moment" of interfluence, he goes on, "between the best that is being thought and written on one hand, and a very large popularity—great sales, great circulation, massive readership—on the other" (45). Now, in contrast, from "the Gutenberg revolution as we now know it," he concludes, we have clearly passed on to "the information revolution" (47), one that "will touch every facet of composition, publication, distribution and reading" (47). As a consequence, "reading in the old, archaic, private, silent sense may become as specialized a skill and avocation as it was in the libraries of the monasteries during the so-called Dark Ages" (48).

Neil Postman, so too, in an application more pertinent to our immediate purposes, citing both McLuhan and Steiner, proposes that this transformation might be most accurately thought of simply as *Amusing Ourselves to Death*. Indeed, as to exploding nonprint technologies, McLuhan's "The Medium is the Message" should now, if anything, be updated to "The Medium is the Metaphor," with metaphor defined mainly as "image."[5] We have all now experienced, he concludes, surely "the most significant American cultural fact of the second half of the twentieth century: the decline of the Age of Typography and the ascendancy of the Age of Television" (8).[6]

In assessing '60s reading and writing in America, this may be the most telling measure of all of what in the moment was so overwhelmingly gained and also so irrevocably lost. For of all the genealogical propositions that may be advanced regarding the '60s generation of youth—and in the following section an array of them will be brought forth in summary and critique—one, at least, can be advanced with great certainty: it was the last great American reading culture to identify itself as such, the finest productions and, in a way, the culminating glory of the People of the Word. Ideologically, the '60s generation claimed in the printed word affirmation of its special status as the fulfillment of the promise of America, the old dream of the conquest of time; and materially, in that same identification as "Youth," they sat waiting to devour it in endless prospects of ecstatic consumption. "Feed your head," the Jefferson Airplane proclaimed. In ways never dreamed, the word had become the last great American item.

Institutionally, moreover, such logosophic-demographic consummation could not have taken place for youth in conditions more ripe for mass-cultural apotheosis. On one hand there was the phenomenon of nearly absolute material textual availability—itself triggered by the techno-cultural revolution embodied in the rise of the twentieth-century paperback. The word had become an ultimate cultural commodity in circumstances of unprecedented textual production, promotion, and distribution. On the other were market conditions of significant mass prosperity and appetite across a large cross section of Americans and including especially American Youth—with Youth, in fact, perhaps actually positioned at the center of the greatest mass-market consumer society in history.

Yet as far as the role of youth was concerned, even this could only have achieved the kind of cultural focus it did through a particular intersection of all these vectors at a crucial site, a position, so to speak, of critical mass. And, without a doubt, that site was American education. Specifically, the '60s generation of youth was discernibly the last generation of a reading and writing society to have access—through the availability of public schooling on an unprecedented mass scale *and* in a continuum now extending from the primary and secondary through the college and university levels—to the print-related competencies.[7] Moreover, instruction in such competencies, particularly in language and literature, humanities, the arts, and the social sciences, was itself *in turn* fueled and facilitated by the mass availability of attractive, textually reliable, relatively inexpensive paperbacks, required frequently in huge numbers for participation in the educational process. Accordingly, for the book industry the educational system became a primary focus of major initiatives in such special textual promotion and distribution.

The way had been opened, as John Dessauer writes, for mass production of what was called the "quality" paperback. "These titles of serious nonfiction and literary classics," he writes, "while enjoying a certain vogue with the general consumer, found their prime markets in education. Most were used in college courses." Then, "during the late fifties, when secondary school programs were upgraded, high schools also contributed to their consumption." And, he concludes, "as time went on, both quality and 'mass market' paperbacks enjoyed increased educational uses" (Atwan 126). The marketing and the consuming habits, moreover, demonstrably caught on.

Throughout the late '60s and early '70s, for example, *The Chronicle of Higher Education* ran a regular feature entitled "What They're Reading on the Campuses." And astonishingly, at the turn of the decade, to show how far youth-marketing had progressed, *Publishers Weekly* was even detailing the logistics of paperback distribution along unsecured highways in Vietnam.

As I have suggested, however, the exploding demographics of '60s reading and writing marked for the printed text a moment at once of both culmination and crisis. Or, as we have become fond of saying, there was a downside as well—in this case one so precipitous that its consequences are even now only beginning to be understood. If '60s youth was in many ways the last generation of a reading and writing society, it was also the first generation of a mass-media society in which discourse overnight would become visual, aural, electronic, even cybernetic. In the defining moment of their cultural education, '60s youth had crossed the boundary from an information culture based on reading and writing to one radically nonverbal in terms of the interpretive "processing" or "use" to which information would quickly come to be put.[8]

Still, in the cultural moment described here, '60s reading and writing marked the Generation of Youth with something like an ultimate cultural appurtenance in idea as well as in fact: at once a means of ideological identification and an identifying material adjunct, what we would now call a political statement and a fashion statement. The '60s youth-text became a scripture, an available cultural icon of magical potency, a way of knowing and being. It was a reified presence important in its very physical thing-ness, as important in its way as long hair, bell-bottoms, a vintage Volkswagen bus, or a handcrafted roach clip. And at the same time, cut free from its quasi-official tetherings in education or criticism, it could also become, in the words of Carlos Castaneda, a separate reality—in its access, that is, to alternative forms of consciousness, a mode of redemption from the more general, consumerish thing-ness of our lives.

It mattered little that what '60s youth took to be radical statement or new mythic imagining turned out to be a matter of curriculum or a marketing concept done up into the latest consumer commodification. Sixties reading and writing in its teeming energy and plenitude would always manage to overflow its educational adoptions and market shares to find new spiritual openings. How many people got their first Camus in a pedagogically useful sophomore French encounter with *L'Etranger*? How many got Heller's *Catch-22* or Pynchon's *The Crying of Lot 49* from some assistant professor's contemporary literature syllabus? How many people cultishly read Tolkien, Vonnegut, or Brautigan in standard paperback on the basis of well-engineered publishing promotions? We will never know these things. Furthermore, it no longer matters. What we do know is that '60s reading and writing became for a last cultural moment a working, corporate experiment in the relations between printed language and ideology: for one last instant, it seemed, the traditional packaging of the "product" might still give way before the genuine article, the possibility of true cultural critique.

THE NEW GENERATION

The new generation they were called, and even the "now" generation, as if this time it would not suffice to be merely new. The first phrase they assimilated from the inaugural rhetoric of an idolized young president. (Never mind that the "new generation" referred to there had been the president's own, the junior officers of World War II taking over command from their elders. On the New Frontier, everything about America seemed young again.) The second they accepted—even as they pretended to despise it—from the apparatus of commerce and advertising, which promoted images of their own glamor and desirability. Their mythic identifications proliferated as fast as popular phrasemaking could spin them out. They were the generation of hope, the generation of love, the generation of peace. They were the Revolution, the counterculture. They were the Generation of Youth. Particular epithets seemed to come and go as quickly as their gurus or their gaudy fashions. Beats, Hippies, Yippies, Freaks. Flower Children and Street People. SDS and SNCC, Black Panthers, Weathermen, Winter Soldiers. Woodstock Nation and Women's International Conspiracy from Hell. There were the hard core and the hangers-on, the committed ones and those mainly along for the foolishness and the social ride. Some ran to the life with crazy desire and never came back; others went for a season or a year and came out on the other side. Many people who were young then remember themselves with bemusement, but just as often they look back with fondness. There for once, amid all the frantic nonsense and the anger that was often just down the street, their lives, at least as they remembered them, seemed more real and immediate than they would ever be again.

More than anything else, the music carried the message. "It's a beautiful morning," one song sweetly proclaimed. "Something's happening," announced another, its whisper of menace building to an edgy hope. In one moment the air sang in Aquarian joy; in the next, it caught the chill of prophetic admonition. "You don't have to be a weatherman," it said, "to know which way the wind blows." Sometimes the song became just a cry of pure, angry defiance. "Up against the wall, motherfucker," it shrieked. "We won't get fooled again."

Whatever the pitch or the lyric, one thing was clear for this generation, the new generation, the now generation: as the decade evolved, they found they had seen enough of it, all of it: racism, poverty, materialism; environmental pollution, sexism, and beyond everything, of course, war—*the* war, any war, all war. Sixties youth had had enough of everything from their parents' tight-assed boredom to a techno-corporate apparatus plotting geopolitical death, it seemed, in every boardroom, command post, and cabinet chamber around the world. It was time for Volunteers of America, time to face the Monster and see the business through. Day had dawned on the Revolution, America's last great utopian dream. And they would bring it off because the new energy of its making was already in their hands.

It would be so because they *were* the Revolution, they themselves: the most advanced beneficiaries of the Republic. To be sure, youthful activists of the era often found their radicalism by identifying with others on the social margins.[9] At the same time, there can be no question now that the major work of cultural revision performed by '60s youth against the established order was performed from within by its own progeny. The real business of change lay not with shock formations or radical cadres although these got most of the headlines in the March on the Pentagon, the Chicago riots, the Moratorium, Cambodia, Kent State, and the Days of Rage. Neither did it rest with the cultural types, denizens of urban and university-fringe hippiedom or agrarian communards escaped to the country to catch the organic vibes. The demographics of what came to be called the Woodstock Generation would continue to be fairly reflected by the varied cross section of youth that seems actually to have showed up for Woodstock the *event,* not to mention those who claimed attendance at that ceremony of body and spirit while flocking to the movie or listening over and over to the album.[10] In myriad choices and degrees of engagement, membership in the Generation of Youth and its participatory enterprise of making a new culture seemed to be conferred naturally upon those born within the American family as its own bright and comely inheritors. The real blows against the empire would begin with sons and daughters arguing politics around the breakfast table or writing home from college for tuition money.

Indeed, in demographic hindsight, one of the few things we can say with fair certainty about the youth-generation of the American '60s and '70s is that it was probably none of the particular mythological things it called itself or allowed itself to be called. As to age, for instance, generational data reveal an unprecedented proportion who would now be categorized as "student." On the other hand, those whom the student movement would claim as its radical celebrities—Mario Savio, Abbie Hoffman, Jerry Rubin, most of the early SDS cadre, black firebrands such as Stokely Carmichael and H. Rap Brown and such emergent feminist heroines as Gloria Steinem—were well beyond college age by the height of the decade. Similarly, the figures cited as new philosophical authorities by '60s youth might have been properly called their intellectual grandparents—Paul Goodman, Norman O. Brown, Herbert Marcuse, C. Wright Mills, J. R. R. Tolkien, Simone de Beauvoir, Marshall McLuhan not to mention departed spirits such as William Blake, Henry Thoreau, Hermann Hesse, Karl Marx, and Sigmund Freud.

As to performance models on the scene, many of these were of the generational vintage of hip uncles and aunts: Timothy Leary, Richard Alpert, R. D. Laing, Alan Watts, Betty Friedan, Michael Harrington, Kenneth Keniston, and Leslie Fiedler. And similarly, the era's earliest literary idols—authors of the very books whereby '60s youth-culture first came to identify itself—were to a significant extent members of the generation of World War II and the early '50s: Kurt Vonnegut, J. D. Salinger, Jack Kerouac, Joseph Heller, Allen Ginsberg, Ken Kesey, Sylvia Plath. In all these respects, then, what styled itself a "now" generation might as easily be described as a deeply historical, even history-engendered state of mind.

Nor was '60s youth-culture, on any corresponding scale of social distribution, a separate or "alternative" culture of any *particularly* identifiable sort, let alone the "counterculture" monolith so frequently presumed. In the early stages especially, "alienated" or "dissenting" youth, to use Kenneth Keniston's phrasings, was, if anything, a mirror of its conventional origins: it was dominantly male, almost exclusively white, largely college-oriented, and generally drawn from the great American middle class. Sixties youth came from American parents who had ridden out economic depression and world war with an unquenchable resolve that the world of their children would be a good, safe, and happy one; and who ironically, in the prosperous and tranquil years of the late '50s and early '60s, often actively encouraged the legatees of that world to try to make it even better.

To ensure that possibility, parents and children alike participated in extraordinary developments in educational access and delivery. Urban and blue-collar, small-town and rural, new representatives of the laboring middle classes competed successfully for traditional college and university scholarships and found ready access to student loans. Sixties students also flocked to newer, local institutions, junior colleges, community colleges, state and regional colleges and universities.

They were wooed by the political and the academic intelligentsia. Almost as if part of a curriculum, they found themselves launched amongst sundry activisms, which even down to their acronyms, often seemed as programmatic and institutional as the social and political formations they opposed: ADA, SANE, NAACP, CORE, ERAP, SNCC, SDS, YIP, PL, RYM, LID.[11]

Moreover, even as they sought some mythic solidarity, they also sowed the myriad fragmentations whereby they would shortly find themselves coming apart. By mid decade the transformation of civil rights into Black Revolution left no room for a white liberalism, let alone one involving a college-educated middle class. The women's movement arose directly out of its betrayal by the New Left, not to mention the patronizing sexism of supposedly hip culture at large. Counterculture radicalism splintered into Yippies, Weathermen, and other strange bands specializing in armed robbery and blowing themselves up. With troop withdrawals from Vietnam, the antiwar movement found itself reduced to a kind of impotent spectatorship, protesting the occasional resumption of bombing in the North, but mainly consigned to a few more years of watching Vietnamese kill each other. Environmentalists, commune-dwellers, and visionaries of countless other utopian persuasions quietly set out to tend their own gardens. Religious questings slid off into slimy hucksterisms: TM, est, Rolfing, Sufism, gestalt therapy, bioenergetics. Some people found Jesus. A lot more just went back to graduate school or resigned themselves to getting the jobs they had promised themselves they would never take. By 1974, there wasn't even Nixon left to hate.

On the other hand, enormous things had been accomplished: indeed, things that constituted fundamental *and* unprecedented changes in American life. Because of environmental and consumer activism, a traditional industrial economy attuned itself to a new climate of regulation and accordingly began to chart its movement after two centuries into a new age of information, service, and applied technology. In an initiative unparalleled in any modern nation, crucial first steps were taken toward establishing equality between the sexes. Before the entire world, a nation committed itself by both attitude and law to the extirpation of institutional racism. Bold commitments were likewise made by government to massive programs of social action and public assistance. America ceased involvement in the most nationally divisive and painful armed conflict it had faced since the War between the States.[12]

Who were the members of the youth-revolution responsible for bringing most of this about? How many people actually went to a demonstration, lived in a commune, slept in a crash pad, did macramé, or got into a natural diet? How many small-town kids ran off from home after hearing Janis Joplin or reading Hermann Hesse? How many college students read Thoreau, bought some bib overalls, and went to the country to watch the food grow? Were there innumerable boarding-school romantics making secret communion with Salinger or Plath? Did droves of sons and daughters of blue-collar families in ugly small cities across the continent hear the siren song of America in Ginsberg or Kerouac? How many first-generation college students, with unprecedented educational access to the American Dream, elected to make part of their curricular repertoire a close encounter with New Left, activist ideologies? How many fraternity or sorority members really got radicalized? How many young black Americans were actually reading Malcolm X and Eldridge Cleaver? How many people really *got lost* in the '60s? How many people even got involved enough to notice that they were there? If such enormous numbers of people smoked that much dope, drank that much beer and wine, showed up at that many demonstrations, went to that many concerts, blew off that many classes, and struck that many blows against the system, how come so many of the same people are now teaching school, practicing law or medicine, running for public office, making movies, performing farm or factory work, supporting political action efforts, serving on boards, working with community groups, preserving the environment, painting, sculpting, potting, drawing, designing, acting in plays, doing standup comedy, or writing books? At the same time, how many in this latter stage in their lives still keep waiting with secret hope for a whole nation full of young people to rise up and call themselves a "new" generation, a "now" generation, a generation of hope, love, peace, and youth?

The answer to the latter question seems to lie at a remarkable intersection of the imaginative and the actual once played out in countless personal histories that still makes such hope possible. For the '60s Generation of Youth became what it said it was through a capacity to believe in what it said it could be. What it was, to put this another way, resulted directly from its own immense capacity for self-mythologizing, its gift for creating itself in imaginative presence. Sixties youths created themselves precisely as facts of consciousness, and it was in that dimension that they were enabled to do the work of a kind of collective shamanism, cultural magic on a vast scale, a realized power of belief to achieve alterations in the very fabric of reality itself.[13]

My chief interest here, as I have said, will be in the print productions—the scriptures for a generation, I have called them—that often helped to make such conjunctions of belief and event actually come about. Through such texts, it becomes possible to show, I believe, that the '60s Generation of Youth, for perhaps the last time in history, truly envisioned itself as a generation looking for the Word; and that in the communitarian experience of the word comprised by '60s reading and writing, it often magically found, perhaps also for the last time in history, a culture's true texts of becoming.

THE '60S TEXT

Mythologizing the '60s: Robin Williams to the contrary, the problem turns out most often to be not amnesia but overload. Yet, as to the memory of a certain structure of consciousness, a complex of historical *and* mythic associations, it is hard to say one doesn't get the picture when something is styled a " '60s" this or " '60s" that. Any single reference seems to invoke all the others. For people who remember '60s reading and writing, such is certainly the case with favorite authors or titles.[14] Thus, in this sense at least, we may still surely speak of something called the '60s text.

At the same time, however, as I have noted, we must take care not to assume too much about either its literariness *or* its popularity. The real cultural importance of the '60s text would always lie elsewhere: in a dimension of imaginative presence often beyond both the discourses of conventional criticism and the demographics of the marketplace.

One notes, for instance, that few '60s youth-favorites ever won the Pulitzer Prize, the National Book Award, or any of the other traditional honors in fiction, poetry, or drama. As late as 1981, the American Academy and Institutes of Arts and Letters included in its membership but three certified '60s idols: Allen Ginsberg, Joseph Heller, and Kurt Vonnegut; one other claimed by adoption from the old underground, Henry Miller; and two more, Norman Mailer and James Baldwin, both exemplary of the difficulty experienced by members of the '60s literary intelligentsia in gaining the favor of the youth-illuminati.

Equally few youth-writers of the '60s were officially embraced by academia. Scholarly comment was confined to resource volumes mainly oriented toward student needs, with titles like *The Vonnegut Statement* or *A Catch-22 Casebook*. A few figures would eventually merit substantial notice in articles and books: Joseph Heller, Thomas Pynchon, Sylvia Plath. On the other hand, equally familiar names from '60s reading and writing—Vonnegut, Kesey, Friedan, Wolfe—even now have hardly become academic bywords in *American Literature, American Quarterly, Contemporary Literature, Modern Fiction Studies,* or *PMLA.* Standard scholarly overviews may consider the occasional '60s writer or '60s text. Such recognitions as may occur, however, are nearly always contextualized by the somehow more definitive achievements of a Barth, a Bellow, or a Nabokov.[15]

So from the '60s onward the curricular case seems largely to have stood still. Indeed, assimilations have seemed often to say as much about the fashions of literary academics as about the interests of their students. A good example is one classic 1978 study, in which a wide sampling of college and university professors was asked to supply reading lists from contemporary fiction courses offered at their institutions. As might be expected, Heller's *Catch-22* and Salinger's *The Catcher in the Rye* ranked significantly high among the top ten choices, placing respectively third and fifth. On the other hand, coming in at fourth was Pynchon's *Gravity's Rainbow*—even by then surely having outrun *Ulysses* or *The Faerie Queen* as the all-time champion of unread masterpieces among persons holding the Ph.D. in literature. The rest of the top ten included the following: Ellison's *Invisible Man,* Nabokov's *Lolita,* Bellow's *Herzog,* Warren's *All the King's Men,* and Mailer's *The Naked and the Dead* and *An American Dream.* Down in the twenties appeared finally Kesey's *One Flew Over the Cuckoo's Nest*—albeit serenely bracketed by Updike's *Rabbit Run* and Hemingway's *The Old Man and the Sea.*

Similar in result was Richard Ohmann's survey of the contemporary canon conducted six years later. Ohmann wished to explore further, he said, the ongoing "interaction between a large audience and gatekeeper intellectuals" (385). To do so, he used the earlier data as a baseline and then educed a new, parallel listing from *Contemporary Literary Criticism.* Of forty-eight figures identified as those most discussed, the vast majority were again canonical literati such as those named above. They were also joined by new mass-market celebrities such as Richard Condon, Peter de Vries, Erica Jong, Ross MacDonald, and Larry McMurtry. Most illuminating again, however, was the continuing lack of critical interest in what we would now consider '60s favorites. Indeed, beyond Salinger, Heller, and Pynchon, only three names had been added: Plath, Brautigan, and Vonnegut.

As with inflated assumptions about the critical and curricular status of much '60s reading and writing, so we must take care with ideas of actual market popularity. Here, information from the publishing industry confirms the perils of nostalgic generalization about the pervasiveness of most '60s texts as mass-market phenomena. As to all-time hardbound sales, for instance, not a single youth-classic of the era ranks among the top fifty.[16] Even mass paperback figures, where much more significant visibility might be expected, reveal cumulative success only for *Catch-22* and *The Catcher in the Rye,* both with sales of about six million; Hannah Green's *I Never Promised You a Rose Garden,* with roughly five million; and William Golding's *Lord of the Flies,* with slightly over two million. Combined listings add a few familiar titles, albeit scattered and decidedly eclectic: Betty Friedan's *The Feminine Mystique;* Eldridge Cleaver's *Soul on Ice;* the anonymously published *Go Ask Alice;* Charles Reich's *The Greening of America;* and Arthur C. Clarke's *2001: A Space Odyssey*—itself the "novelization" of a film.

Certain marketing flurries, to be sure, occurred as well. Nineteen sixty-six and 1967 saw massive promotions of all the J. R. R. Tolkien texts in the first of what would become a succession of uniform paperback editions. Nineteen sixty-six also produced large new paperback sales for William Golding's *Lord of the Flies,* as did 1967 for Hermann Hesse's *Siddhartha.* Nineteen sixty-eight and 1969 paperback favorites included *The Autobiography of Malcolm X,* Eldridge Cleaver's *Soul on Ice,* Frank Herbert's *Dune,* Robert A. Heinlein's *Stranger in a Strange Land,* and Hannah Green's *I Never Promised You a Rose Garden.* Nineteen sixty-nine also saw the era's sole appearance of a certified youth classic on an annual bestseller list: Vonnegut's *Slaughterhouse Five.*[17]

On the other hand, a larger survey of the market during the same years quickly sets even this information in sobering relief. In 1959, for instance, on the eve of the era, the nonfiction bestseller was Pat Boone's *Twixt Twelve and Twenty.* Nineteen sixty-three gave us Morris L. West's *The Shoes of the Fisherman* as the fiction leader and as its nonfiction counterpart, Charles M. Schulz's *Happiness is a Warm Puppy.* In 1964, four exemplary bestsellers were Saul Bellow's *Herzog,* one of Ian Fleming's 007 thrillers entitled *You Only Live Twice,* Bel Kaufman's *Up the Down Staircase,* and Terry Southern's *Candy.* Nineteen sixty-five paired Jacqueline Susann's *Valley of the Dolls* with Dan Greenburg's *How to be a Jewish Mother.* In 1968—the year of the Tet Offensive, the My Lai Massacre, the

Poor People's March on Washington, the assassinations of Martin Luther King Jr. and Robert Kennedy, and the riots at the Democratic National Convention—those same two positions were occupied by Arthur Hailey's *Airport* and the *Better Homes and Gardens New Cook Book*.

By 1970, the decade as a period of youth-expression already seemed largely a forgotten echo. Bestsellers for the year included Richard Bach's *Jonathan Livingston Seagull;* James Dickey's *Deliverance;* Ernest Hemingway's *Islands in the Stream;* Eric Segal's *Love Story;* and Dr. David Reuben's *Everything You Always Wanted to Know About Sex But Were Afraid to Ask.* Over the next few years, a handful of new youth-classics gained further notice: *The Last Whole Earth Catalog; Our Bodies, Ourselves;* Annie Dillard's *Pilgrim at Tinker Creek;* and Robert Pirsig's *Zen and the Art of Motorcycle Maintenance.* Vonnegut struggled on. But mainly '60s reading and writing in America seemed already to have become history.[18] Indeed, by 1975, when '60s figures had been added in with those of prior decades, the all-time bestseller continued to be Dr. Benjamin Spock's *The Common Sense Book of Baby and Child Care.* The next four places on the list were occupied by two cookbooks, a dictionary, and a book of world records. In sixth place was Mario Puzo's *The Godfather.*[19] Other favorites high on the list included Eric Berne's *Games People Play,* Thomas Harris's *I'm OK, You're OK;* Robin Moore's *The Green Berets;* William Blatty's *The Exorcist;* Ira Levin's *Rosemary's Baby;* James Michener's *Hawaii;* and Harold Robbins's *The Carpetbaggers.* The '60s text was not merely dead; according to market figures, it had hardly ever been alive.

Thus the verdict of criticism *and* the record of the marketplace. And thus, in spite of both, we still remember something distinctly called '60s reading and writing. Moreover, I would submit, the reflex really does have its own kind of validation—in a dimension of consciousness, that is, even now still created largely *by* such texts themselves. For members of the Generation of Youth, the '60s will always be a bookshelf and a curriculum, the curriculum founded on that extraordinary production called the '60s text.[20]

So now the second portion of this text proceeds to examine that putative '60s bookshelf in fuller detail. And so now also, as in the first place, the reader is asked to participate: to add, subtract, amend; to substitute, arrange, or reconfigure; to make the study of '60s reading and writing itself a new experience of relationship. One is asked, in sum, actively to help reconstruct and reimagine a curriculum. Build a consensus. Make a dissent. Register the full range of possibilities.

Already I can hear the voices of fellow trippers and askers. "How can he possibly talk about Hesse," someone will be saying, "without discussing *Demian?*" "How can he fail to see that the *real* Kesey is in *Sometimes a Great Notion?*" "Where is Bob Dylan's *Tarantula?* Frederick Exley's *A Fan's Notes?* Frances Fitzgerald's *Fire in the Lake?* Tom Robbins's *Another Roadside Attraction?*" My only response can be to repeat an invitation intended as political in the fullest sense. From beginning to end, debate the authority of the textual arrangement, restructure the system, and try to imagine it the way you might see it. To do so, you will be participating in constructions of knowledge unavailable to any of us alone. In a very '60s phrase, follow your head.

'60s Texts and '60s Writers

The title of this, the main part of my study, suggests its relation to the rest. Here I attempt an illustrative guide to '60s reading and writing, something like a curriculum of the illuminati; youth-texts and youth-authors granted special wisdom-status; visitations of the Word upon a community of initiates. In many instances, one might call the works described scriptures for a generation. In others, the better phrase might be pre-texts and co-options. Whatever the fates of individual works and authors, the community in question remained, as I have said, perhaps the last real American community of the word, seekers through the printed text of a common gift of illumination.

My entitling implies a plan of discussion as well. My object is a composite critical overview, compartmentalized enough to allow for easy reference and topical focus yet also sufficiently cross-connected to allow for discursive relations.

For these reasons the idea of a *'60s Omnigathering* seemed too ambitiously comprehensive. A *'60s Checklist* sounded too modestly descriptive. A *'60s Encyclopedia* seemed too, well, encyclopedic. On the other hand, there *was* the figure suggested by Michel Foucault, by way of Jorge Luis Borges, of the heterotopia: a field of knowledge rewritten through the restructuring of the categories of knowledge, with the field in turn changed by any restructuring of categories. This seemed a complicated way of saying, however, what is by now accepted by most theorists of knowledge: that all fields on the outside are protean and that all fields on the inside are porous; that any field, in fact, is reconfigured by any rearrangement, within *and/or* without. But I wanted at least the spirit of that. The result is what follows, something that might be called a working heteropedia.

Here, then, is the attempt to create a field comprising at once the figure of the writer enshrined *in* or *through* the '60s text, the text canonized as '60s scripture, and the figure of the reader also enlisted *in* or *through* the text as fellow illuminatus in the community of the word. It contains the odd crossovers from the literati and the mass market, as well as from journalism, music, film, television, and other information and entertainment media. At the same time it attempts to link the idea of '60s reading and writing to an actual body of texts—to what an E. D. Hirsch of the counterculture might have called a program of cultural literacy. It attempts realistically to catalog '60s texts likely to have been known by large numbers of the Generation of Youth. It also addresses the '60s writer explicitly in many ways *as* cult figure, although cult is only the right word here to the degree we connect it with culture—a vital subset of the dominant culture in this case that itself in many ways, as I have already proposed, rewrote that culture. It addresses the '60s text, then, as cult classic and cultural icon. Accordingly, it addresses writing itself as a particular form of cultural iconography in a last great historical moment of print production and consumption. It addresses the writer in relation to the text and the text in relation to the reader in the cultural provenance of issues of mass popularity, critical status, visibility in advertising and review media, and frequency of scholarly attention. It makes many of its so to speak hard cultural claims on the basis of sales figures (hardbound, paperback, and combined); numbers of printings; and new editions and adaptations to other media. It addresses circulation on college and university campuses, evidence of curricular adoption, appearance in co-ops and bookstores, and frequency of citation in credible discussions of the era.[1]

Finally, a few notes on practical composition. Discussions of individual authors usually focus on one or two representative selections. Certain entries deal with freestanding texts, in some cases of unattributed authorship, in others of multiple authorship or editorship. There will be grounds for disagreement here. All one can say is that books, and especially books about books, have to end. Still, a number of figures and texts not individually discussed deserve mention as at least constructive of the general conversation. These may be grouped into three broad categories.

First, there were the semiofficial authors and titles in general intellectual circulation, found mainly in college and university course descriptions, comprising something like a counterculture background readings list: Beckett, especially *Waiting for Godot;* Camus, *The Rebel, The Myth* of *Sisyphus,* and *The Stranger;* Sartre, *No Exit* and *Nausea;* Borges, *Labyrinths;* Nathanael West, *Miss Lonelyhearts* and *Day of the Locust* (in a single, skinny, no-frills Grove Press volume); dark Twain; freaky Melville; Buber, *I and Thou;* Dostoyevski, *The Idiot, Notes from Underground,* and "The Grand Inquisitor" from *The Brothers Karamazov;* Huxley, *Brave New World* and, of course, *The Doors of Perception;* Orwell, *1984* or *Animal Farm;* Freud, *Civilization and Its Discontents,* perhaps *Totem and Taboo,* but almost never the "primary" Freud, the case studies, and the theoretical fragments; Nietzsche—like Freud, in the '60s on the eve of postmodern enshrinement—but for the moment the Nietzsche of *Also Sprach Zarathustra* or *Beyond Good and Evil;* Kafka, "The Metamorphosis," "The Penal Colony," and *The Trial;* Marx, *The Communist Manifesto* and selections from *Das Kapital;* Kierkegaard, *Fear and Trembling* and *The Sickness Unto Death.*

These were joined by assorted other moderns and postmoderns: Lorca, Robbe-Grillet, Pinter, Pirandello, Brecht, Rilke, Rimbaud, Grass, Malraux, Woolf, Joyce, e. e. cummings, Anaïs Nin, T. S. Eliot, Gertrude Stein, Ralph Ellison, Richard Wright, Simone de Beauvoir, D. H. Lawrence, and Henry Miller. Further in vogue was a subset of what might be described as literary outlaws, old and new: Genet, de Sade, Céline, and Henry Roth. Also, beyond such newly semiofficial figures as Kerouac and Ginsberg came other Beats and affiliates including William Burroughs, Gary Snyder, Gregory Corso, Peter Orlovsky, and Kenneth Rexroth. Finally, mixed liberally into the general curriculum were certain earlier figures— Blake, Thoreau, Tolkien, Hesse—discussed in separate listings below, now newly enthroned by a generation as its true prophets and oracles.

A second category comprised what might be called members of the curriculum-at-large, figures possessing a kind of iconic textual authority but for the most part seen, heard, or read *about* rather than read:[2] Mohandas Gandhi, Che Guevara, Mao Tse-tung, Mort Sahl, Lenny Bruce, Woody Allen, Pete Seeger, Bob Dylan, Muhammad Ali, Lily Tomlin, Joan Baez, John Lennon, Jane Fonda, Jim Morrison, Rex Reed, Dotson Rader, Timothy Crouse, Paul Krassner, Mark Rudd, H. Rap Brown, Bobby Seale, Stokely Carmichael, Dick Gregory, Guru Maharaj Ji, Tom Hayden, Angela Davis, Huey Newton, the Maharishi Mahesh Yogi, Andy Warhol, Daniel Berrigan, Philip Berrigan, Cesar Chavez, William Sloan Coffin, Daniel Ellsberg, Francine du Plessix Gray, Erika Huggins, Carl Oglesby, Phil Ochs, Adelle Davis, and Euell Gibbons.[3]

The last orbit in the curriculum was also occupied by a pantheon of figures, most of them somewhat older, best described as Trusted Explainers: Elders, Scribes, Exegetes, in some few cases, genuine Evangelists. Some, discussed individually below, seem to have enjoyed substantial readership and discussion among '60s youth. These include Norman O. Brown, Paul Goodman, R. D. Laing, Norman Mailer, Herbert Marcuse, C. Wright Mills, and Alan Watts. Others, also to be discussed, were authors of the topical classic; Rachel Carson for *Silent Spring,* for instance, or Frantz Fanon for *The Wretched of the Earth.* Figures of more general influence were equally numerous: Wilhelm Reich, Kenneth Keniston, Edgar Friedenberg, Leslie Fiedler, Erich Fromm, Noam Chomsky, Marshall McLuhan, John Kenneth Galbraith, Michael Harrington, David Riesman, Daniel Bell, William Whyte, D. T. Suzuki, Eric Hoffer, Ralph Nader, Arthur C. Clarke, and R. Buckminster Fuller.

As to views of the youth-culture of the era now themselves assuming classic status, I must pause here to note my indebtedness to earlier, groundbreaking studies such as Theodore Roszak's *The Making of a Counter-Culture* and Morris Dickstein's *The Gates of Eden.* As for '60s scriptures themselves, still the best way to know the experience and the community of the word they engendered is to go back and experience the reading and writing firsthand. The modest heteropedia below, one hopes, is at least a serviceable place to begin.

Alpert, Richard [Baba Ram Dass]. The surname Alpert appears suggestively in my '60s alphabet just before "anonymous." Were another such listing possible, it would also just precede "archetypal." By Richard Alpert's original name, he is most often identified by '60s initiates and historians as the other Harvard psychological researcher dismissed with Timothy Leary for consciousness-raising drug experiments with students. Whoever Alpert was entering the decade, he surely measured the East-West journey undertaken by many '60s thinkers who returned toward the end only to meet themselves going the other way.

Beginning as a serious academic, Alpert produced a 1957 Stanford dissertation bearing the sober title "Anxiety in Academic Measurement Situations: Its Measurement and Relation to Aptitude." At the height of his drug notoriety, he became known for his work with Leary and Ralph Metzner on a volume entitled *The Psychedelic Experience: A Manual Based on the Tibetan Book of the Dead.* (For true cognoscenti, he was also co-author, with Sidney Cohen, of a widely known but now virtually unavailable book entitled *LSD.*) By the late '60s and early '70s, he had reinvented himself, somewhat in the vein of the Maharishi Mahesh Yogi or the Guru Maharaj Ji, as a text and a product called Baba Ram Dass, author of a handbook on meditation, *Be Here Now, Remember,* and California cohort of various other high priests of New Age spiritualism, psychic energy, and human potential movements such as Arthur Janov and Werner Erhard.[4]

The latter work, Alpert/Ram Dass's magnum opus, traces his spiritual odyssey. It begins with a section entitled "Journey," detailing "The Transformation of Dr. Richard Alpert, Ph.D., into Baba Ram Dass." This is followed by "From Bindu to Ojas," subtitled "The Core Book," and best described as a New Age gospel combining the visual style of the '60s poster or underground comic with a kind of running catechism, drawn equally from various hip oracles and spare parts of the world's major religions. Next is a discourse on method, "Cookbook for a Sacred Life," or "A Manual for Conscious Being." Finally, along with a glossary of religious terms, is appended a bibliography-reference section. Itself entitled "Painted Cakes," it is further apportioned into "Books to Hang Out With," "Books to Visit Now and Then," and "Books to Have Met."

Inside and out, *Be Here Now, Remember* is the quintessential high-'60s production. The physical text, flat and square, looks like a paperbound craft book or lab manual. The cover shows the title in mantra-like arrangement around a string art sphere. Contained within the sphere is the drawing of a simple caned chair. The back cover, in contrast, features a far-off horizon of mountains looking vaguely Himalayan. The copyright notice righteously announces 1971 as "Year of the Earth Monkey" and the sponsorship (documented with cost-profit breakout) of "The Lama Foundation" of San Cristobal, New Mexico.[5] The opening section of spiritual autobiography, illustrated with personal snapshots, is printed a Third World bluish white. In its line drawing and primitive typography, the core text gives the impression of hand-printed art. The paper is brown in color like a grocery sack and like rice paper in feel (perhaps it is brown rice paper). The drawings are pure '60s flashback: "The Big Ice Cream Cone in the Sky" (37); the twinned erect phalluses flanking "That Urge," "That Desire," "That Unfulfilled Thing," and "Just Let It Be" (22); "The Divine Mother Which is Nature" with her upward flowing earth-and-heaven hair, the downward pointing body of the standard, wet dream, freak-art nude with the perfect pencilled-in pubic triangle (48). We admire the swift, yin-yang brushstroke curve of "Time and Space" (65). We contemplate the perfection of the Rhode Island Red Rooster under "The Chicken Sees" along with the moral: "When I met my Guru who knew"

> everything
> in my head,

> I realized
> that he knew
> everything
> in my head
> whether 'I' liked it or not.
> He knew it. (67)

Eventually the manual on practice appears in a pale beige and sepia. The further reading section concludes in brown and ocher. The general impression is of an earnest silliness. We confront a surfing swami (32). We approach the door of the Magic Theater from Hesse's *Steppenwolf* (102). We find invoked all manner of authority: Siddhartha, St. John of the Cross, Meher Baba, Buddha, the Tao, Jesus Christ, Mother Kali, Maharaj Ji, Lao-tzu, Hermes Trismegistus, the Incredible String Band, Ecclesiastes, Ouspensky, St. Paul, Jacob Boehme, the Bhagavad Gita, Thomas Merton, Blavatsky, Gandhi, and Bob Dylan. Once they might have been a catalog of what the '60s looked for. Now, in this text of hip assimilation, they become a benchmark, as sure as any geologic survey monument of the strange world of New Age hucksterism into which so much of the spirit of the '60s had vanished.

Anonymous, *Go Ask Alice.* This widely known 1971 text announces itself as "based on the actual diary of a fifteen-year-old drug user." It concludes with notice of the author's death, three weeks following the last entry, of an overdose, either "accidental" or "premeditated." The latter issue, the editors aver, "isn't important." Rather, they conclude simply, "she died," and "she was only one of thousands of drug deaths that year." "The difference," the jacket copy tells us, "between *Alice* and a lot of other kids on drugs" is textual: "Alice kept a diary."

As to readership and influence, *Go Ask Alice* has much in common with a comparable text, Joanne Greenburg's pseudonymous *I Never Promised You a Rose Garden,* the intimate account of a teenage girl's struggle with schizophrenia. But while publishing figures are available, reliable reading information on both is hard to find. As in a long Anglo-American tradition of texts written by women about women's concerns and issues, one suspects that both texts enjoyed unrecorded hand-to-hand circulation. Since they focused on teenagers, they were likely read by a high school and public library audience not generally counted in formal surveys. General information suggests that both, however, attracted considerable attention.

Rose Garden became the basis of a feature film, and *Alice* was adapted for television; both today can still be found in libraries as young adult staples.

The contemporary visibility of *Go Ask Alice* in particular was evidenced by its multimedia connections. The title, as any '60s listener would have known, comes from the Jefferson Airplane's song, "White Rabbit," itself a '60s drug-classic of major status. The Alice, of course, is the Alice of Lewis Carroll's *Alice in Wonderland.* Meanwhile, blazoned on the dust jacket even while the book remained in hardback came notice of its dramatization as an ABC "Wednesday Movie of the Week."

As the song goes, one pill makes you larger, one pill makes you small. So goes the text also, amidst an otherwise poignantly typical "dear diary" accounting of the elations and travails of young womanhood. Working out sex confusion; moving to a new town and school; finding and losing boyfriends, best girlfriends, confidantes and accomplices: this everyday teenage chronicle of American loneliness crowds upon itself. Soon, Alice winds up in her own bad movie. A game called "button button who's got the button," played to the old routine of spin-the-bottle, produces a first LSD experience, at once terrifying and ecstatic. Shortly comes the linear acceleration into the drug vortex. The Rabbit Hole yawns. Alice lists the stops on the way down: missing school, increasing reliance on friends and lovers with drug connections, brushes with the law, hospitalizations, runaway vagabondage, flashbacks, nightmares, and periodic reunions and attempts to make a new life at home.

Then, suddenly, home is always somewhere else, and Alice is someone we don't know. "Another day, another blow job," she writes:

> The fuzz has clamped down till the town is mother dry. If I don't give Big Ass a blow he'll cut off my supply. Hell, I'm shaking on the inside more than I'm shaking on the outside. What a bastard world without drugs! The dirty ofay who wants me to lay it on him knows my ass is dragging, but he's doling out the only supply I know about. I'm almost ready to take on the Fat Cats, the Rich Philistines, or even the whole public for one good shot. Goddamn Big Ass makes me do it before he gives me the load. Everybody is just lying around here like they're dead and Little Jason is yelling, "Mamma, Daddy can't come now. He's humping Carla." I've got to get out of this shit hole. (84)

Diary Number Two (90) records one last try at home and school. There is pressure from the drug crowd, then acid planted on some candy she eats while baby-sitting. As in Greenburg's chronicle and in Sylvia Plath's as well, there follows a season in the Therapy Unit. At home again, we hear about hope of reunion with a special boyfriend (152). There are small choices now: Tampax or kotex? (152).

The time seems also to have arrived to abandon the diary—They're "great when you're young," she says, but "when a person gets older she should be able to discuss her problems with other people" (158). Now comes a seeming emergence. "I shall thank you always," she tells the text, "for sharing my tears and heartaches and my struggles and strifes, and my joys and happinesses. It's all been good in its own special way, I guess."

"See ya'," she concludes. Farewell, writes the author to her book. Three weeks later, we are told, she makes her farewell to life. Yet as the author *of* her book, Alice also held onto life in ways that few authors ever dream of. One will never know how many young people were saved by *Go Ask Alice*. If the continuing status of the text as young adult classic is any indication, the number would seem to be substantial.

Baldwin, James. One of the most curious stories of '60s reading and writing in America is that of the disappearance of James Baldwin. Indeed, on the basis of celebrated fiction and nonfiction volumes like *Go Tell It On The Mountain* (1953), *Notes of a Native Son* (1955), *Nobody Knows My Name* (1961), *Another Country* (1962), and *The Fire Next Time* (1963), it would have once been nearly impossible to overestimate the promise with which Baldwin came to be invested as the literary voice of early '60s black America. Deeply involved in the struggle for civil rights, he combined the homiletic appeal of his contemporary Martin Luther King Jr. with his own distinctly literary eloquence. Coupled with such political recognition was his status among postwar literati at home and abroad—the *Paris Review comitatus* of George Plimpton and Peter Matthiessen along with such other expatriates as James Jones, William Styron, and Irwin Shaw; the New York cognoscenti; the East Village Beats; the Harlem arts communities; and Jewish intellectuals such as Norman Mailer, Bernard Malamud, and Saul Bellow. As a major black intellectual, Baldwin had both the political and the literary credentials to speak with immense public visibility.

What then happened to ensure the overnight waning of Baldwin's influence from the mid '60s onward? On Baldwin the philosopher of black identity, Henry Louis Gates Jr. is surely correct in observing that Baldwin was simply too complex, too philosophical, to be rhetorically appropriated to the needs of an increasingly activist, media-oriented agenda. What he had to say, that is, on the dialectic of self and other simply could not reduce itself to succinct political formulation, platform or podium statement, or radical shibboleth or slogan. When Baldwin spoke, for example, as he frequently did, on the "need" of white and black America for each other, he was accused of a tired conciliation or accommodationism. In fact—and here loomed large his expatriation to the milieu of post–1945 France—Baldwin was pointing toward the larger redefinitions of the very boundaries of cultural knowledge and discourse soon to become the project of literary and philosophical postmodernism. The quest for freedom and individuality defined by Baldwin was thus not anything nearly so naive as interracial "communication," "dialogue," or "understanding." Rather, it was tied up with questions of white and black identity and consciousness as *forms of cultural discourse,* deeply reflexive and interrelated, with each requiring the other as a basis for dialectical movement.

Thus he described the problem movingly in a section from *The Fire Next Time* entitled "Letter from a Region of My Mind":

> In short, we, the black and the white, deeply need each other here if we are really to become a nation—if we are really, that is, to achieve our identity, our maturity, as men and women. To create one nation has proved to be a hideously difficult task; there is certainly no need now to create two, one black and one white. But white men with far more political power than that possessed by the Nation of Islam movement have been advocating exactly this, in effect, for generations. If this sentiment is honored when it falls from the lips of Senator Byrd, then there is no reason it should not be honored when it falls from the lips of Malcolm X. And any Congressional committee wishing to investigate the latter must also be willing to investigate the former. They are expressing exactly the same sentiments and represent exactly the same danger. (456–57)

Here indeed, for the era especially, was a brilliant meditation on the reflexive politics of identity. The real problem of boundary-challenging, however, most crucially involved in Baldwin's precipitous undoing as the voice of young black America, lay beyond. That, of course, was his homosexuality. To be sure, there had been the explicit content of *Giovanni's Room* (1956). But given a climate of general refusal and Baldwin's increasingly focused racial indignation, this dimension of his work was for the moment gently ignored. Meanwhile, however, with the rise of the Nation of Islam and black power movements, black leadership became increasingly young, angry, deeply revolutionary, and intensely male. The old civil rights people were Toms. Baldwin was worse, a double anathema: he was a Tom and a Queer.

From the mid '60s onward, Baldwin kept trying to navigate back into the ideological action. But his status as a cultural spokesman was behind him. His voice would be drowned out in the streets by Eldridge Cleaver, H. Rap Brown, Bobby Seale, and Huey Newton. On the page, it would be superseded by texts from Malcolm X, Amiri Baraka, or Ishmael Reed, and with the rise of black women's writing, by the work of such new stars as Toni Morrison and Alice Walker.

Now, on the other hand, it has become possible for Henry Louis Gates Jr., the W. E. B. Du Bois Professor of Cultural Studies at Harvard, to produce an important text about his own experience of the late '60s and early '70s entitled, "Remembering James Baldwin." At once memoir and homage, it eloquently stakes out the crucial place that the Baldwin of the '60s has now come to occupy in the '90s. Accordingly, it also becomes something of a parable of our own attempts to understand the era at large. Much of the story of '60s reading and writing has to do not only with where the '60s came from but also with where they went; those they emplaced as cultural icons and those they also discarded. Of the latter especially, as will be seen, Baldwin proves but the first of many whom it is now time again to remember.

Blake, William. Were there ever to be built a hall of '60s prophets and oracles, William Blake—albeit for particular reasons that no single discussion can identify—would likely get one of the main places of honor. Blake's power over the era was one of complex and inspired example. One can of course spotlight the more obvious genealogies of allusion, such as Blake's figure of the "doors of perception," used by Aldous Huxley to entitle the record, itself a cult-text of the era, of his experiments with psilocybin and other hallucinogens, and in turn adopted as the name of the legendary rock group featuring Jim Morrison. ("If the doors of perception were cleansed," the original lines read in *The Marriage of Heaven and Hell*, "everything would appear to man as it truly is, infinite" [154].) Direct homage was also paid by Allen Ginsberg, Jack Kerouac, and the other Beats. For these, who styled themselves his most direct, self-appointed legatees, Blake became the great Western ancestor incarnating the period's great Eastern incantatory adjective: Holy.

More important was the generalized affinity of Blakean visionary mysticism with the revolutionary spirit of the times. In its profound moral concerns, it was deeply Manichean; in its moments of ultimate insight, it was spectacularly apocalyptic. Then, of course, there was also direct political genealogy, the utopian romantic of the great age of revolution, still showing the way against "blind world-rulers of this life." "I must Create a System," spoke the master in *Jerusalem,* "or be enslav'd by another Man's" (629).

On the other hand, for many '60s readers, deeply appealing as well was the private, internalized, meditative intensity to be found in Blake. Profound, oracular, obscurantist, the Blakean vision seemed especially to connect with new forms of alternative consciousness contemporarily being sought in non-Western mysticism—Zen, the Tao, Hinduism.

Indeed, nearly every adjective applied to the spiritual aspirations of '60s consciousness seemed somehow to make its way back to Blake: mystic, epiphanic, hermetic, gnostic. The plain, short texts bespoke the wisdom of a homely beatitude. The long, cryptic strains of prophecy revealed systems, structures, orders, endlessly proliferating into antisystems, antistructures, antiorders.

As '60s reading, the pieces themselves were something to get into: hermetic, willfully and elaborately encoded yet heavy with the promise of epiphany. As in "Auguries of Innocence," one could seek eyeblinks of creation:

> To see a World in a Grain of Sand,
> And a Heaven in a Wild Flower,
> Hold Infinity in the palm of your hand,
> And Eternity in an hour. (43)

In other texts and cycles, *Songs of Innocence* and *Songs of Experience,* for instance, or *The Marriage of Heaven and Hell,* one could voyage into explorations of multifold oppositions and irreconcilabilities—what Blake himself elaborated as the doctrine of "Contraries." In *The Book of Thel, The Daughters of Albion, The Four Zoas,* and *Jerusalem,* one could further explore such themes into the labyrinthine constructions of complex allegories. At every turn, then, Blake seemed to fulfill someone's '60s reading and writing expectations: deeply moral, but visionarily ecstatic; contemplative, but revolutionary; eccentric, but accessible; gentle, but "heavy."

Also important as '60s influences were the conflations in Blake's mystical art of verbal and visual modes. Blake the painter, the illustrator, was the twin of Blake the poet, setting forth his complex literary creations and his extraordinary copperplate engravings and watercolors to be read, as with the great medieval and Renaissance emblemists, in a fullness of textual complementarity. Accordingly, the Blakean mode reproduced itself in everything from posters and comic books to exquisitely handprinted texts, illustrated editions, collections of engravings, and poetry chapbooks and led to the revival of Book Arts itself as a cultural pursuit.

Finally, one must acknowledge the visibility in the '60s of the academic Blake. In the hands of influential figures such as Meyer Abrams, Northrop Frye, and Harold Bloom, here too Blake became a part of the official literary curriculum, the romantic prophet of revolution celebrated in a revolutionary rewriting of scholarship itself, a turning away from the cerebral technicalities of high modernists such as Eliot and the priestly celebrants of the New Criticism with its privileging of the English Metaphysicals and their neoclassical inheritors over the passionate, unruly Romantics. Accordingly, Morris Dickstein in *The Gates of Eden* would reflect fondly on an undergraduate Blake course he taught several times "in which even those who came to get high stayed on to sweat out the intricacies of the system" (13). And so Theodore Roszak, the other celebrated chronicler of the era, would feel compelled to generalize in a bibliographic note to his final chapter of *The Making of a Counter-Culture* (itself headed by an epigraph from Blake and entitled "Eyes of Flesh, Eyes of Fire"): "Anything Blake ever wrote," he concluded, "seems supremely relevant to the search for alternative realities" (302).

So across the spectrum of culture, the '60s honored Blake as a mythic progenitor, and so the records of the era would continue to invest the vision of Blake in the '60s with the new aura of mythic remembering.

Boston Women's Health Book Collective, *Our Bodies, Ourselves.* From the standpoint of both ideology and publishing practice, one of the most noteworthy features of the '60s women's movement, particularly in the last years of the decade and on into the '70s, was its truly revolutionary redefinition of writing and authorship themselves as forms of cultural production. Issues of the cultural status of the text—problems of language, power, genealogy, and authority now familiar to criticism— seem often in fact to have been commonplaces of '60s and '70s women's reading and writing, forms of radical critique realized in feminist texts well in advance of their elevation to the status of poststructuralist topoi.

By asking what is a woman, feminist writing indeed expressly challenged existing categories of consciousness and voice. What is an author? it asked, frequently offering in reply volumes of multiple authorship or editorship. What is a text? it also asked, frequently copyrighting volumes in the name of discussion groups and collectives. What is a subject? What is an audience? What are the cultural terms of textual production, distribution, consumption?

No feminist text of the era asked these questions more completely as matters of theory *and* practice—and continues to do so in an evolution extending to the present—than the Boston Women's Health Book Collective's *Our Bodies, Ourselves.* Beginning in 1969 as *Women and Their Bodies,* then becoming *Women and Our Bodies,* and finally adopting the title by which it is now universally known, the text has unfolded through nearly a quarter century of revising, correcting, expanding, and updating to incorporate information across the whole range of contemporary women's health concerns: issues of physiology, sexuality, gender identity, hygiene, reproductive choice, pregnancy, childbearing, menopause, and institutional health care. (Other texts, similarly innovative in their authorship and production, include *Ourselves and Our Children,* subtitled "A Book By and For Parents," and *Ourselves, Growing Older.*)

On the other hand, no need has been found to change the familiar crayon scrawl on the original cover billing the text as "A Book By and For Women" or the joyous adjacent photograph of three women, one elderly and two of college age, together holding a sign that says "Women Unite." And—precisely because from the outset it has been the collaborative work of women, beginning with a dozen and now growing to number in the hundreds and thousands—neither has it ever found any reason to change its attribution of authorship. It is, as it always has been, "By The Boston Women's Health Book Collective."

To say it succinctly, *Our Bodies, Ourselves* is a '60s communitarian text that puts its money where its mouth is. Like the huge, sprawling, collectively produced *Last Whole Earth Catalog,* the other work of the era *Our Bodies, Ourselves* most closely resembles, it creates authorship through common ownership, claims voice by sharing it. *Our Bodies, Ourselves,* reads the title. And so reads the corporate body that is the text.

An opening theoretical reflection on "Our Sense of Self," for instance, turns out to be the only portion of the book by a single author. (On the other hand, even here the "Our" of the title enforces the theme of rhetorical pluralism.) Within the ensuing text, all other sections are of multiple authorship, listing two, three, five names, often with further acknowledgment of friends or supporters.

A second chapter then proceeds to the explicitly clinical, an "Anatomy and Physiology of Sexuality and Reproduction." And thereby is established the basic rhythm of the book, a calculated alternation between the spiritual and the physical. "Sexuality" is succeeded by "Living With Our-selves and Others—Our Sexual Relationships." An ideological meditation entitled "In Amerika They Call Us Dykes" is succeeded by a series of quite pragmatic, informational entries under the heading of "Taking Care of Ourselves."

Similarly, within the essays, discursive sections are interspersed with individual women's testimonies, one voice succeeding another and join-ing eloquently with all the others. These are combined with photographs, poems, cartoons, charts, diagrams, glossaries, technical and scientific ref-erences, bibliographies, and detailed lists of suggested further readings.

Yet to emphasize excessively from a literary standpoint the work's bril-liant synthesis of the ideological and the rhetorical would also be to slight the real, experienced, communitarian drama and excitement of this and comparable feminist texts of the era such as *Sisterhood Is Powerful* and *Radical Feminism:* the adventure of women setting forth through language to revise the very categories of cultural understanding. As the preface of *Our Bodies, Ourselves* says in its original edition, the book is above all "A Good Story." "The history of this book, *Our Bodies, Ourselves,*" it asserts, "is lengthy and satisfying" (11). How lengthy and satisfying even these pioneers could only have begun to know. What they had created for them-selves, and for all the others seeking admission to the discourse of culture, was a truly revolutionary publishing success.

Brautigan, Richard. The emergence in the late '60s of the San Fran-cisco writer Richard Brautigan quickly elevated him among the youth-culture to the status of a Tolkien, a Hesse, or a Vonnegut. A study of that process, on the other hand, becomes a demoralizing exposé of the textual promotions often attending such enshrinement.

Closer in generational and literary affiliation to the Beats than to the '60s and early '70s youth who crowned him their hippie-laureate, Brauti-gan had secured a West Coast following on the basis of productions such as *A Confederate General from Big Sur, Trout Fishing in America,* and *In Watermelon Sugar.* Meanwhile, according to biographer Keith Abbott, the publishing industry had come casting about San Francisco for "a *Catch-22* of the Hippie" (67). Mass-market republication of the early texts ensued, along with the rapid appearance by 1971 of works such as *The Abortion,* a novel; *The Pill versus the Springhill Mine Disaster* and *Rommel Drives Deeper into Egypt,* both collections of poetry; and *The Revenge of the Lawn,* a collection of short stories. These were followed within a decade by five more novels and two poetry collections. For a time, the author was also adopted by the academy. Articles appeared in journals, and even monographs were produced. Meanwhile, Brautigan sank into alcohol and despondency, and in 1984 took his own life.

On the other hand, for faithful devotees of '60s reading and writing, Brautigan would surely stay alive in memory and imagination for his chief contribution to the era: a book, to be sure, yet somehow at once a character *and* a text; a brilliant experiment entitled *Trout Fishing in America.* In spite of all its hip currency—the allure of the Day Glo metaphor and the easy epiphany, for instance, or the expression of serious environmental concern—the text also aspired to the literary. It lightly invoked Ishmael upon the deep, Jake Barnes at Burguete, Hemingway himself at Ketchum, and Thoreau at Walden. Description of "A Walden Pond for Winos" (17–18) also contained a Walt Whitman afoot with his vision. Indeed, in all these respects, *Trout Fishing in America* closely resembled that other tremendously literary hip-classic of the era, Robert Pirsig's *Zen and the Art of Motorcycle Maintenance.* It was a physical *and* metaphysical odyssey covering America and attempting to connect—with the Zen component equally pronounced—the spheres Asiatic, the self, and the world. And, as with Pirsig on his motorcycle, it was not uninformative on trout fishing either.

Other literary echoes came from the Beats—Kerouac, Ginsberg, Gary Snyder. As with Kurt Vonnegut, the stylistic signature often seemed to be the starburst simile. In one short stretch, a creek resembles "12, 485 telephone booths in a row with high Victorian ceilings and all the doors taken off and all the backs of the booths knocked out" (55). "The smell of coffee" hangs "like a spider web in the house" (61). A campsite has "a big wooden table with benches attached to it like a pair of those Benjamin Franklin glasses, the ones with those funny square lenses" (62). Similarly, one finds the Vonnegut-, Heller-, Pynchon-like Chinese-boxing of texts within texts. Interpolated narratives include a cookbook (11–12), a catalog of fishing treatises (29–30), and the trout-fishing diary of one Alonso Hagan (83–85). As with these writers also, there assembles before our eyes a spectacle of American clutter: Benjamin Franklin, Andrew Carnegie, John Dillinger, Maria Callas, Ed Sullivan, Nelson Algren, Charles Lindbergh, Ernest Hemingway, Adlai Stevenson, Deanna Durbin, Lewis and Clark; "C. C. Rider," Chubby Checker, Kool Aid, Woolworth's, Metrecal, Nixon buttons, a ukelele.

On the great landscape of American writing, we are somewhere between Huck's river and Hashbury. The perfect Trout Stream lies somewhere between a Zen version of itself and the Cleveland Wrecking Yard. It has to be here somewhere.

Trout Fishing in America, then, like many of its classic American an-
cestors, pushes what we might call "the package" toward the limits of
language itself. A narrative whim is a good pretext, origin enough for any
"concept." "Expressing a human need," the narrator tells us toward the
conclusion, "I always wanted to write a book that ended with the word
Mayonnaise" (111). This is a good concept, something almost always on
the American menu—downhome food, the latest version of Joel Barlow's
Hasty-Pudding. And sure enough, there follows the Mayonnaise chapter,
in this case another American antiepic that turns out to be a personal
communication, to "Florence and Harv" from "Mother and Nancy," a
February 3, 1952, sympathy note about "the passing of Mr. Good," with
the postscript, "Sorry I forgot to give you the mayonnaise" (112). Continuing the joke at the conclusion, one suddenly realizes, is the voice of that
great conjoiner of everyday American words and things, William Carlos
Williams. "This is just to say," the note reads, practicing American humor
in the best sense of the term, letting the air out of the drama, looking for
a laugh with the would-be consumer. And there *it* is, of course, the joke-
word at hand, having itself as the last word, on the back of the back cover.
This is just to say, in case you missed it: "Mayonnaise."

Brown, Claude. Claude Brown's 1965 *Manchild in the Promised Land,*
in the lineage of Richard Wright, Ralph Ellison, and James Baldwin, took
black autobiography into the streets of the urban ghetto with a documentary bleakness that seemed to bankrupt political or artistic visions of
human possibility. As a representation of the lives of black Americans, it
challenged the hip rhapsodizing of a Kerouac or a Mailer on the romance
of blackness. As a social document, it also confirmed the visions of social
nightmare advanced in contemporary works such as Robert Coles's *The
Children of Poverty,* Jonathan Kozol's *Death at an Early Age,* and Michael
Harrington's *The Other America.* As a text of witness, it also seemed to
mediate between the evangelical exhortation of a Martin Luther King Jr.
and the revolutionary anger of a Malcolm X or an Eldridge Cleaver.

As promised in the title, the particular history it writes is the transformation of the rural black from the backwoods of the South into the
new, Northern, urban version for rough weather (47, 122, 278–79). Along
the way, however, it becomes a chronicle of '60s struggles for black identity at large. It sketches an ideology of soul (166), the Coptic quest for an
Afrocentric vision of origin (228), its displacement in turn by the Black
Muslims (316–37) with their radical affirmation of blackness in a world
of the "white devils" (326). It records the tortured relations of black men

and black women (109, 157, 270), their common hatred of the Jew: the urban exploiter, the new "cracker" (43), "Goldberg" (284). Crime is a perfect genocide, the endless misery of black on black (330). Harlem is a place where there are no childhoods (285), where someone is old at twenty-one if he is male and alive, something like a survivor of "the plague" (355).

Most disturbingly at the last, we are served prophetic notice here of a particular American tragedy of race, poverty, and violence that continues unabated into our own decade, when today's epidemiology data now identify the leading cause of death among young black males as homicide. The witness of survivorship continues to be the distinctive legacy of life in black America. On any given day, Brown's narrator tells us, "you might see somebody get cut or killed. I could go out in the street for an afternoon, and I would see so much that, when I came in the house, I'd be talking and talking for what seemed like hours. Dad would say, 'Boy, why don't you stop that lyin'? You know you didn't see all that. You know you didn't see nobody do that.' But I knew I had" (415).

Brown, Dee. A *New York Times Book Review* (May 3, 1992) was headlined by an essay on some twenty new texts by Native American writers about Native American subjects. Over the past decade, college literary surveys have attempted serious integration of Native American materials into their texts. As to such late cultural recognitions of native peoples, surely, one assumes somewhere back in counterculture nostalgia, this must have begun to happen some time ago. Where were the texts of '60s reading and writing to this effect? The answer is that there were relatively few to speak of among the youth-scriptures of the era, save the odd graduate student copy of John G. Neihardt's *Black Elk Speaks,* Theodora Kroeber's *Ishi in Two Worlds,* Oliver Lafarge's *Laughing Boy,* perhaps Thomas Berger's cult masterpiece *Little Big Man,* or, toward the end of the decade, N. Scott Momaday's *The House Made of Dawn.* Nineteen sixty-nine marked the appearance of the first of Carlos Castaneda's chronicles of the Yaqui medicine man Don Juan, and also of Vine de Loria's indictment of Bureau of Indian Affairs policies in *Custer Died for Your Sins.* However, the first text to devote effectively to Native Americans the kind of attention achieved on behalf of American women by Friedan's *The Feminine Mystique* or black Americans by Cleaver's *Soul on Ice,* was Dee Brown's 1971 *Bury My Heart at Wounded Knee.*

To be sure, '60s youth-culture fancied itself tuned in to native cultures in a variety of ways. Varieties of ritual, magic, meditation, spiritualism, and nature-reverence fed easily into the ongoing romance of the '60s with alternative states of consciousness and nontraditional religion. People going back to the land styled themselves once again tribal and animistic, adopting the flowing hair, the jewelry, the body decoration, the holy nakedness. Here, in a set of gestures trading on yet another chapter in an egregious history of racial guilt, seemed at once the recapture of a ritual purity of relation to the world and a blow against the techno-corporate apparatus responsible for destroying so much of it.

Sixties cultural commentators rhapsodized over beads, bells, and amulets as symbolic rejections of corrupt social values, and about the quests of new communitarians for mentors instructing them in the ancient ways. Native Americans, on the other hand, seemed frequently less than enthusiastic, having considerable acquaintance, in those intervals when they were not being exterminated, with right-minded white people trying to feel virtuous by association.

Anger at such patronization would shortly boil over in de Loria's *Custer Died for Your Sins*. But as the quality of polemic in that work would reveal, political anger meant little without political history. That became the work of Brown's *Bury My Heart at Wounded Knee*. And when the job was finished, both Native American history and American history at large would never be able to see themselves *or* each other in the same ways again.

The revisionary genius of Brown's project is imaged in his choice of epigraph introducing a photo section of Indian portraits. "They made us many promises," it reads, "more than I can remember, but they never kept but one; they promised to take our land, and they took it." The speaker is noted as "an anonymous Indian." In the eyes of the speaker, "They," one suddenly understands, truly are someone else. Even as we prepare to look at "them," "They," it turns out, will here be read accusingly as "we."

This strategy of writing other presides over Brown's book from the first pages onward. The title, for instance, we discover in an epigraph, comes from a sentimental lyric entitled "American Names" by the popular twentieth-century poet, Stephen Vincent Benét. "I shall not be there," the lines read. "I shall rise and pass./Bury my heart at Wounded Knee" (4). In contrast, the subtitle supplies a quick, unsentimental corrective: "An Indian History of the American West."

So, in the introduction, Brown also speaks explicitly of the new rhetoric of alternative history that will comprise his revisionary project. It is time to talk again, Brown writes, of "the 'opening' of the American West," as it is called. Particularly, it is time to write the history of the crucial years between 1860 and 1890 out of which "came virtually all the great myths of the American West—tales of fur traders, mountain men, steamboat pilots, goldseekers, gamblers, gunmen, cavalrymen, cowboys, harlots, missionaries, schoolmarms, and homesteaders" (xi). What it really comprised *as history* was the methodical destruction of the continent's native peoples. Having memorialized, he writes, "an incredible era of violence, greed, audacity, sentimentality, undirected exuberance, and an almost reverential attitude toward the ideal personal freedom for those who already had it" (xi), we must now write at last of those who comprised the other of the mythic predication: those deemed in the interests of an advancing civilization politically unworthy of personal freedom on *their terms,* and those thereby rendered politically voiceless in any argument then or now that might have been mounted to the contrary. The time has come, he says, to recover for history the discourse of the native other.

As the narrative proper begins, Brown quickly moves to an enactment of the textual politics described. The first thing we see is a chapter title reading "Their Manners are Decorous and Praiseworthy," which turns out to derive from one of Columbus's first communications about "them" back to the king and queen of Spain who had financed his venture. Just below, we find an epigraph from Tecumseh of the Shawnees. *"Where today are the Pequot?"* he begins. *"Where are the Narragansett, the Mohican, the Pokanoket, and many other once powerful tribes of our people? They have vanished before the avarice and the oppression of the White Man, as snow before a summer sun"* (1).

Brown's own opening sentences conflate the rhetorics to redefine the vision of a familiar historical moment. "It began with Christopher Columbus," he writes,

> who gave the people the name *Indios.* Those Europeans, the white men, spoke in different dialects, and some pronounced the word *Indien,* or *Indianer,* or Indian. *Peaux-rouges,* or redskins, came later. As was the custom of the people when receiving strangers, the Tainos of the island of San Salvador generously presented Columbus and his men with gifts and treated them with honor. (1)

Already we see that we are reading "it," this thing that "began with Christopher Columbus," not in one text but two texts. The one, largely a discourse-event, so to speak, will be the familiar narrative we learned in school about Europeans trying to deal generously with strange people in a mythic place we call America. The other, a properly historical event, albeit hitherto not admitted into historical discourse, will be the unfamiliar one we learn here. And by this unmasking of official narrative, as with our other great dark crime of race—chattel slavery—we will newly learn to speak the name America and to know it again, like Ahab's *Pequod*, as a factory burning a corpse.

Tribe by tribe, region by region, year by year, name by name, we at once unlearn and newly learn it all. For context we are supplied by the author with an outline of national and world events roughly contemporaneous with those of a given installment. Often the facts are momentous, the names weighty, the figures staggering. Invariably, however, they pale before the succeeding narratives of particular destructions: "The Long Walk of the Navajos," "Little Crow's War," "Red Cloud's War," "The War to Save the Buffalo," "The War for the Black Hills," "The Last of the Apache Chiefs." Finally, they have all passed before us and gone, all the names and stories. The tribes: Sioux, Ponca, Nez Perce, Cheyenne, Arapaho, Commanche, Ute, Kiowa; and the leaders: Manuelito, Spotted Tail, Cochise, Captain Jack, Kicking Bird, Sitting Bull, Crazy Horse, Joseph, Geronimo, Dull Knife, Little Wolf. By the end only two more installments are left: "Dance of the Ghosts" and "Wounded Knee." Then it is over.

What has risen to meet us on the page is nothing less than history itself. The word newly materializes in testimonies, songs, anecdotes, eyewitness accounts, facts and figures. The slightest correction in a sense rewrites everything. We learn, for instance, that General Philip Sheridan, the great Union cavalry leader turned Indian fighter, did not really say *The only good Indian is a dead Indian.*" Rather he seems to have said, "The only good Indians I ever saw were dead" (170–72). Then we suddenly realize that the precise wording of the aphorism never mattered at all so much as the fact that such a phrasing could have become an aphorism. The point of *Bury My Heart at Wounded Knee* is just here. The business of history is to get the quotes straight, to be sure, as a matter of record, but more crucially it is a lesson of language and power, an attempt to recover for history the voices consigned to silence.

Brown, Helen Gurley. If only for the title, one suspects, Helen Gurley Brown's *Sex and the Single Girl* will always carry for many readers the aura of the quintessential early '60s item. As to the then controversial concept of women's identity it tried to promote, the title still pretty much says it all: "sex" and "the single girl." Abandoning the quasi-scientific sobriety of the Kinsey volumes on male (1948) and female (1953) sexuality, it brought the unmarried woman's sexuality out of the closet and celebrated it. On the other hand, it framed a putative discourse of sexual liberation in terms decried by feminist readers then and now as basically recapitulating the culture's traditional sexual politics. Especially demoralizing in this respect was the wedge it drove between unmarried women and their married sisters.

Cute, smirking, hush-hush; "giggly-poo," one source described it: at our remove, the sexist adjectives just seem to pile themselves on for this text by the founding editor of *Cosmopolitan.* At the same time, the publication figures tell the story: translation into twenty-three languages, an estimated readership of ten million.

Opening with a boldly punctuated challenge, "Women Alone? Oh Come Now!", the book quickly went on to describe "The Availables: The Men in Your Life," and gave instructions on "Where to Meet Them" and "How to Be Sexy." Other how-to-do-it chapters dealt with the workplace, money management, the apartment, food and drink, physical conditioning, the wardrobe, and kisses and make-up. Finally came advice on "The Affair: From Beginning to End" and a eulogy on "The Rich, Full Life."

"If you are worried about being single," the author wrote near the end, "or, more importantly, uneasy about being *you* all your life (as I was and still am), intermittent forays into dressing, cooking, looking, flirting, and flattering better can help you rout the trembles" (266–67). Further,

> you may marry or you may not. In today's world that is no longer the big question for women. Those who glom on to men so that they can collapse with relief, spend the rest of their days shining up their status symbol and figure they never have to reach, stretch, learn, grow, face dragons or make a living again are the ones to be pitied. They, in my opinion, are the unfulfilled ones.

The "rich, full life possible for the single woman today" is "a good show" Brown exhorted. "Enjoy it from wherever you are, whether it's two in the balcony or one on the aisle—don't miss *any* of it" (267).

By today's accounting, the message here is certainly mixed. One cannot deny, however, its importance as Brown's contribution to an enduring iconography of the sexually independent woman.[6] As everyone from semioticians to tennis stars seems to tell us these days, image is everything. Accordingly, in 1992, as we should not be surprised to learn, Helen Gurley Brown, author of *Sex and the Single Girl,* is still the editor of an extremely successful women's magazine called *Cosmopolitan.*

Brown, Norman O. In the lengthening memory of '60s reading and writing, Norman O. Brown retains his status as exemplary elder, an intellectual prophet with only a few other analogues—Paul Goodman, Herbert Marcuse, perhaps Alan Watts or R. D. Laing. Then and now Brown can be said to remain one of the era's true oracles. "I can recall no public event more inspiriting and electrifying at that time," writes Morris Dickstein in *The Gates of Eden,* "than Brown's vatic, impassioned Phi Beta Kappa oration at Columbia in 1960 (later published under the title, 'Apocalypse: The Place of Mystery in the Life of the Mind')" (81).

Indeed, Brown's appeal to the era is basically contained in the foregoing adjectives: "vatic" and "impassioned." In works such as *Life Against Death* and *Love's Body,* this classics professor from Wesleyan University sought nothing less than the total resacralization of Western culture and consciousness: a post-Freudian writing of civilization out of its neuroses—its sublimations, exclusions, substitutions, and evasions—and back into a new, holy relationship with the original body. As Allen Matusow writes, here was "a Freudian who reshaped the ideas of the master to provide a happy ending." (277). In the psycholinguistic coinages of "pan-sexualism, 'polymorphous perversity,' the union of many bodies," Brown wrote nothing less than a new dream of "erotic life based on the pre-Oedipal Eden" (279).

Cultural schizophrenia was what R. D. Laing would call his version of this disease of personality artificially rifted by the traditions of culture in the West. "Consciousness III" is what Charles Reich would eventually call at least one version of a cure. They both meant essentially what Brown meant in isolating the need to work out of a basic pathology and what Goodman meant in a title like *Growing Up Absurd* or Marcuse in *Eros and Civilization* or *One-Dimensional Man.* It was all the same project.[7] As with the dense, meticulous dialectics of Marcuse—whose more explicit attempts to synthesize Freud and Marx Brown's thinking often oddly approached—Brown's rhapsodic neo-Freudianism was never easy to read. Still, it was an unlikely '60s paperback collection that did not contain a copy of at least *Life Against Death.*

There, from the title on, Brown definitively stated the problem and the project: the need to confront, in Nietzsche's phrase, "the disease called man" (10), "neurosis" as "an essential consequence of civilization or culture" (10), and "the need to develop a concept of a 'normal' or a healthy culture by which to measure the neurotic cultures recorded by history" (14–15). More specifically, he went on, "in spite of two thousand years of higher education based on the notion that man is essentially a soul for mysterious accidental reasons imprisoned in a body, man remains incurably obtuse and still secretly thinks of himself as first and foremost a body" (31). Further, "all Freud's work demonstrates that the allegiance of the human psyche to the pleasure-principle is indestructible and that the path of instinctual renunciation is the path of sickness and self-destruction" (57).

It was exactly here that matters had to be brought to the present and Freud rewritten. The occasion for new work had to become this false division embodied in our conventional understandings of repression and sublimation:

> If psychoanalysis is right, we must radically change our attitude toward human culture. The concept of sublimation includes the most outrageous paradoxes, all of them asserting a connection between higher cultural activities and lower bodily regions, between adult 'rational' procedures and infantile irrational prototypes, between 'pure' mental constructs and sexuality. (134)

Accordingly, Brown goes on (much in the vein of R. D. Laing), the proper activity of therapeutic response to a mind in the shackles of culture may very well be to "blow it." Moreover, the doors to this remedy are already opened, Brown asserts, by the model of repression given us by Freud himself in *Totem and Taboo*. "The neuroses exhibit on the one hand striking and far-reaching points of agreement with . . . art, religion and philosophy," observed Freud. "But on the other hand they seem like distortions of them." Hence, "it might be maintained that a case of hysteria is a caricature of a work of art, that an obsessional neurosis is a caricature of religion and that a paranoiac delusion is a caricature of a philosophical system" (142). Accordingly, within a new, post-Freudian model, therapy can thus be nothing less than radical in a new as yet undreamed sense. The aim of psychoanalysis—still unfulfilled and still only half-conscious—is to return our souls to our bodies, to return ourselves to ourselves and thus to overcome the human state of self-alienation.

Yet to speak of the body in this way after Freud, Brown tells us, now very much in the vein of Marcuse, is also to speak of it after Marx. Accordingly, the spiritual self-alienation of consciousness must simultaneously be corrected in a new, *historically* material key as well:

> The alienated consciousness is correlative with a money economy. Its root is the compulsion to work. This compulsion to work subordinates man to things, producing at the same time, confusion in the valuation of things (*Verwertung*) and devaluation of the human body (*Entwertung*). It reduces the drives of the human being to greed and competition (aggression and possessiveness, as in the anal character). The desire for money takes the place of all genuinely human needs. Thus the apparent accumulation of wealth is really the impoverishment of human nature, and its appropriate morality is the renunciation of human nature and

desires—asceticism. The effect is to substitute an abstraction, Homo economicus, for the concrete totality of human nature, and thus to dehumanize human nature. (237)[8]

Hence, "the ultimate category of economics" at present "is power." On the other hand, power "is not" and need not be "an economic category" (251). Indeed, "if there is a class which has nothing to lose but its chains, the chains that bind it are self-imposed, sacred obligations which appear as objective realities with all the force of a neurotic delusion" (252). And "psychoanalysis" thus "takes the final step of showing the origins of the myths which sustain social power and power struggles in the repression of the human body" (252).

"Here," truly, "is the point of contact between Marx and Freud," Brown writes: "I do not see how the profundities and obscurities of the 'philosophic-economic manuscripts' can be elucidated without the aid of psychoanalysis." He goes on:

> Psychoanalysis, mysticism, poetry, the philosophy of organism, Feuerbach, and Marx—this is a miscellaneous assemblage; but, as Heraclitus said, the unseen harmony is stronger than the seen. Common to all of them is a mode of consciousness that can be called—although the term causes fresh difficulties—the dialectical imagination. By 'dialectical' I mean an activity of consciousness struggling to subvert the limitations imposed by the formal-logical law of contradiction. (318)

"Body mysticism" Brown finally called it, this new dialectical imagination that might conquer dialectic by making us newly at one with ourselves. And chief among its promises, as Brown's own text revealed, will be the liberation of language itself from "that general deflection of libido from sexual to social aims which, according to psychoanalytic theory, is sublimation and culture" (65). "The ineffability of beauty," he concludes,

> and the connection between beauty and what Valéry calls the integrity of sensuality, together constitute a measure of the repression of Eros in civilization, as well as a measure of the difference between men as they are today, with their neurotic addiction to their neurotic speech, and men as they might be if they attained their proper perfection as an animal species and recovered the power of sensual speech. (73)

What Rilke set as "the goal of mute speech, 'essentially natural speech by means of the body,'" (73) can become, Brown proposes, the new language of grace.

Here and in a succeeding '60s classic aptly entitled *Love's Body,* Brown thus envisioned a world existing somewhere at once before modern dissociations and already beyond some hyperintellectualized crisis of postmodern desire. Like so many other '60s thinkers, Brown opted for holy mystery become new magic, the ultimate vatic and impassioned text that would celebrate the great, ongoing human performance called creation.

Carson, Rachel. On any list of books that made a difference or changed the world, one will always find Rachel Carson's *Silent Spring.* To use an appropriate adjective, its appearance was nothing less than earthshaking.

At least initially however, it still strikes the reader as an unassuming performance and one continuous with a series of productions by a popular explainer of science hardly theretofore considered a controversialist. By the late 1950s, indeed, Carson had gained household respect with two companion texts, *The Sea Around Us* and *The Edge of the Sea.* The first had won the National Book Award, had been a Book-of-the-Month-Club main selection, and had been condensed by *Reader's Digest.* The second was serialized by the *New Yorker,* enjoyed large sales, and won Carson further awards from the American Association of University Women and the National Council of Women in the United States. Thus when *Silent Spring* appeared, it was greeted as the work of a revered public figure, and a voice, it turned out, that the assembled authorities of science, industry, and even government found impossible to silence.

Hence, the double significance of the rhetorical figure in the title. The obvious image is, of course, that visually and aurally rendered of a blossoming earth now in dead soundlessness.[9] Yet we also sense what the author, a woman laboring in the doubly marginalizing fields of writing and science, must have meant us to see as a deeper textual significance of the scene as well: the symbolic power of silence as an emblem of human powerlessness in the face of cosmic destiny.

One might say then that it took a certain kind of writer to give us *Silent Spring.* At the very least, it took someone who had spent a career, according to her own observations, developing a uniquely conscious sense of nonegocentric relation to the subject. One souce of this, no doubt, lay in the fact that she was a scientist, trained in effacement of the authorial self. But it went further than that. Carson knew herself also to be a *writer* of a very special sort. "The writer must not try to impose himself on his subject," she wrote, even down to the pronouns a good self-effacing soldier of standard usage.

He must not try to mold it according to what he believes his readers or editors want to read. His initial task is to come to know his subject intimately, to understand its every aspect, to fill his mind. Then at some turning point the subject takes command and the true act of creation begins ... The discipline of the writer is to learn to be still and listen to what his subject has to tell him. (2)

One is tempted to read such figures of self-negation, submissiveness, even silence, as stereotypical feminine categories. But one must also note how they here facilitate images of replenishment and new creation. Expressing itself with new authority is the relational consciousness of a scientist who also happens to be a woman and vice versa. The object of science, as of writing, is too often to make the other into the same. Here is offered a feminist correlative for addressing same exactly from the perspective of other.

So, in *Silent Spring,* from the first page on, we are chilled by the new vision of the greatest of all our familiars: nature itself, now defamiliarized and void, a cosmic allegory of death made everyday. "The most alarming of all man's assaults upon the environment," Carson asserts,

is the contamination of air, earth, rivers, and sea with dangerous and even lethal materials. This pollution is for the most part irrecoverable; the chain of evil it initiates not only in the world that must support life but in living tissues is for the most part irreversible. In this now universal contamination of the environment, chemicals are the sinister and little-recognized partners of radiation in changing the very nature of the world—the very nature of its life. (6)

Now we literally shower ourselves, she continues, with chemical "elixirs of death" and insecticides especially, in full confidence of our ability to stage-manage these and all our other manipulations in what we take to be "natural" control. In fact, she warns, "in the less than two decades of their use, the synthetic pesticides have been so thoroughly distributed throughout the animate and inanimate world that they occur virtually everywhere" (15).

The remainder of the book comprises the anatomy of death that may already become the planet's autopsy: through water, soil, and air; among birds, fish, other animals, and plants—through all the animal and plant products consumed by humans. In everything, she notes, even now we have passed "beyond the dreams of the Borgias." Already, we pay "The

Human Price," in cancer especially, not to mention the grim mutations whereby "Nature Fights Back" in strange extinctions and proliferations.

There is still a chance, however, she proposes at the end, to take "the other road." What it will cost, however, as with so many other '60s prophetic postmodernists, is as startling as it is simple: the revolutionary redefinition of knowledge in the West, the faith in the unholy triad of reason, science, and nature that has led us to our dreadful hubris in the face of cosmic mystery. "The 'control of nature' is a phrase conceived in arrogance," she says in a final paragraph,

> born of the Neanderthal age of biology and philosophy, when it was supposed that nature exists for the convenience of man. The concepts and practices of applied entomology for the most part date from that Stone Age of science. It is our alarming misfortune that so primitive a science has armed itself with the most modern and terrible weapons, and that in turning them against its insects it has also turned them against the earth. (297)

We now know all this to be true. At the time, however, it was largely indicted as fantasy and Carson labeled, naturally—with emphasis on the gendered adjective—a hysterical doomsayer. Rebuttals were mounted by agencies and lobbying groups. A public health scholar at Harvard described her work as "baloney." Another from Vanderbilt said, "this book should be ignored" (296).

Indeed, it is difficult now to recreate the virulence of reaction, the extent of its hostility, ridicule, and aggressive vengefulness. Parodies were written. *Time* magazine featured the author in a dismissive cover article. *Reader's Digest* this time elected not to publish anything from the book but rather an abridgment of the *Time* story.

What had Carson done? In a word, she had taken on the real "system." Chemical pesticide producers, whose products she indicted, were a very small albeit lucrative segment of American industry. The Department of Agriculture, whose policies and dicta she declared disastrously uninformed, was hardly Defense, Justice, or the Treasury. Together, however, they comprised a node in a massive network of industrial-bureaucratic affiliations. And when one strongpoint was attacked, the whole apparatus responded.

In this instance, of course, the system failed, and a bravely imaginative scientist was vindicated. Environmental awareness and protection activities were launched on a scale previously inconceivable. Today we may seem to make minor progress against a spectacle of planetary devastation. What we must remember, however, is that before Rachel Carson, there was virtually nothing. People engaged in traditional conservationism, plant and wildlife management, agricultural science, and public health data collection. *Silent Spring* literally made ecological science global.

We often use the word prophetic too easily. At most we describe texts that inspire future belief. Here was a text that literally dictated the future by being simply and irrefutably true.

The bravery and genius of Carson's achievement in *Silent Spring* are still perhaps best imaged in a Charles Schulz cartoon of the period. There, Lucy Van Pelt is chided for her frequent invocations of Rachel Carson. "Girls need heroes too," she declaims in response. The cartoon, even down to the available linguistic conventions, remained like Rachel Carson a product of its times. The language would change as the needs of sense-making changed. What counted for the moment was the challenge of the scientific imagination to public discourse. There, already, *Silent Spring* had become part of us all.

Castaneda, Carlos. Of major cult-fantasists—Tolkien, Hesse, Vonnegut, Castaneda—the last had for the youth audience of the '60s and early '70s the special appeal of the contemporary. Best known as the author of a trilogy including *The Teachings of Don Juan, A Separate Reality,* and *Journey to Ixtlan,* Castaneda had begun his career as a '60s graduate student at Berkeley, pursuing doctoral studies in anthropology. Moreover, his work seemed to conflate a number of topics of timely interest. Devotees of fantasy and of chronicles of the spiritual quest relished a narrator's recounting of adventures in the ritual world of an elderly Yaqui *brujo,* or sorcerer/medicine man, Don Juan, and particularly the magical new possibilities of experience afforded through the latter's instructions in the use of native hallucinogens. Moreover, for '60s academics, Castaneda's work, published first by the University of California Press, also carried the cachet of the new human sciences, of poststructuralist issues of language, power, and knowledge, and of theories of alternative consciousness increasingly catching on with American intellectuals from the mid '60s onward.[10] Here seemed cultural anthropology as creative statement on the postmodern cutting edge.

At the same time, the style of narration was breathlessly diaristic and the compelling presence of the central figure almost irresistible. The *brujo* was at once real-life cultural shaman, amalgam of "medicine man, curer, witch, sorcerer" and also *"diablero"* or daimon-wizard enlisting the dark magic of the universe. Lending further interest and authority to the experience of the text was the quite specific attention given to three hallucinogenic plants in conjunction with the magic described. These included "peyote (*Lophophora williamsii*), Jimson weed (*Datura inoxia* syn. D. *meteloides,*) and a mushroom (possibly *Psilocybe mexicana*)" (21).

Within each pairing of hypnotic narration and sober "structural analysis," the reader too might venture upon the "nonordinary reality" (47) that is the ground of the "ally," the "power capable of carrying a man beyond the boundaries of himself" (45), which "takes you out to give you power" (53). But the path is perilous and crowded with enemies: "fear" or self-doubt (79); "clarity," or lack of self-doubt, which often blinds (80); "power" itself (81); and "old age" (83).

Still, at the end of the "Yaqui way" may lie great reward: relief from alienation between the self and the other and entry into "the world of happiness where there is no difference between things because there is no one there to ask the difference" (153). "The particular thing to learn," the wizard tells us near the end of the first narrative, "is how to get to the crack between the worlds and how to enter the other world." He continues:

> There is a crack between the two worlds, the world of the *diableros* and the world of living men. There is a place where the two worlds overlap. The crack is there. It opens and closes like a door in the wind. To get there a man must exercise his will. He must, I should say, develop an indomitable desire for it, a single minded dedication. But he must do it without the help of any power or any man. The man by himself must ponder and wish up to a moment in which his body is ready to undergo the journey. That moment is announced by prolonged shaking of the limbs and violent vomiting. The man usually cannot sleep or eat, and wanes away. When the convulsions do not stop the man is ready to go, and the crack between the worlds appears right in front of his eyes, like a monumental door, a crack that goes up and down. When the crack opens, a man has to slide through it. (185)

At the climax of the decade of Tolkien, Vonnegut, Leary, and Hesse, not to mention LSD, TM, est, and a host of other '60s preoccupations with alternative structures of consciousness, Castaneda had come up with a total package. And as the new decade began, new concerns of ethnicity focused on both Native and Hispanic American cultures gave his works even further political appeal.[11] From the initial trilogy on, new titles—

Tales of Power, The Second Ring of Power, The Eagle's Gift, The Fire from Within, and *The Power of Silence*—extended the cultural fiction, even as Castaneda's research claims were increasingly called into doubt.[12]

The body of Castaneda's work assumed a life of its own, at once mythic and material. Simon and Schuster became its hardbound publishers, and Pocket Books developed a uniform paperback series that has remained consistently in print. Into text and world, the crack stays open. With each new title and cover design in the latest desert hyperrealism, the separate reality offered by Castaneda thus remains one of the era's total bibliographic triumphs, the tale of power purveyed as the purest material reification.

Cleaver, Eldridge. Most of the voices of '6os black America were known better for their speaking than for their writing. This included authors such as Martin Luther King Jr. and the Malcolm X of the *Autobiography,* as well as such media celebrities as Bobby Seale, Stokely Carmichael, and H. Rap Brown.[13] Then upon the scene suddenly appeared what would become one of the most ubiquitous texts of the late '6os, a collection of writings by a black California convict, Eldridge Cleaver, entitled *Soul on Ice.* And *how* this happened was itself a vivid lesson not only in the evolution of '6os racial awareness but also in the history of a production now increasingly known as the '6os text.

The property in question here was an eclectic blend of spiritual autobiography and sociopolitical meditation by a self-taught criminal-intellectual-revolutionary who had spent the better part of his life in prison, first on marijuana possession charges and then later for rape. The trail of discovery had led from *Ramparts* magazine to a hardbound contract with McGraw-Hill and then shortly into a bestselling Dell paperback,[14] complete with a laudatory introduction by the venerable American critic Maxwell Geismar. The latter, noting the risk of "excessive praise," gave it anyway. He described Cleaver as "simply one of the best cultural critics now writing." "And I include in this statement," he went on, "both the formal sociologists and those contemporary fictionists who have mainly abandoned this province of literature in the cultivation of the cult of sensibility" (9–10).

In the crossing of constituencies so described was the secret of the success. In genre, theme, and topic, there was something for nearly everybody: memoir, novel, essay, and manifesto; treatise on race, sexuality, politics, and economics. There was an indictment of the legal and penal systems, of sexuality as an instrument of oppression dividing both male and female and black and white, of the impotence of national government to solve social problems at home, of the racist murder being perpetrated abroad in Vietnam. With a kind of guilty pleasure, white liberal culture got to feast on observations of their own fatuity by a professional "Ofay watcher" (69); on the other hand, the young especially were praised for their brave new revolutionary alliances with black Americans and other people of color the world round. Here finally, Cleaver asserted, was "a generation of white youth that is truly worthy of a black man's respect" (84). And so too, in a moving conclusion, Malcolm X was eulogized for his final bravery of acceptance, the renunciation of a politics of hate described eloquently by Cleaver as "the true white man's burden" (65).

Coupled with the text's other rhetorical appeals was its appearance in the form of that properly revolutionary genre, the prison-letter. Cleaver was a real prisoner at real war with the real system and in the same moment writing with a serious literary-intellectual provenance. Dean Moriarity was a jailkid, just as Randall McMurphy was the eternal prisoner-inmate. Thoreau had written *Civil Disobedience* in response to going to jail. Gandhi also wrote most powerfully from there, as did Martin Luther King Jr. (Unfortunately, of course, so did Hitler.) Modernist classics heroicizing the political prisoner abounded, ranging from Kafka's *The Trial* and Koestler's *Darkness at Noon* to Ellison's *Invisible Man*.[15] Prominent white counterculture figures such as Timothy Leary and Abbie Hoffman would also be at pains to publish prison writings. And shortly, *Soledad Brother: The Prison Letters of George Jackson*—edited by Cleaver's own revolutionary attorney-lover, Beverly Axelrod—would bring Jackson the criminal sainthood that Cleaver would deny himself through a series of postprison histrionics including Algerian exile, hip entrepeneurship, and born-again Christianity.

Discussed most fervently at the time, however, was the work's claim to a new politics of racial consciousness based on original sociocultural analysis: its status, that is, as a serious *structural* critique of conventional structures of such consciousness. The argument was dense with revolutionary pronouncement and studded with new ideological coinages. General readers were shocked by the author's identification of himself as a rapist, apprenticing, by his own admission, with women of his own race, and then graduating to white women as a vocational speciality. Good revolutionaries, on the other hand, suddenly saw the idea of rape transmogrified into a more generalized politics of oppression, related to a myth of white womanhood—here called "the Ogre"—and the "sickness" of desire for her visited upon the black man as at once sexual temptation and signifier of cultural impotence. By this logic, it became possible for Cleaver, he confesses, to assert "rape" as "an insurrectionary act," a "defying and trampling upon the white man's law, upon his system of values" (26) as well as additionally expiating "the historical fact of how the white man has used the black woman" (27).

Yet this was also a blind turning, he now admitted, the symptom of deeper hatreds of sex *and* race that propel the cycle of victimization. Now writing expiates those hatreds at last (27), breaks the deadly cycle, and pays the price of "loving oneself less" (29).

The story is a long one, beginning in what Cleaver calls "The Allegory of Black Eunuchs": "The myth of the strong black woman" that "is the other side of the coin of the myth of the beautiful dumb blonde." There follows "The Primeval Mitosis": the division of the male into "The Omnipotent Administrator" (the white male power structure) and "The Supermasculine Menial": the division of the female into "The *Ultrafeminine*"—"the elite woman"—and "The *Subfeminine*"—"the woman below" (167). From these divisions soon follow the relationships of desire *and* the administrations of control. The Supermasculine Menial, fearing homosexual castration, is brought as "psychic bridegroom" (170) to his "dream girl" (172), the Ultrafeminine in her role as "Ogre of Frigidity" (170). The Subfeminine, relegated to the household domestic, despises the Supermasculine Menial as prisoner of white-inculcated desire. Meanwhile, "the Omnipotent Administrator," by "usurping the Supermasculine Menial's mind," enjoys "all sovereignty"; and further, "because of his monopoly on sovereignty, he is the psychic bridegroom of the Amazon. In another sense, however, being also attracted to the body of the Supermasculine Menial, the Amazon is lost between two worlds" (173).

The problem all seems properly dialectical and deeply theorized. And so does the outline of a solution, in a next-to-final chapter entitled "Convalescence," which proposes that a society managing to cleanse itself sexually from the demon of class will also cleanse itself sexually from the demon of race, and vice versa. Thus, as with so much '60s thinking and writing: as we have struggled into the self-imprisonment of a false dialectics, we may now begin to write the better one of a redemptory reunification.

At the end, the Lazarus who has written this text of the death of soul begins to arise. In a final letter entitled "To All Black Women From All Black Men," he writes, "I, the Black Eunuch, divested of my Balls, walked the earth with my mind locked in Cold Storage" (191). But now, he goes on, it is time to reassume the original energy of the race, to break the old dialectics of systematic exploitation, black and white, male and female, by embracing creation at the source: "put on your crown, my Queen," he exhorts, "and we will build a New City on these ruins" (192).

With the invocation of Eliot's *The Waste Land,* Cleaver put a concluding literary signature on an eclectic, often obscurantist pastiche of textual meditations. Like the rewritings of Freud and Marx by Goodman, Brown, Marcuse, and others, it seemed at once alternative history and world-historical critique. At the same time, it also proved of considerable appeal to new revolutionary constituencies of late '60s youth—black militants, radical feminists, and rising postcolonialists espousing everything from global Maoist insurrection to various other Third World internationalisms. Of particular significance to them all was Cleaver's identification of the historical common enemy: a class-bound, patriarchal, deeply Western hegenomics of power, in which anyone not white and male seemed condemned to endless cycles of repression and exploitation.

To be sure, Cleaver remained controversial among many of the same constituencies. Women rejected the political rationalizations of rape as well as the constructions of women white *and* black as racist and sexist caricatures of long cultural standing. The white liberal intelligentsia found hard to stomach Cleaver's insistence on their need to luxuriate in unlimited historical guilt. Youth on the other hand, from the title onward, took *Soul on Ice* as a kind of total ideological product, at once revolutionary icon and exposition of a collective plight. These were prison-letters in a new key: written from someone in the big house, published under the gaze of the keepers, and addressed to all the other inmates. For '60s readers, Cleaver's definition of soul enlarged to become a message to every other enchained spirit in the prison-house called America.

Dillard, Annie. One opens any reading of Annie Dillard's *Pilgrim at Tinker Creek* with a cliché of origin that the author openly invites. As Thoreau authorizes the alternative spirit of so much of '60s thought and writing, so Dillard's early '70s classic explicitly reauthorizes the Thoreau of *Walden* in a new key of difference decidedly her own. The secret is even in the titles: *Walden, Pilgrim at Tinker Creek.* Here is not the transcendental confidence of the unitary term, the self that is a world and the world that is a self. Here it is always self and other. Of our daily apprehensions of the world, Dillard writes, "something pummels us, something barely sheathed. Power broods and lights. We're played on like a pipe; our breath is not our own" (13).

That other, moreover, is here distinctly sexual. The book in fact opens and closes with the same bedroom scene. On a hot summer's night, the narrator sleeps by an open window. She is awakened by a cat of hers, "an old fighting tom," she calls him, "stinking of urine and blood." "Some nights he kneaded my bare chest with his front paws, powerfully, arching his back, as if sharpening his claws, or pummelling a mother for milk," she writes. "And some mornings I'd wake in daylight to find my body covered with paw prints in blood; I looked as though I'd been painted with roses" (1). "What blood was this," she asks, "and what roses? It could have been the rose of union, the blood of murder, or the rose of beauty bare and the blood of some unspeakable sacrifice or birth" (1–2).

Nature, in *Pilgrim at Tinker Creek,* is always a sexual assault, a ravishing scene in which we are at once astonished interpreters and erotic participants. Moreover, it is in this programmed otherness of our being that we most keenly bear the blood stigmata of our loss. "It is ironic," Dillard writes, "that the one thing all religions recognize as separating us from our creator—our very self-consciousness—is also the one thing that divides us from our fellow creatures. It was a bitter birthday present from evolution, cutting us off at both ends" (80). "Illumination," she writes, "comes to those who wait for it," but "it is always, even to the most practiced and adept, a gift and a total surprise" (34–35). On the other hand, "experiencing the present purely" is equally "being emptied and hollow; you catch grace as a man fills his cup under a waterfall" (82).

At best, nature is a Heisenbergian tease, a hopped-up blur of variety. "Look, in short, at practically anything," she writes, "—the coot's feet, the mantis's face, a banana, the human ear—and see that not only did the creator create everything, but that he is apt to create *anything.* He'll stop at nothing" (139). "The creator," she gloriously concludes, "loves pizazz" (140). And so, she asserts shortly, "what stands revealed" most frequently "is the Chesire cat's grin" (206). "The electron is a muskrat," she continues; "it cannot be perfectly stalked. And nature is a fan dancer born with a fan; you can wrestle her down, throw her on the stage and grapple with her for the fan with all your might, but it will never quit her grip. She comes that way; the fan is attached" (207).

At worst, it is a love song gone bad, an "unholy revulsion" (65). "Fish gotta swim and birds gotta fly," writes Dillard with a hard disingenuousness about nature's fecund couplings and destructions: "insects, it seems gotta do one horrible thing after another. I never ask why of a vulture or a shark, but I ask why of nearly every insect I see" (65).

"What makes Iago evil, some people ask," writes Joan Didion's Maria Wyeth. "I never ask" (Play 1). Dillard brings even this shiver of cold acceptance down to closer range. "I love the wild not less than the good"

(140), pronounced Thoreau. "Chomp or fast" Dillard notes in sterner echo of brutal acknowledgement. It is the same nature. Still, one rewrites the other.

Out of the search for transcendental harmony arises a new celebration of the rank, chaotic rifeness of difference. "There is more day to dawn," writes Thoreau in his last sentences. "The sun is but a morning star." They are justly celebrated because they are so exact a concluding conceit. In Dillard, instead, we discover something even beyond the seamless transcendental figure, a true erotics of epiphany. "I used to have a cat, an old fighting tom, who sprang through the open window by my bed and pummelled my chest, barely sheathing his claws," Dillard begins anew at the end; and, once again, as before, she *goes on* in every sense of the phrase:

> I've been bloodied and mauled, wrung, dazzled, drawn. I taste salt on my lips in the early morning; I surprise my eyes in the mirror and they are ashes, or fiery sprouts, and I gape appalled, full of breath. The planet whirls alone and dreaming. Power broods, spins and lurches down. The planet and power meet with a shock. They fuse and tumble, lightning, ground fire; they part, mute, submitting, and touch again with hiss and cry. The tree with the lights in it buzzes into flame and the cast-rock mountains ring. (278)

With his new morning, the sage of Walden invites us into the beautiful, deeply aesthetic silence of metaphysical closing and departure. With hers, the Pilgrim at Tinker Creek records but the hubbub and clangor of the latest ecstatic awakening.

Fanon, Frantz. For youth-readers of the '60s, Frantz Fanon emerged late in the decade as the era's great theorist and prophet of what we would now call Third World postcolonialism. The text by which Fanon came mainly to be known to American audiences, *The Wretched of the Earth,* although published in France in 1961 and again in 1963, did not appear in a Grove Press English edition until 1966. (A translation followed of an earlier work, *Black Faces, White Masks,* and also a posthumous collection entitled *The Revolutionary Thought of Frantz Fanon.*)

Anecdotally, at least, one can assert the emergence of *The Wretched of the Earth* in the youth-culture of the era as a topic of conversation.[16] One suspects for a number of reasons, however, that it may have been more talked about than read. Unlike the pronouncements of other favorite oracles of international revolution such as Mao Tse-tung or Che Guevara, for instance, *The Wretched of the Earth* does not break itself down into easily exportable "sayings." It is a meticulous, systematic analysis of the origins and justification of revolutionary violence as a weapon against colonial oppression. It is also a handbook on revolutionary development; a discourse on method, planning, and organization; and a set of injunctions against new postrevolutionary forms of political self-betrayal, cults of leadership, false nationalism, and tribal nostalgia. In sum, it is a very dense readerly undertaking, then or now, a brilliant psychiatrist's foray into complicated social analysis and political argument. Moreover, although speaking to the plight of Third World peoples around the globe—it suggests early on, for instance, that a victory such as that of the Viet Minh over the French at Dien Bien Phu is a victory of one colonialized people for the sake of all colonialized peoples—its focal emphasis is on the rise of postcolonial revolution in Africa in general and on the Algerian struggle for national liberation against the French in particular.

Similarly, the work may identify the United States as a patron of post-colonial capitalist hegemony, urging its European counterparts "to decolonise in friendly fashion" (62); and it may also note the increasing legitimation of revolutionary violence within an American domestic politics of race. For the most part, however, the colonialist-imperialist other in the text is clearly identified as European, with the particular example of horror being as noted above, that of France in Algeria during the late 1950s and early 1960s.

Why, then, did *The Wretched of the Earth,* upon its Grove Press appearance, become such an American item? For one thing, in gloss and imprimatur, it bore a lengthy preface by Jean Paul Sartre, by 1966 one of the most visible international critics of U.S. policy in Vietnam. "We find our humanity on this side of death and despair," he writes; Fanon, on the other hand, "finds it beyond torture and death. We have sown the wind; he is the whirlwind. The child of violence, at every moment he draws from it his humanity. We were men at his expense, he makes himself man at ours: a different man, of higher quality" (20). By pointing "the way forward," Sartre argues, Fanon "has gained his end" as far as we are concerned: "when we have closed the book, the argument continues within us, in spite of its author; for we feel the strength of the peoples in revolt and we answer by force. Thus there is a fresh moment of violence; and this time we ourselves are involved, for by its nature this violence is changing us, accordingly as the 'half-native' is changed" (20).

Here, then, lay a text of postcolonial revolution conceived as global political action. But most compelling for U.S. readers involved in the often Manichean politics of anti–Vietnam War struggle was Fanon's new idea of

Third World liberation, of the possibility of people's revolutions defining themselves independently of both an international capitalism and an international socialism (albeit availing themselves, nonetheless, of many of the latter's postcapitalist aims). For exactly this reason, it gave American critics of U.S. colonialism abroad and racism at home a new choice. Passionate support for wars of national liberation around the globe became possible without the totalizing embrace of international socialism. Or, as Fanon himself enjoined, one might seek socialism but not communism, communalism but not collectivism. One might equally seek liberationism but not by simple displacement to some other, localized African-ism, Negro-ism, or Arab-ism.

For those involved in the programmatics of revolution, *The Wretched of the Earth* also translated this spirit of eclectic opportunism into a thoroughgoing emphasis on utility. It offered a handbook of revolutionary practice *and* social reorganization even down to the headings of its major argumentative sections: "Concerning Violence," "Spontaneity: Its Strength and Weakness," "The Pitfalls of National Consciousness," "On National Culture."

Given the global heft of the arguments developed in these sections, one responds with some surprise, therefore, to a concluding chapter. A set of case studies centered on the topic of "Colonial Wars and Mental Disorders," it may strike us as appropriate for a psychiatrist but somewhat off the point. Then we see exactly the point. The chief patient is culture itself; the global state of things is itself a madness. America, especially, apes its own early imperial masters: here "the taints, the sickness and the inhumanity of Europe have grown to appalling dimensions" (253). Here has come indeed "a permanent dialogue with oneself and an increasingly obscene narcissism" (253).

The predicament of the colonial has always been, "In reality, who am I?" (203). This is now the predicament of people around the world. A new dialectic of self and other must begin that moves beyond the tired old dialectics of ideological conflict. A Third World rises now to speak with the new authority of the other and marches forward to "try to set afoot a new man" (255).

Fariña, Richard. A somber editor's note prefacing the paperback edition of Richard Fariña's *Been Down So Long It Looks Like Up to Me* attempted to parlay the tragic reciprocity of art and life into instant '60s hagiolatry. "On the night of April 30, 1966, returning from a party celebrating the hardcover publication of his book, Richard Fariña was thrown from the back of a motorcycle and killed. It is our great loss that so vital and authentic a voice has been stilled forever. Mr. Fariña was 29."

It was all too mythic to be true: the creator of Gnossos Pappadopoulis, killed in a motorcycle accident on his way home from a party; the Cornell campus legend, husband of Mimi Baez, friend of Thomas Pynchon, dead before he was thirty.

Fariña's text, on the other hand, has proved a good deal less securely enshrineable. Once it seemed a truly original portrait of the artist as campus iconoclast and madman-saint, complete with an attendant panoply of zanies, drugheads, rich-kid proselytes, shadowed confederates, and assorted other bizarre academic types: the sinister Dean Magnolia; the unattainable Kristin McCleod; Mojo, Motherball, Pamela Watson-May; the Buddha, Aquavitus, Heffalump, Fitzgore, Heap; Juan Carlos Rosenbloom, Judy Lumpers, Calvin Blacknesse, G. Alonso Oeuf, George and Irma Rajamuttu. Likewise irresistible, from the first breathless rush on, seemed its dubious, paranoiac plot: the return to academe of Gnossos Pappadopoulis "from the asphalt seas of the great wasted land;" visits of occult figures from a shadowed past; the swirl of sex and politics in the local academy; the dark Monkey Demon menacing Gnossos at every hallucinatory turn. Such becomes the network of intrigue and counterintrigue that finally comprises the novel's strange allegorical plot, somehow stretching from idyllic campus precincts into the far reaches of international conspiracy and back.

"To Athené then." So begins Gnossos's progress, liberally laced with booze and drugs, through the uptight late '50s and early '60s. And, like much popular fiction of the era, it now seems at once part *Odyssey* and part A. A. Milne; part visionary quest and part hipster comic book; part revolution and part panty raid. It covers the whole terrain: the student scene, the faculty and administration scene, the sex scene, the race scene, even, for a moment in pre-Castroite Cuba where the book turns serious with suddenly mortal consequences, the Third World revolution scene. And it does so with what still strikes the reader as immense original energy: the bizarre erudition, the queer verbal fecundity, the mockings and invocations piling all over each other in manic plenitude. "See me loud with lies, big boots stomping, mind awash with schemes," brags the Whitmanesque hero. "Home to Athené, where Penelope has lain in an exalted ecstasy of infidelity, where Telemachus hates his father and aims a kick at his groin, where old patient Argus trots out to greet his weary returning master and drives his fangs into a cramped leg, infecting with the froth of some feral, hydrophobic horror" (17). "Oh, welcome," he declaims:

for home is the madman,
home from his dreams
and the satyr
home to make hay. (17)

There is the legend of Gnossos's miraculous escape:

No one has seen him (or if they have, there has been no acceptance of the impossible sight, for rumors have him dead of thirst, contorted on his back at the bottom of Bright Angel Trail, eyes gnawed out by wild Grand Canyon burros; fallen upon by tatooed pachucos and burned to death in the New Mexico night by a thousand cigarettes dipped in aqua regia; eaten by a shark in San Francisco Bay, a leg washed up in Venice West; G. Alonzo Oeuf has him frozen blue in the Adirondacks), he stumbles back from its lakes now (found sitting on a bed of tender spruce boughs, his legs folded under him in the full lotus, a mysterious caste mark where his third eye would be, stark naked with an erection, discovered by the St. Regis Falls D.A.R. out on their winter bird walk). (17–18)

And likewise, in present consciousness, there is the teeming energy of his own inspired dementia:

I am invisible, he thinks often. And Exempt. Immunity has been granted to me, for I do not lose my cool. Polarity is selected at will, for I am not ionized and I possess not valence. Call me inert and featureless but Beware, I am the Shadow, free to cloud men's minds. Who knows what evil lurks in the hearts of men? I am the Dracula, look into my eye. (18)

At the same time, much of the business now increasingly strikes us as minor '60s literary collage. Both the totally Beat title—"been down so long it looks like up to me"—and the quote attributed to Benjamin Franklin serving as the book's epigraph ("I must soon quit the Scene") strike us as heavy with the posturing of doomed prescience. And so, all the way from his fondness for alcohol and other controlled substances to a set of decidedly primitive attitudes toward women, the protagonist remains all too visibly Kerouac- or Kesey-like in his basic construction for anyone's good. Indeed, like Heller's Yossarian, Gnossos Pappadopoulis's chief source of heroism throughout the novel seems to lie chiefly in his capacity to *make scenes*. "'I am King fucking MONTEZUMA, that's who,'" he screams at a cashier rejecting one of his treasured silver dollars as payment for three Red Cap ales, "'and *this* is the coin of my kingdom. . . . And if you fail to honor the symbol of my realm, I will have your heart torn out, right?! OUT OUT OUT of your body.' She gasped. 'At the top of a pyramid.' She reeled. 'And I will eat it RAW!' " (32).

As to particular literary impersonations, the author has found several other too easily identifiable idols as well. Pynchon, for instance, is so completely there—the names; the whacked-out plots; the strangely adolescent jocularity; the fondness for the literary sideswipe, the verbal riff, the mock-epic cataloging and itemization—that one occasionally flashes on the truly paranoiac suggestion that perhaps Fariña is Pynchon or vice versa. On occasion, one can nearly say the same of the John Barth of *The Floating Opera* and *The End of the Road,* not to mention a picaresque sendup of truly original genius, published just a few years earlier, entitled *The Sot-Weed Factor.* More perniciously, the author has also surely embraced the J. P. Donleavy of *The Ginger Man.* Adoring Sebastian Dangerfield mimicries abound in the stage directions, the smirking double takes, the ditty chapter endings, the lyric fadeouts. Fariña's protagonist has even mastered the Donleavy Pukka put-on, not to mention the swinish habits of seduction: "Ian Evergood"; "Mountbatten blood in the family"; "Smashing tea this. Pamela what?"

Meanwhile, the indescribable, paranoiac plot unfolds. Amidst mysterious returns and congruencies, Paps attempts to outrace the past by seeking his own manic version of a total present. Along the way, in Cuba, losing a friend to death, he instead finds the revolutionary future. And back home, things have come to a rather nasty impasse as well. Dean Magnolia has managed to engineer a vacuum of power into a campus takeover. In the process, as trumpeted in a marriage announcement, he has also claimed the sorority princess Kristin McCleod as his consort. Her nasty little wedding gift from Gnossos turns out to be a heroin suppository up the ass. His nasty little wedding gift from the Dean turns out to be a military induction notice. In strange '60s prophecy, the fun sours in uniquely vicious ways. The Revolution fails. The System wins. The Movement Hero falls back on an old misogyny, a casual way with drugs, and the latest race with the draft board. In a larger sense, it is also capsule history in a way that the author, could he have outlived the '60s, would have surely recognized. "This book comes on like the Hallelujah Chorus done by 200 kazoo players with perfect pitch," exclaimed Fariña's old friend Pynchon in an ecstatic cover blurb at the time. "I mean strong, swinging, skillful and irreverent—but also with the fine brassy buzz of irreverence in there too. Fariña has going for him an unerring and virtuoso instinct about exactly what, in this bewildering Republic, is serious, and what cannot possibly be." So, the cult figure soon to publish his own attempt at the '60s hip-classic, *The Crying of Lot 49,* applauded the creator of Gnossos Pappadopoulis. Meanwhile, in spite of both Fariña's and Pynchon's best efforts, Gnossos and his book would quickly get old. The artist-iconoclast would shortly come to be seen as the latest case of arrested development, the prodigy of the revolution as campus clod.

Ferlinghetti, Lawrence. As a beat insider, Lawrence Ferlinghetti became a key figure in the San Francisco literary scene. The owner of the City Lights Bookshop in North Beach, he became publisher of a poetry series devised as a serious countercultural alternative to the dictations of the academy and the eastern literary establishment. Most importantly, in the latter role he would also become the publisher of Allen Ginsberg's *Howl,* engineering a legal and literary scandal whereby the Beats would shortly become a new force in mainstream literary production. As an author, on the other hand, Ferlinghetti will always, one suspects, be remembered as much for a poster as for his poetry. Among '60s wall decorations, the blownup cover photo from the New Directions *Coney Island of the Mind* was virtually ubiquitous. As to the poems, most people remember a handful, perhaps just one. That poem, on the other hand, one truly remembers. For it was a poem that really seemed to say it all, whatever "it" happened to be at the time. For the initiate, the bottom line in a Ferlinghetti poem became the gift of identification: a slogan, a motto, a creed.

A classic production, for instance, appeared in a much favored section of the book entitled "Pictures of the Gone World." "The world is a beautiful place/to be born into," it begins,

> if you don't mind happiness
> not always being so very much fun
> if you don't mind a touch of hell
> now and then
> just when everything is fine
> because even in heaven
> they don't sing
> all the time. (88)

Never mind, it goes on, the "dying" and "starving," "dead minds," "a bomb or two," "our Name Brand society,"

> its men of distinction
> and its men of extinction

and its priests
and other patrolmen
and its various segregations
and congressional investigations
and other constipations
that our fool flesh is heir to. (89)

Perhaps, one may object, there are also better things—

making the fun scene
and making the love scene
and singing low songs and having inspirations
and walking around
looking at everything
and smelling flowers
and goosing statues
and even thinking. (89)

"Yes," perhaps, the poet concludes,

but then right in the middle of it
comes the smiling
mortician. (89)

Thematically, the poem is pure Ferlinghetti, a masterpiece of chastened resignation. Who was the smiling mortician. Death? God? Nixon? Billy Graham? A cop? The Dean? Your father?

Here also, literarily and philosophically, as in all Ferlinghetti's work, honor was given to worthies of a new hip curriculum. Favored name-droppings included Goya, Blake, Keats, Christ, Saint Francis, Buddha, Dante, Kafka, Yeats, Chagall, Brancusi, Emmett Kelly, Picasso, and Praxiteles. Allusion was heavy with doomed irreverence: "HORSEMAN, PASS BY!"; "In God We Trust;" "SPITTING IS FORBIDDEN." The studied lack of mechanical correctness, the jazzy line placement, the spontaneous, just-off-the-typewriter look of the page, attempted, as with Kerouac, Ginsberg, and other Beats, to make print a conduit for spontaneous performance.

Thus paperback poetry could be for the people and still supply the needs of the spiritual cognoscenti. The experiment—a kind of counterculture version of cultural literacy—was a success. Successive printings mounted into the hundreds of thousands. Accompanying blurbs made no apology. "It is easy to understand Lawrence Ferlinghetti's popularity," confided his publishers: "his material, his tone, and phrasing, are taken from everyday life, from the 'Coney Island' of ideas and feelings in all our minds, and he transmutes them into poetry of satiric bite and lyric beauty." Here, at the intersection of art and commerce, poetry created its new ground of celebration.

Friedan, Betty. *The Feminine Mystique* certainly sounded like the title of one of "those" women's books, 1963 readers must have thought. Their credulity was quickly dispelled. Apace, so was nearly everyone's conception of women's writing in America.[17] Friedan's title, like her text, began by precisely constructing the icon it proposed to rewrite; and it used that construction to drive a feminist wedge at exactly the point in women's publishing where it could have the widest revolutionary effect: at the intersection of ideology and commercial print. The popular poetics of gender in America was challenged to rewrite itself into a new politics of public discourse. "The Feminine Mystique" became "The Problem That Has No Name."[18]

That, of course, was the point of Friedan's own duplicitous naming. The problem itself literally lay beyond words. Where could naming itself even begin, Friedan asked, when one American critic had dismissed Simone de Beauvoir by saying "she obviously 'didn't know what life was all about,' and besides, she was talking about French women. The 'woman problem' in America no longer existed" (14). The issue in America, that is, lay in a silence encoded into the national discourse itself. *The Feminine Mystique* had to come on like just another women's book exactly so that it might become *the other* women's book—the one in fact that changed women's writing and thinking in America forever.

"Is this all?" (11). At midcentury, said Friedan, such was the question forming on virtually every middle-class American housewife's lips. Or, perhaps as often, they just spoke of the problem as "the problem" (15): the "mystique of feminine fulfillment" that from 1945 onward "became the cherished and self-perpetuating core of contemporary American culture" (14); "the problem," that is, called "Occupation: housewife" (14). Ironically, in the most affluent country in the world, the problem was precisely affluence and the adjustment it facilitated to convenient social roles. Moreover, especially for women of advanced educational status in the best-educated country in the world, it was even more ironically a problem of education. As Friedan's fellow Smith College graduate, Sylvia Plath, was concurrently noting in *The Bell Jar,* the time had come for women to resist the standard wisdom doled out by their own most prestigious colleges and educators: "that sixteen years of academic training is realistic preparation for wifehood and motherhood" (18).

But the chief problem preventing discussion of particular issues was the one that had already been posed. As yet, *there existed no discourse,* social, educational, or otherwise, to describe the problem, save "in the generally accepted terms by which scientists have studied women, doctors have treated them, counselors have advised them, and writers have written about them" (22). Out of the discourse of repression itself, then, had to be written anew the very "standards of feminine normality, feminine adjustment, feminine fulfillment, and feminine maturity by which most women are still trying to live" (26).

This Friedan set out to do by deconstructing the popular mythology implied in the "straight" construction of her title. She begins with the image of "The Happy Housewife Heroine" of post–World War II magazine lore, itself unwriting the earlier social drama of American women's victories of the century—in the voting booth, the workplace, literature and the arts, the Hollywood screen, and, most recently, the production lines of war industry. Suddenly the new American woman welcomes home the soldier-husband and retreats into a mystique of wifehood, motherhood, and happy domesticity that quickly creates, as Friedan brilliantly phrases it, "its own fiction of fact" (53). "Why did women go home again?" (61) she asks. And why now again must they find themselves and their identities in crisis?

The proximate story can only be told, Friedan shows us, by retracing another larger one as the truest measure of what has been lost. That story she calls "The Passionate Journey," the progress of Anglo-European feminism that once seemed so close to having brought twentieth-century women to the edge of real historical identity. Along the way, however, it also ran headlong into new constructions of countervailing myth: "The Sexual Solipsism of Sigmund Freud"; "The Functional Freeze, the Feminine Protest, and Margaret Mead"; and "The Sex Directed Educators." Yet even these might have been surmounted save for that crucial bad turning in the wake of World War II, which Friedan elects simply to call "The Mistaken Choice." For then, in the arena of domestic entrapment created by the postwar marketplace, came shortly the onslaught of new mass-cultural myths designed exquisitely to enforce the choice: "The Sexual Sell," or "Housewifery Expands to Fill the Time Available." "Sex-Seekers" sublimate what remains of desire into their coddled children; they all adjust, somehow, to the happily "Progressive Dehumanization" peculiar to what Friedan calls "The Comfortable Concentration Camp." The result: that same "Forfeited Self" that for women, as for all the other political victims of the century, has now become not an intellectual conceit but a realized existential fact.

What must now therefore be written, Friedan proposes at the end, is "A New Life Plan for Women" that will no longer structure itself according to any of the fictions currently comprising the "mystique": fictions passing themselves off as fact through "women's magazines, sociologists, educators, and psychoanalysts" or fictions perpetrated equally by a woman's "husband, her friends and neighbors; perhaps her minister, priest, or rabbi; or her child's kindergarten teacher; or the well-meaning social worker at the guidance clinic; or her own innocent little children" (338–39). "The time is at hand," she concludes, "when the voices of the feminine mystique can no longer drown out the inner voice that is driving women on to become complete" (364).

Friedan herself drove on into the '60s and beyond, helping to create new texts of political action—The National Organization for Women; a proposed Equal Rights Amendment; and debates over abortion, pornography, sexual harrassment, and gender in the workplace that now continue to structure the everyday discourse of women's lives. Meanwhile, the Passionate Journey continues: a step or two forward, a step backward perhaps, but now mainly forward. And not backward at all really, since a homemaker-writer named Betty Friedan decided to set in motion a new history of discourse-events that would rewrite history and discourse forever for American women. The first, *The Feminine Mystique*, would be followed by others with more direct titles such as *Sexual Politics; Sisterhood Is Powerful; The Female Eunuch; Radical Feminism;* and *Our Bodies, Ourselves.* But the directness of all of them had been made possible only through the radical duplicity whereby the first had succeeded in opening up the discourse from within.

Gibran, Kahlil. In a *Newsweek* article of October 31, 1960, the Insomniac Bookshop of Hermosa Beach, California, reported its sales leader for the first ten months of that year to be Kahlil Gibran's *The Prophet.* According to composite figures at the end of the decade, it continued to rank in sales popularity between *Catch-22* and *The Catcher in the Rye.*

Now as then, *The Prophet* remains for us an ultimate '60s curio, the archetype of counterculture kitsch. People seduced each other by it. People got married to it. Thirty years later, Gibran's name tops any nostalgia list of individual figures.[19] The book itself is an indelible picture of memory. The dust jacket, in brooding tones of beige and sepia, carries a haunting portrait, a charcoal study or pencil-drawing of a face, sensitive, solitary, haunted, looking somewhat like a Sunday School Christ but also decidedly Eastern. Beneath, and enhancing the air of mystery, is the author's name. The title page bears the august imprint of Alfred A. Knopf.

The outside of the volume is slim, spare, well-crafted. Inside, it beckons from the outset as dense with meanings. The table of contents is portentous, beginning with "The Coming of the Ship," moving through twenty-six other pregnant chapter headings (On Love, On Marriage, On Children, On Self-Knowledge, On Pleasure, On Beauty, On Religion, On Death), and ending in "The Farewell."

The text proper is prose poetry with wide margins and short paragraphs that look like stanzas, often single lines set alone. It is also interspersed with twelve mystical illustrations, distinguished by nudity of a chaste, prepubescent vagueness. The total effect suggests some strange conflation of *The Rubáiyát of Omar Khayyám* and *The Marriage of Heaven and Hell*. It is a total presentation.

In mode or genre, it also fulfilled the '60s penchant for a very particular kind of allegory: at once easily reducible yet resistantly amorphous, something obvious enough for the average reader to "relate to" yet vague enough to facilitate true cosmic epiphany. And best of all, of course, it *was,* actually, prophetic. Published first by the author, an obscure Lebanese Christian mystic in 1924, it was literally about a prophet, a young visionary named "Almustafa, the chosen and the beloved," come to speak to the people of a mystical city before his departure on a waiting ship for a voyage of going and return. And what he spoke, page after page and heading after heading, seemed to spill forth as a storehouse of epigrammatic wisdom on '60s topics. *Someone,* rhapsodized convert after convert, had dreamed it all in advance.

"Love":

> Like sheafs of corn he gathers you unto himself.
> He threshes you to make you naked.
> He sifts you to free you from your husks.
> He grinds you to whiteness.
> He kneads you until you are pliant;
> And then he assigns you to his sacred fire,
>   that you may become sacred bread for God's sacred feast. (12)

"Love gives naught but itself and takes naught but from itself," the Prophet continues with heavy scriptural echo. "Love possesses not nor would it be possessed;/For love is sufficient unto love" (13). ("Marriage," a version of the same story, may well have served as the most widely borrowed set of alternative wedding vows in the era.)

"Children": "Your children are not your children," the Prophet intones. "They are the sons and daughters of Life's longing for itself."

You may give them your love but not your thoughts,
For they have their own thoughts.
You may house their bodies but not their souls,
For their souls dwell in the house of tomorrow,
    which you cannot visit, not even in your dreams. (17)

"Giving": "You give but little when you give of your possessions," says the Prophet. "It is when you give of yourself that you truly give./For what are your possessions but things you keep and guard for fear you may need them tomorrow" (19).

The topics go on like this for nearly a hundred pages, a complete guide to alternative *kultur:* "Work," "Clothes," "Buying and Selling," "Laws," "Freedom," "Reason and Passion," "Self-Knowledge," "Teaching," "Friendship," "Good and Evil."

"Pleasure":

Go to your fields and your gardens,
    and you shall learn that it is the pleasure of the bee
    to father honey of the flower,
But it is also the pleasure of the flower to yield its honey to the bee.
For to the bee a flower is a fountain of life,
And to the flower a bee is a messenger of love,
And to both, bee and flower, the giving and receiving of
    pleasure is a need and an ecstasy. (73)

"Beauty":

People of Orphalese, beauty is life when life unveils her holy face.
But you are life and you are the veil.
Beauty is eternity gazing at itself in a mirror.
But you are eternity and you are the mirror. (76)

"Religion": "Have I spoken this day of aught else?" replies the Prophet to a questioner (77).

All your hours are wings that beat through space from self to self.
He who wears his morality but as his best garment
    were better naked.

The wind and the sun will tear no holes in his skin.
And he who defines his conduct by ethics imprisons
 his song-bird in a cage. (77)

Toward the end, there is even "Death." But it too is now but a movement in the voyage toward cosmic epiphany. "If these be vague words," the
Prophet says on the eve of departure,

 then seek not to clear them. Vague and nebulous
  is the beginning of all things, but not their end,
 And I fain would have you remember me as a beginning.
 Life and all that live, is conceived in the mist and not in the crystal.
 And who knows but a crystal is mist in decay? (92)

At present, we may look back with amusement at the pretentious bombast, the homogenized religiosity, the vapid metaphysics. If we do so completely, however, we will have missed the point of much '60s reading and
writing as *total production: The Prophet* was at once text and commodity,
a thing to hold onto; a literal medium of transport for the voyagers assembling themselves along the shore.

Ginsberg, Allen. With the 1956 publication of *Howl and Other Poems*
by Lawrence Ferlinghetti's City Lights Books, the poet Allen Ginsberg
rose to lasting visibility as one of the two or three best known of all writers
associated with the '60s Generation of Youth. Accordingly, it is appropriate
to the literary and commercial conditions of the times that the enterprise
had risen out of the avant-garde poetry equivalent of a corporate merger.
Or, to use a current figure, the Eastern Beats had finally begun networking
with the San Francisco Renaissance.

The scenario itself stood in a worthy lineage of earlier American textual
self-promotions.[20] Ginsberg, having found employment in San Francisco
as, of all things, a market researcher, had shortly set up the celebrated Six
Gallery reading where, on the program with poets Michael McClure, Gary
Snyder, Philip Whalen, Philip Lamantia, and Kenneth Rexroth, dean of
the San Francisco group, he brought the house down with his first public
presentation of *Howl*. Ferlinghetti next supposedly telegraphed him, playing Emerson to the new Whitman, "I greet you at the beginning of a great
career. When do I get the manuscript?" (Smith 202–3).

Howl and Other Poems was duly published by City Lights in a sold-out
edition of fifteen hundred copies. Contributing to the success, moreover,
were the San Francisco police, the U.S. Customs Service, and the federal

courts. The issue was obscenity.[21] Ferlinghetti, it turned out, had contracted for the book to be printed in England, thus requiring importation. Predictably, it was seized. Anticipating the seizure, Ferlinghetti had earlier provided a text to the ACLU, who had agreed to support him should trouble arise.

With seizure in effect, Ferlinghetti quickly circulated the volume in a local photo-offset edition, and as a reviewer for the *San Francisco Chronicle*, called *Howl* the greatest long poem since World War I, perhaps since Eliot's *Four Quartets*. Meanwhile, he was being topped by the judge in the federal lawsuit, whose opinion in favor of the defendants concluded with a vindication itself almost Ginsbergian in the poetic eloquence of its political statement. "It ends in a plea for holy living," he concluded of the poem. *"Honi soit qui mal y pense."* By the end of 1957, ten thousand copies of *Howl and Other Poems* were in print, in a familiar flat, portable, no-nonsense volume, just narrow enough to fit in a hip pocket, just wide enough to stand out on a shelf. It has not stopped selling.

After a long career, Ginsberg has finally been celebrated and, at some length, officially canonized. Yet for most readers of the Generation of Youth, it's likely he will always be mainly the author of that squarish white paperback in a black frame: "Number Four," as announced by the border legend, in the "Pocket Poets Series"; *"Howl and Other Poems";* "Allen Ginsberg"; "Introduction by William Carlos Williams."

"Hold back the edges of your gowns, Ladies, we are going through hell" (8). Thus Williams warns us at the end of his terse page and a half, having passed on the Blake-Whitman-Rimbaud mantle to the young inheritor. Then, already, we are into the layers of descent. "HOWL" is the title, "for Carl Solomon" the dedication, "I" the peremptory pronoun of person and voice that launches us forth.

> I saw the best minds of my generation destroyed by madness,
>   starving hysterical naked,
> dragging themselves through the negro streets at dawn
>   looking for an angry fix,
> angelheaded hipsters burning for the ancient heavenly connection
>   to the starry dynamo in the machinery of night,
> who . . . (9).

"Who . . . , who . . . , who . . .": the poetry drives on, outrunning the line, the syntax, the categories: "who poverty and tatters and hollow-eyed and high sat up smoking in the supernatural darkness of cold-water flats floating across the tops of cities contemplating jazz, . . . with dreams, with drugs, with waking nightmares, alcohol and cock and endless balls" (9). Six wide, dense, teeming pages later there is still not a period in sight. The first interruption beyond a comma or simple white space follows "with mother finally ******," and a few lines later, after "a hopeful little bit of hallucination—" (15) and a short apostrophe to the hero, "ah, Carl, while you are not safe I am not safe, and you're really in the animal soup of time—" (15–16). Only after that, a page later, does the single frantic sentence find its end.

But this is not just a howl of personal outrage; it is also a cry of political and economic indictment that knows just where to drive the opening of dialectical critique. "What sphinx of cement and aluminum bashed open their skulls and ate up their brains and imagination?" begins the second section. "Moloch!" is the answer. "Moloch! Solitude! Filth! Ugliness! Ashcans and unobtainable dollars! Children screaming under the stairways! Boys sobbing in armies! Old men weeping in the parks!/Moloch! Moloch! Nightmare of Moloch! Moloch the loveless! Mental Moloch! Moloch the heavy judger of men" (17).

Exactly in such pluralizations, a vision arises of common resistance to outrage against our kind. We are all in it together. "Carl Solomon I am with you in Rockland where you're madder than I am . . . ," the third section begins. And so it continues to declaim in its concluding lines two pages later: "I'm with you in Rockland in my dreams you walk dripping from a sea-journey on the highway across America in tears to the door of my cottage in the Western night" (20).

"Shantih, Shantih, Shantih," concludes the Eliot of *The Waste Land*, seeking closure and benediction. Here, in "FOOTNOTE TO HOWL," the new poet of the body and the soul, barely pausing for breath, instead plunges forward into the latest openings of his epic rant. "Holy! Holy! Holy!" cries the poet, and then repeats the triplet four more times. "The world is holy!" the chant continues. "The soul is holy! The skin is holy! The nose is holy! The tongue and cock and hand and asshole holy."

> Everything is holy! everybody's holy! everywhere is holy!
>   everyday is in eternity! Everyman's an angel!
> The bum's as holy as the seraphim! the madman is holy
>   as you my soul are holy! (21)

"Holy forgiveness! mercy! charity! faith!" concludes the holy-madman, the one, inimitable Ginsberg: "Holy! Ours! bodies! suffering! magnanimity!/Holy the supernatural extra brilliant intelligent kindness of the soul" (22).

This was the Ginsberg the early trippers and askers would always remember. Those coming later would know others. The youth-revolution would cherish the vision of Allen Ginsberg at the great January 1967 San Francisco Be-In with his wild hair, his flowing Indian shirt, his funny little glasses, his incantations. The antiwar movement would know him as the indefatigable activist, the Vietnam poet. The environmental movement would revere him as the author of *Planet News*. The Ginsberg of *Howl* and *Kaddish* eventually won the National Book Award, he reached the *Norton Anthology of American Literature*,[22] and with the *Collected Poems, 1947–84* he assumed standard author status.

Most importantly, however, Ginsberg in this century had made American poetry political in a way it had never been before. Indeed, from his first bold, ecstatic utterances on, *all* the old poetico-political commonplaces went by the board. It was one thing for Shelley to describe poets as the unacknowledged legislators of mankind, or Pound to call them the antennae of the race. In the introduction to *Howl,* however, Williams, himself the inheritor of Blake and Whitman, caught *his* successor's new key. "Poets are damned but they are not blind, they see with the eyes of the angels," he wrote. "This poet sees through and all around the horrors he partakes of in the very intimate details of his poem. He avoids nothing but experiences it to the hilt. He contains it. Claims it as his own—and, we believe, laughs at it and has the time and affrontery to love a fellow of his choice and record that love in a well-made poem" (8).

The politics expressed by Ginsberg over the years have been simply that: love indited through poetry into the true transformative work of the world, love expressed for the sake of the madman, the mother, the nigger, the queer, and thereby expressed for the sake of us all and for the sake of the planet. This is not poetry, then, as political statement but as itself political action. To put it simply, Ginsberg made radical poetry and politics indistinguishable as forms of art. In the last great era of mass-print literacy he propelled the poetic word beyond the printed page into new communal experiments of language *as vision,* and at the same time he returned its magic to the oldest ground of political origin: the voice.

Shaman was a word that seemed increasingly to appear in the '60s argot, especially as the decade moved on. R. D. Laing would understand it in relation to a new, divine madness. Carlos Castaneda and other students of Native American anthropology would understand it in relation to an ancient magic. Ginsberg seemed to know it from the start going both ways. Here truly was the madman-poet and the holy poet-shaman returning us to ourselves and the cosmos.

Golding, William. William Golding's *The Lord of the Flies,* published first in 1954, like works by post–World War II American contemporaries such as Salinger and Vonnegut, found new life as a '60s scripture. Upon reexamination, one sees that it could have hardly failed to catch. For an American youth-audience, it was the kind of allegorical truth-fantasy that seemed to have everything. It told dramatically of a group of preadolescent schoolboys, marooned by war on an uninhabited island, first divided into biguns and littleuns, firekeepers and hunters, a ruling council and a *polis*— the semblance of a new democracy—but eventually returned into some old tribal dance of original murder. At the same time, its heavy existential and mythic resonances made it a favorite in college literature, philosophy, religion, and social science courses.

The book combined youth-appeal with the educational benefits of a high modernist field trip. Everyone seemed to be there: Conrad, Eliot, Freud, Levi-Strauss. At the same time, it seemed a parable deeply rooted in '60s experience. A children's experiment in self-governance, beginning in a brave new world where suddenly there are no adults, struggles from the outset against a paranoiac dream, somehow at once remembered and invented, of some pure, dark other. The Beast, they call it. For a while they imagine it living in the forest or perhaps slithering forth from the sea. For a while, by virtue of a strange, plummeting arrival they have observed, they think it may come from the air. Some mysteries are unriddled—the jungle creatures turn out to be beasts, for instance, and the dead body of a parachutist, presumably from the war zone outside, gets discovered. But mainly mystery breeds new mystery and new horror.

The hunter-boys, attempting to propitiate whatever it is out there—the Beast—ritually slaughter a huge female pig and place its impaled head at the center of a jungle shrine. There, Simon, a charmed, mad boy, the seer of the lot, encounters it covered with flies, and hears the voice, for the first time named, of The Lord of the Flies. For his discovery, his merging with the madness, he too is ritually killed in a wild dance to the hunting chant that has somehow become the ritual group slogan, *"Kill the beast! Cut his throat! Spill his blood!"* Then, as the feeble ruling council makes one last attempt to reason with the tribe, follows shortly yet another murder, this time of Piggy, the fat boy with the glasses whose one unbroken remaining lens is the only fire-tool on the island. Piggy now washes somewhere at sea, his head split open by a boulder. The glasses hang on the belt of Jack, the new chief. The old chief, Ralph, is solitary, hunted, the final outcast. " 'Cos I had some sense" (186), he says to himself.

All along, some remembered work of civilization has made its feeble attempts to countervail. Fire-making, for the sake of rescue, has become a religion. Hunting has been delegated to a warrior-class. But as quickly as a structure is built, it all breaks down, first into accidents, then into divisions, blood frenzies, murders. The Lord of the Flies knows why. "You're a silly little boy," he says to frightened, mad Simon, "just an ignorant, silly little boy" (186). Simon does not answer. "Well then," the voice says, "you'd better run off and play with the others. They think you're batty. You don't want Ralph to think you're batty, do you? You like Ralph a lot, don't you? And Piggy, and Jack?" Simon finally says something: "Pig's head on a stick." The voice replies: " 'Fancy thinking the Beast was something you could hunt and kill!' " said the head. For a moment or two the forest and all the other dimly appreciated places echoed with the parody of laughter. " 'You knew, didn't you? I'm part of you? Close, close, close! I'm the reason why it's no go? Why things are what they are?' " (143).

Then, just at the end, just when Ralph too is about to go the way of Simon and Piggy, an adult in a uniform arrives, a naval officer from a cutter anchored offshore to effect their rescue. Their world will consist, for those who are left, of the restoration of a reason for things, an order and organization according to age and function. The savage world is again made historical and dignified under the name of civilization. It is now called war.

Liberal academics canonized the text as eagerly as it was embraced by their youth-constituents. Here was a complete apparatus, something that really made evil relevant to issues of resistance versus complicity, power versus powerlessness. Philologists noted "Lord of the Flies" as itself an English translation of the Hebrew *ba'al zĕbhūbh* (*Beelzebub* in Greek). Political theorists examined the governmental model, the attempt at democracy, the bespectacled intellectual as advisor on policy, the well-intentioned organizer as helpless victim of the old instinct for disorder. Students of contemporary youth-activism jumped in with the no-adults business, the ritual killing and blood-consciousness business, the war business. Updating *Gulliver's Travels* or *Robinson Crusoe* into *Heart of Darkness,* official exegetes found Golding to have written a latest young people's version of the shipwreck book gone horribly wrong. The young people, on the other hand, listened to the allegorical explanations but remembered the primal scene: the impaled Head, the Beast, the Lord of the Flies, Simon and his Madness, now all somehow became one. And they knew what Simon knew.

Goodman, Paul. For American memory, World War II marked the defeat, by "free" or "democratic" governments, of various totalitarianisms. Membership by the Soviet Union in the mythic aggregation was quickly rescinded with the lowering of the Iron Curtain and the onset of the Cold War. Concurrently, a new dialectics of fear stalked the nation from within. The work of the House Un-American Activities Committee and the Army-McCarthy hearings awakened American liberalism from the sleep of the '50s. Soon, left-looking intellectuals were locating the subtle totalitarianisms peculiar to advanced capitalist democracy. Political homogenization, they noted, brought immense pressures of social conformity; generalized affluence and material comfort were used to suppress spiritual dissent. Thinkers such as William Whyte Jr., C. Wright Mills, Norman O. Brown, Herbert Marcuse, and Paul Goodman revealed in the titles of key texts their anxieties about the increasing lack of critical openings in mainstream American culture—the kingdom of what Marcuse called in *One-Dimensional Man* "the Happy Consciousness"—"the belief that the real is rational and that the system delivers the goods" (84). *The Organization Man, White Collar, Life Against Death, Eros and Civilization, Growing Up Absurd:* in all of these the subject was, again according to Marcuse, "the new conformism which is a facet of technological rationality translated into social behavior" (ODM 87).

Of the figures named, Whyte and Mills concentrated on the social aspects of institutional behavior. Brown and Marcuse attempted to integrate their social observations into a theoretical matrix arising out of European modernist intellectualism, with emphasis on the ongoing dialog between the psychological politics of Freud and the economic politics of Marx. Psychological inquiry became the critique of material relationship and vice versa.

Goodman, a social psychologist, attempted something of a conflation of these various projects but with a distinctly existential yearning, a lyric, visionary desire, acknowledging its genealogy in late romanticism. Like Norman Mailer in particular, Goodman early on found a special promise in the Beats through what he saw as their continuities with the European intellectual tradition. Goodman's chief importance, however, now and then, was blazoned in the title of the book for which he became famous: *Growing Up Absurd.* The Americans who were going to pay the real price of the Happy Consciousness, the exchange of spiritual adventure for social conformism and material complacency, he said upfront, were the current nation of the young.

In fact, it might be said of Goodman what can be said of few other late '50s and early '60s figures: as an advanced intellectual, he explicitly appointed himself the ideological Prophet of Youth, their advocate *and* their cultural theoretician; and he did so before they themselves may be said to have existed. On the other hand, once they did exist, it is also likely that not many of them actually read him. For one thing, *Growing Up Absurd* seemed very much a '50s production with large portions of it having appeared prior to the book's 1960 publication in various intellectual journals. By the middle and latter portions of the decade, it must have seemed even more dated, especially in light of the with-it exhortations of an Abbie Hoffman, a Jerry Rubin, a Timothy Leary, or a trendy successor such as Charles Reich (in *The Greening of America,* for instance). For another, Goodman's most famous book as well as his other writings required a certain kind of cultural memory peculiar to the Western liberal intellectual tradition. They carried, that is, a dense philosophical legacy, and they also demanded a willingness to invest that legacy in ambitious new configurings and syntheses. All this notwithstanding, Theodore Solataroff was probably still right as late as 1967 in describing Goodman as holding the status of "a sort of Pied Piper who has caught the ear of the college students and asks all sorts of embarrassing questions about the education they receive and the lives they are being prepared to lead" (211).

Of the postwar generation of elders, it was Goodman, after all, who first told youth of the pain *he* felt at that terrible thing happening to *them* amidst unprecedented peace, happiness, and prosperity; that thing they too already felt and—like Friedan's happy housewife—felt constrained not to speak; that thing they knew wrenchingly within their souls and just needed a name for; that thing called growing up absurd.

Goodman's first sentence in *Growing Up Absurd* at once announces the enormity of the problem and predicts the complexity of the address. He describes the collection of essays comprising the text as an attempt to unite reflections on "the disgrace of the Organized System of semimonopolies, government, advertisers, etc., and the disaffection of the growing generation." "In the rush of books on the follies, venality, and stifling conformity of the Organization," Goodman goes on, one still looks for "a book on Youth Problems in the Organized System" (ix). This one will fill that need; it will also, moreover, attempt to move from a framing of issues to an envisioning of necessary response. "I assume," he concludes, that the young *really* need a more worth-while world in order to grow up at all, and I confront this real need with the world that they have been getting. This is the source of their problems. *Our* problem is to remedy the disproportion. We can. Our inheritance, our immense productivity, has been pre-empted and parceled out in a kind of domainal system; but this grandiose and seemingly impregnable feudalism is vulnerable to an earnest attack. (xvi)

What follows is, if nothing else, earnest to a fault. At the time, indeed, it stood by itself as a brave, lonely tour de force.[23] "Faith," he says, in a blazingly ironic core chapter, is no longer future, not even present, but meanly present perfect. "Business, government, and real property have closed up *all* the space there is," he says. "Public speech" even now "quite disregards human facts." "And so forth." In such circumstances, he concludes, "is it possible, being a human being, to exist? Is it possible, having a human nature, to grow up? There would be a kind of metaphysical crisis" (133). He goes on: "Or, to put it another way. These conditions are absurd, they don't make sense; and yet millions, who to all appearances are human beings, behave as though they were the normal course of things" (133–34). No wonder then, in what ensuing chapters describe as "An Apparently Closed Room," young people in particular separate themselves into "The Early Resigned"—Beats and other forms of sanctioned Rebels—and "The Early Fatalistic"—other young persons already deemed officially sociopathic. These groups of the young themselves constitute a proximate social problem, Goodman asserts. But more importantly, they also represent nothing less than the failure of our collective promise as a human community. *"It is the missed revolutions of modern times,"* he italicizes, "*—the fallings-short and the compromises—that add up to the conditions that make it hard for the young to grow up in our society*" (231). Still, he concludes, there remains time for the battle to be joined, if only the generations can again be newly joined:

> Now the organized system is very powerful and in its full tide of success, apparently sweeping everything before it in science, education, community planning, labor, the arts, not to speak of business and politics where it is indigenous. Let me say that we of the previous generation who have been sickened and enraged to see earnest and honest effort and humane culture swamped by this muck, are heartened by the crazy young allies, and we think that perhaps the future may make more sense than we dared hope. (241)

This was 1960, and such a concluding exhortation on behalf of the youth-culture and its adult compatriots obviously partook of a liberal hope that was already failing to acknowledge a diversity of marginalized constituencies—blacks, women, Hispanics, Native Americans, and other non-white, non-Western subcultures, not to mention persons on the margins of sexuality, where Goodman himself had spent his life in silence. Nonetheless, the prospect outlined here could never have begun to be fulfilled had it not begun in the shiftings of generational perspective and alliance, which Goodman said it would have to take. In Goodman and others like him, the youth-revolution found the intellectual and ideological sanction among the established liberal intelligentsia (carrying with it at times the unrecognized threats of some old co-options) that would be required before any of its serious work could be undertaken in the culture at large.

Greenburg, Joanne [Hannah Green]. It is astonishing to count the number of '60s youth-scriptures that are about somebody going crazy in America.[24] Significantly, the somebody in question is often a young person, sensitive, intelligent, well brought up (as they used to say), born to a comfortable life, sometimes actually privileged. Yet that same young person invariably finds himself or herself estranged to a deep heart's sickness from a culture that seems to have offered virtually everything possible materially and institutionally and virtually nothing morally and spiritually. Models of the juvenile head-case, described as the "over-sensitive," "troubled," or "disturbed" adolescent or young adult would surely include J. D. Salinger's Holden Caulfield and Sylvia Plath's Esther Greenwood but also such spiritual compatriots as Charles Webb's Benjamin Braddock, the young "Exley" protagonist of *A Fan's Notes,* and the titular heroine-victim of *Go Ask Alice.* An outlaw variation on the model is the young adult sociopath, a jailkid deviant like Dean Moriarity, for instance, or a manic genius of disruption like Gnossos Pappadopoulis. Finally, there is the madman boy-granddaddy of them all, the ultimate antiauthoritarian wiseacre, Ken Kesey's Randall McMurphy.

In Joanne Greenburg's *I Never Promised You a Rose Garden,* the '60s reader encountered a true, albeit even to this day largely unacknowledged, classic of the genre. At the same time, it is a classic with a difference. Specifically, it seems to have been one of the few '60s youth-scriptures by a contemporary writer to achieve massive circulation, mainly without public notoriety, through steady paperback sales over an extended period.[25] Published in 1964, as late as 1967 and 1968—the equivalent of an eternity for a largely unheralded book—it continued to appear on lists as a top ten paperback bestseller. In a 1977 accounting of combined hard- and paperbound bestsellers, Greenburg's work appeared fourth, among texts regarded as '60s youth-classics, following only *Catch-22, The Prophet,* and *The Catcher in the Rye.* By that time, sales had risen to five million.

Where did the book find its large readership? As with *Go Ask Alice,* a later text that proved similarly successful, the answer seems to be that it appealed to young women of precollege age who found in its chilling depiction of a contemporary's battle with clinical schizophrenia something beyond metaphor: some deep analogue to their own strivings in a culture where they found themselves doubly mute and invisible in a dread otherness of age *and* gender.

The incredible success of *I Never Promised You a Rose Garden* thus lay in its appeal not so much as an underground classic but as a *secret* classic, at once a function of genre and gender, the wisdom-text of a largely invisible culture-within-a-culture-within-a-culture. It spoke out of the silent world of adolescent schizophrenia to the silent solitude that was often the consequence of young women's own cultural positioning. As social thinkers such as Paul Goodman, Norman O. Brown, Herbert Marcuse, R. D. Laing, and others addressed various theories of madness as the only forms of sane response to an insane world (what Laing described as the condition of trying to live with an existential broken heart) and as literary idols inscribed visions of a redemptory nuttiness through figures such as Joseph Heller's Yossarian, Kurt Vonnegut's Billy Pilgrim and Eliot Rosewater, and Ken Kesey's Randall McMurphy—all along the way, Greenburg's readers must have smiled with their secret knowledge.[26] As young people in America who also found themselves young women in America, they had already been there. Theirs would be a truly existential gift of vision.

In just this existential vein, *I Never Promised You a Rose Garden* is a text at once hallucinatory, terrifying, heartbreaking, and exalting. There is no moral to the story; there is no metaphor save the story. It describes a harrowing ride to the end of consciousness and language in the waking forms whereby we know them. It is a world-voyage as haunted and phantasmagorical as anything out of Tolkien; it is a self-imprisonment as claustral in its dreamlikeness and as agonized in its hermetic solitude as anything inside Hesse. It is the whole strange silent world of, to use Michel Foucault's phrase, imperial unreason.

And what a quiet, demure white-knuckler it turns out to be. Even today one finds the harmless sounding title sitting innocuously on the young adult shelf. What one reads, on the other hand, is a passage to the ultimate region of the soul. The subject is Deborah Blau, daughter of Jacob and Esther Blau. The workup is succinct: "16 yrs. PREV. HOSP: None. INITIAL DIAG: SCHIZOPHRENIA" (18). The physician is Dr. Fried. She remembers a young girl named Tilda once just as lost and mad, with Hitler outside the walls. Now the battle must be joined against the old enemy. "The *hidden* strength is too deep a secret," she admits to herself. "But in the end . . . in the end it is our only ally" (20).

Meanwhile, Deborah has slipped beyond anyone's reach. "Into the vacuum of the Midworld where she stood between Yr and Now, the Collect was beginning to come to life. Soon they would be shouting curses and taunts at her, deafening her for both worlds" (15). One had to be careful. "Over the years the power of the Censor had grown greater and greater, and it was he who had lately thrust himself into both worlds, so that sometimes no speech and no action escaped him. One whisper of a secret name, one sign written, one slip of light could break into the hidden place and destroy her and both the worlds forever" (22). As the doctor speaks, it happens for Deborah in the usual way:

> She began to fall, going with Anterrabae through his fire-fragmented darkness into Yr. This time the fall was far. There was utter darkness for a long time and then a grayness, seen only in bands across the eye. The place was familiar; it was the Pit. In this place gods and Collect moaned and shouted, but even they were intelligible. Human sounds came, too, but they came without meaning. The world intruded, but it was a shattered world and unrecognizable. (33–34).

On the other side, in the Disturbed Ward, Dr. Fried "wanted to tell the stunned-looking girl in front of her that this sickness, which everyone shied from and was frightened of, was also an adjustment; these hidden worlds—all of them—and tongues and codes and propitiations were for her the means to stay alive in a world of anarchy and terror" (71). But Deborah is too far away now to hear, out there on "the edges of terrestrial reality" (73), out of space, out of time, out where language itself, some of it words no one else has ever seen or heard, speaks a separate kind of powerful magic. "*You see what it is . . .* Anterrabae said genially. *We can really do it. Don't toy with us, Bird-one, because we can do it up, down, and sideways. You thought all those descriptions were metaphors: lost one's mind, cracked-up, demented, lunatic? Alas, you see, they are all quite, quite true. Don't toy with us, Bird-one, because we are protecting you. When you admire the world again, wait for our darkness*" (104). Trapped in her gabble of "the wrong-coming words," Deborah measures "the uncrossable expanse between herself and the species called 'human being'" (116). Dr. Fried gets a new name. Furii. Fire-touch.

> "Look here," Furii said, "I never promised you a rose garden. I never promised you perfect justice . . ." (She remembered Tilda suddenly, breaking out of the hospital in Nuremburg, disappearing into the swastika-city, and coming back laughing that hard, rasping parody of laughter. 'Sholom Aleichem, Doctor, they are crazier than I am!') . . . "and I never promised you peace or happiness. My help is so that you can be free to fight for all of these things. The only reality I can offer is challenge, and being well is being free to accept it or not at whatever level you are capable. I never promise lies, and the rose-garden world of perfection is a lie . . . and a bore, too!" (122)

Still, the secret garden of madness remains a circle of power, disqualifying Deborah from the world, insulating her, protecting her, rendering her inviolate from the world. The crisis approaches. The angers pour over into self-mutilations with matches and cigarette stubs. Then, one day, the languages of the other pour forth. "Fear . . . Censor—doing the forbidden . . . destroy me . . . and . . . ," Deborah cries out. "And what is it?" Dr. Fried asks. "Then . . . no. No-ness. Not Yr even. Loud gibberish and just *No. No*! !'"

" 'Not even the gods for friends,' the doctor mused" (210).
Something, however, has begun to change. One evening, Deborah notices, "It was quiet. Yr was quiet and the Collect, for once, was silent also. All the voices in all the world seemed stilled" (223). Then,

> in a slow, oncoming way, widening from a beginning, it began to appear to Deborah that she would not die. It came upon her with a steady, mounting clarity that she was going to be more than undead, that she was going to be alive. It had a sense of wonder and awe, great joy and trepidation. 'When will it begin?' she said to the gradual night. It came to her that it was already beginning. (223)

The voices return, but in different tones, and with a new one among them. Hers. " '*One would have to wait in order to find out,*' Anterrabae said. '*Who knows, this happening may be gone by tomorrow*'" (193). " '*You may not even have to do anything about it,*' Lactamaeon said. '*You may not even have to think about it.*'" " '*Maybe it was just a symptom,*' Deborah said" (224–25).

The time has come to begin a return to the world. There are still voices.

Deborah is still in the hospital. But now she also finds new studies, other thoughts. "*'We could wait until you called us . . .'*" the voices cajole. "*'I will not call,'*" she replies. "*I am going to hang with the world. Full weight.*" A geometry theorem intrudes. Someone is talking on the ward. Phrases catch from history books. "Full weight," says Deborah. (300)

"If I could blow your minds," R. D. Laing exclaims near the end of *The Politics of Experience*. "Then you would see." Deborah *has* seen it. Finally, *we* have seen it too in this brave, terrifying, once-in-a-lifetime book that millions of '60s young people seemed to have found as their secret scripture just at the moment in a lifetime when it was needed to speak to them. Deborah had it just right about the madness: it was a symptom.

Greer, Germaine. An old paperback of Germaine Greer's *The Female Eunuch* provides a classic late '60s and early '70s example of the text as total product. A bold "#1" tops the cover, as if saying it all—at least as far as sales were concerned. "The Ultimate Word in Sexual Freedom," declaims a line just underneath. Then comes the title, framing from above a cameo photograph of the author smiling that wry, knowing Germaine Greer smile. "A saucy feminist that even men like," reads the opening leaf with the excited announcement, "*Life Magazine* puts Germaine Greer on its cover!" A following page fills with dedications to sister-women. The table of contents lists the cosmic heads of discussion: BODY, SOUL, LOVE, HATE, REVOLUTION. These in turn give way to eye-catching lists of particular topics: Curves, Hair, Sex, The Wicked Womb, The Psychological Sell, The Raw Material, Womanpower, Obsession, Romance, The Object of Male Fantasy, The Middle-Class Myth of Love and Marriage, Loathing and Disgust, Abuse, Misery, Resentment, Rebellion.

Finally, we arrive at an introduction, something about the second feminist revolution now upon us. Yet as we actually turn to the remembered text, expecting some old excitement, we find instead opening pages about as arresting as a graduate sociology paper or grant application. The chief conceit of the essay is, to be sure, exactly the same as the flashy one offered by the book's title: the idea of woman as "castrate." This "Female Eunuch," Greer will argue, is now the upshot of The Feminine Mystique; but for the moment, it all seems rather technical and abstract. "Status ought not to be measured for women in terms of attracting and snaring a man," she writes portentously. "The woman who realizes that she is bound by a million Lilliputian threads in an attitude of impotence and hatred masquerading as tranquillity and love has no option but to run away, if she is not to be corrupted and extinguished utterly." Even an exemplary dramatic formulation of the crisis, borrowed from Ibsen, winds up queerly distanced into the oratorical: "Liberty is terrifying but it is also exhilarating. Life is not easier or more pleasant for the Noras who have set off on their journey to awareness, but it is more interesting, nobler even" (10).

As the almost Emersonian phrasing of the last reveals, the call for revolution thus far suggests a mainly visionary urge and one not greatly distinguished from anyone else's feminist politics or rhetoric of the time. But then, suddenly, the fun begins. "Body" gets down to specifics in "Gender" and suggests a possible *genetics* of female dominance (19). "Curves" introduces *its* problem with a righteous candor: "The most popular image of the female despite the exigencies of the clothing trade is all boobs and buttocks, a hallucinating sequence of parabolae and bulges" (26). "Sex" then lays it all anatomically on the line:

> Part of the modesty about the female genitalia stems from actual distaste. The worst name anyone can be called is *cunt*. The best thing a cunt can be is small and unobtrusive: the anxiety about bigness of the penis is only equaled by anxiety about the smallness of the cunt. No woman wants to find out that she has a twat like a horsecollar; she hopes she is not sloppy or smelly, and obligingly obliterates all signs of her menstruation in the cause of public decency. (32–33)

The successive jolts of the prose are interspersed with equally provocative intertexts. Some are directly from the enemy. " 'The finest bosom in nature is not so fine as what the imagination forms,' " offers Gregory's 1809 *A Father's Legacy to his Daughters* (27). Others partake of contemporary discussions. " 'The myth of the strong black woman is the other side of the coin of the myth of the beautiful dumb blonde,' " writes Eldridge Cleaver, quoted, as we have seen, from his 1968 "The Allegory of Black Eunuchs" in *Soul on Ice*. Mary Wollstonecraft is there from the holy record. For shock, there is Valerie Solanis and *The S.C.U.M. Manifesto*.

But mainly one fixes on the text emerging *here* from behind the market stereotype of "a pretty smile, good teeth, nice tits, long legs, a cheeky arse, a sexy voice," the work of a new rhetorical and political self, "sick of the masquerade." She goes on:

> I'm sick of pretending eternal youth. I'm sick of belying my own intelligence, my own will, my own sex. I'm sick of peering at the world through false eyelashes, so everything I see is mixed with a shadow of bought hairs; I'm sick of weighting my head with a dead mane, unable to move my neck freely, terrified of rain, of wind, of dancing too vig-

orously in case I sweat into my lacquered curls. I'm sick of the Powder Room. I'm sick of pretending that some fatuous male's self important pronouncements are the objects of my undivided attention, I'm sick of going to films and plays when someone else wants to, and sick of having no options of my own about either. I'm sick of being a transvestite. I refuse to be a female impersonator. I am a woman, not a castrate. (58)

This act of psychological self-creation becomes the ground for a proposed rewriting of women's history at large. Too long, Greer asserts, women's bodies and souls have served what she calls the old gynolatry: the movement from baby to girl to puberty to the psychological sell, then on to the further conditioning: woman as raw material, woman's body, woman's work. What is now required is the new rewriting of psychology into history that would be true womanpower: a radical critique of all the old taxonomies of sexual behavior and culture. Love must be pressed out of the old ideological filters of The Ideal, Altruism, Egotism, Obsession, Romance, The Object of Male Fantasy, The Middle-Class Myth of Love and Marriage, Family, Security. Hate must be brought down to real Loathing and Disgust, Abuse, Misery, Resentment, Rebellion.

Yet at the same time, dialectical critique must not be allowed to recast itself as negative theology. "Revolution," Greer insists, must be the final word. But it is an energy that itself requires a dialectical check. "Reaction is not revolution," she writes.

It is not a sign of revolution when the oppressed adopt the manners of the oppressors and practice oppression on their own behalf. Neither is it a sign of revolution when women ape men, and men women, or even when laws against homosexuality are relaxed and the intense sexual connotation of certain kinds of clothes and behavior is diminished. The attempt to relax the severity of the polarity in law bears no relation to the sway that male-female notions hold in the minds of real people. (335)

In an atmosphere of sexual polarization created by contemporary women's texts such as Kate Millett's *Sexual Politics,* Robin Morgan's *Sisterhood Is Powerful,* and Anne Koedt's *Radical Feminism*—not to mention the activist models supplied by media figures such as Angela Davis, Valerie Solanis, or Ti-Grace Atkinson—Greer's book and its summary pronouncements were taken as attempts to turn down the dialectical heat. This, in retrospect, turned out to be more a function of marketing than of message. What Greer was attempting to devise, rather, was a new way for people to continue living together in the world, a synthesis of experience and ideology now characteristic of much postmodern thought as a whole: she was attempting, that is, to move beyond a dialectics bred by categorical thinking, to undo bipolar opposition itself as the bedrock of a logic essentially of aggression and confrontation. "What most 'liberated' women do," she complains,

> is taunt the penis for its misrepresentation of itself, mock men for their overestimation of their virility, instead of seeing how the mistake originated and what effects it has had upon themselves. Men are tired of having all the responsibility for sex; it is time they were relieved of it. And I do not mean that large-scale lesbianism should be adopted, but simply that the emphasis should be taken off male genitality and replaced upon human sexuality. The cunt must come into its own. (338)

We not only, then, undo simple-minded functional ideas of sexual difference but the same ideas of pure difference that are the basis for other distributions and conflicts of power. Because the latter are marked particularly by violence and aggression, the benefits of Greer's program would thus be political in the largest sense. "The question of the female attitude to violence," she continues, "is inseparable from this problem. Perhaps to begin with, for instance, women should labor to be genuinely disgusted by violence, and at least to refuse to reward any victor in a violent confrontation, even to the point of casting their lot on principle with the loser. If they were to withdraw their spectatorship absolutely from male competition, much of its motivation would be gone" (338).

That indeed would be the true *political* upshot of the Sexual Revolution: the cancellation of any further history determined by all the old bipolar alliances of sexuality and power. To be sure, along the way women might find plenty of situational changes to enact, such as training in self-defense, redefinitions of marriage and motherhood, or resistance to a female consumerism. The greatest reward, however, would be in the decision to act itself, in what Greer insists in conclusion must and will be "*the joy in the struggle*" (351). That will be the happy point of rupture in the old fabric, the realization that unworking the nexus of sexuality and power in any one place frees everyone everywhere. "The first significant discovery we shall make as we rocket along our female road to freedom is that men are not free," she writes in conclusion, "and they will seek to make this an argument why nobody should be free. We can only reply that slaves enslave their masters, and by securing our own manumission we may show men the way that they could follow when they jump off their own treadmill"

(352). Real liberation, that is, is not a mere rebellion but an acting apart and a leading. "What," she then asks, *will* you do?"

Heinlein, Robert W. The '60s cult celebrity of Robert W. Heinlein's *Stranger in a Strange Land* exemplifies the role played in reading and writing of the era by science fiction and utopian fantasy.[27] The cover of the Berkley paperback—picturing the hero as love-messiah, suspended above a swimming pool in the presence of two unclothed priestesses—billed the text as "The Most Popular Science Fiction Novel Ever Written." The gaudy tale within, actually a merging of science fiction with such other pulp genres as the hard-boiled detective story and the soft-core romance, showed the reasons for such extraordinary '60s appeal.

Valentine Michael Smith, love child of an expedition to Mars who has been reared there as a Martian, is discovered and returned to earth. He is rescued from greedy earthling politicians and bureaucrats who wish to defraud him of his inheritance—possibly Mars itself and total power over the planet—and perhaps even kill him, by Jill Boardman, a nurse in the hospital where he is confined. She is assisted by a muckraking newspaper columnist and would-be lover, Ben Caxton, who shortly disappears in mysterious circumstances. Jill and her ward take refuge with the celebrated gadfly and eccentric, Jubal Harshaw, at a Poconos retreat where Harshaw surrounds himself with cronies and a female staff best described as a kind of interplanetary Charlie's Angels. Here, Mike is reoriented to his earthling legacy and made aware of the beneficent uses of certain extraordinary powers he is discovered to possess: levitation, trans-logical analysis, astonishing literal memory, total loyalty to anyone who has become—through a sacramental sharing of precious (for a Martian) liquid—a "water brother," and the capacity to make threatening persons and objects disappear. Most important, these powers also include "grokking," a capacity for total communication through a kind of consummate merging. Best of all is the discovery that the latter expresses itself, once the innocent, androgynous Michael achieves his new earthling maleness, most fully and enjoyably through sex.

Shortly, Michael has become the love-god of every woman in the house. Once freed from the clutches of the Terran government by the wily Harshaw, he then disappears with Jill, whom he has chosen of all the women as his companion. They travel and enjoy experience of the world, which includes initiation into a cult of erotic worship and eventual work as carnival performers where Mike practices levitation and other mysteries. Soon, the main act becomes the main show, with Mike himself a new love-messiah surrounded by adoring women who have attached themselves to him. At length, nearly all of the novel's main figures become initiates. Finally, however, the whole enterprise comes crashing down. Mike dies a martyr's death at the hands of an angry mob and is somehow translated to a spiritual realm populated by Martian Old Ones and other departed hucksters he has met along the way.

The love-messiah story, of course, the vision of an incarnate Michael the Archangel (283), found an immediate following in its promotion of a group theogamy of actual love transcending traditional concepts of property, ego, and selfish possession. Here was the ultimate cult of the shared holy orgasm, a total merging of divine and human love, something like maximum sex. No longer is there life or death, time, space, or corporeal limitation. One does not die. One simply discorporates and becomes at one with the Old Ones. All living things are food. It is holy to die and to be eaten. Living and dying are a sacrament, as is the ritual taking of water, drinking, bathing, total immersion in fluid, and weightless being.

Not surprisingly, "grokking" quickly entered the '60s argot as sign and index of the cognoscenti, with sex becoming, of course, the ultimate "grok." "Thou art God" (315), initiates of the divine mysteries must have repeated endlessly to each other. "Thou art God, I am God, all that groks is God" (396).

Along the way, the text offered myriad other fine points of portent and prophecy to be marveled over. Michael's apotheosis would come in San Francisco. Among his chief converts would number a powerful astrologer, once consultant to the wife of the World Federation secretary-general. Among Harshaw's gizmos would be something like a fax machine. The music chosen for Michael's grand meeting with the Terran representative would be the Mars movement of Holst's *The Planets* (202).

As to literary connections, Vonnegut worshippers could find a prophecy of their own master's intergalactic classic of 1969, *Slaughterhouse Five*. Michael in many ways is a prediction of the new love-messiah, Billy Pilgrim, and the mysteries of grokking anticipate the latter's Tralfamadorian idyll with Montana Wildhack. Harshaw, the eccentric gadfly-genius, and Caxton, the underground writer-publisher, anticipate seedy iconoclasts such as Eliot Rosewater and Kilgore Trout. The Martian notions of life and death as simply alternative states of being predict the larger patterns of Tralfamadorian time as an infinite number of such possible moments.

Indeed, in the largest sense, one could weave virtually any of Heinlein's speculations on thought, language, time, love, self, property, and religion into the critique of the traditional "earthling" logic of civilization undertaken by the vast body of '60s texts. At issue through language are all categorical conceptions of meaning, knowledge, and value. "Grok," as in any proper new metadiscourse, especially of love, is finally untranslatable as a word or as a conceptual formulation. "You need to *think* in Martian," an aspiring translator (a Muslim philologist and eventual convert nicknamed "Stinky") helpfully explains, "to grok the word 'grok'" (212).

On the other hand, as with a host of supposedly visionary '60s texts, one now needs no language or logic but one's own to see how language in *Stranger in a Strange Land* generally remained very much a prison-house of gender. Like the hip scriptures of Kerouac, Fariña, Pynchon, or Kesey, Heinlein's mode was distinctly male fantasy, involving deeply conservative representations, often literal, of the "position" of women. Thomas D. Clareson is correct in finding "small wonder" at the time "that with the example of Valentine Michael Smith and the authoritative voice of Jubal Harshaw, *Stranger in a Strange Land* became a cult book during a period whose restless youth demanded change" (153). On the other hand, here and elsewhere the kinds of literary sexism practiced by favorite '60s fantasists, including even the seemingly benign evasions of Tolkien, Hesse, Brautigan, or Castaneda, continue to be striking. One sees in literature and life how the existential politics of '60s feminist discourse often arose as a reaction against both the dominant culture and a host of other visions styling themselves "alternative." As to matters of gender, especially, '60s texts like Heinlein's, while attempting to critique the dominant culture, were also in unforeseen ways unwriting many of their own deeply traditional assumptions and attitudes from within.

Heller, Joseph. From its first sentence onward, Joseph Heller's *Catch-22* became the great antiwar novel of the Generation of Youth. "It was love at first sight" (7), begins the text, introducing us to its protagonist, Yossarian, hospitalized "with a pain in his liver that just fell short of being jaundice" (7), and to his infatuation with A. T. Tappman, the Anabaptist (as the latter repeatedly insists) chaplain of his World War II bomber group. But this was no pacifist-absurdist fantasy. It also began and ended by being truly a war novel, as painful, graphic, hideous, and insane as perhaps any other in the language, with destruction on a grand scale and nonstop murder by the numbers. *Catch-22* is a uniform horror with a dirty secret at its core. "'Help him, help him,' Dobbs sobbed. 'Help him, help him.'" So begins the novel's recurrent primal scene:

"Help who? Help who?" called back Yossarian. . . .

"The bombardier, the bombardier," Dobbs answered in a cry when Yossarian spoke. "He doesn't answer. Help the bombardier, help the bombardier."

"I'm the bombardier," Yossarian cried back at him. "I'm the bombardier. I'm all right. I'm all right."

"Then help him, help him," Dobbs begged. "Help him, help him."

And Snowden lay dying in the back. (51–52)

"I'm cold, I'm cold," complains Snowden, somewhere back in the bowels of the plane where Yossarian has crawled to help him, only to find a gaping wound in the thigh and nothing to minister to it with—the contents of the first-aid kit having been taken by M&M Enterprises and cheerily replaced with a note reading, "What's good for M&M Enterprises is good for the country. Milo Minderbinder" (447).

"I'm cold," Snowden said again in a frail, childlike voice. "I'm cold."

"There, there," Yossarian said, because he did not know what else to say. "There, there."

"I'm cold," Snowden whimpered. "I'm cold."

"There, there. There, there." (447)

As it turns out, the slow-motion horror is just beginning. Snowden whimpers. Yossarian comforts. Somehow he contrives to bandage the thigh wound. Then Snowden points to his other wound, the one to the body, on the inside:

Yossarian ripped open the snaps of Snowden's flak suit and heard himself scream wildly as Snowden's insides slithered down to the floor in a soggy pile and just kept dripping out. A chunk of flak more than three inches big had shot into his other side just underneath the arm and blasted all the way through, drawing whole mottled quarts of Snowden along with it through the gigantic hole in his ribs it made as it blasted out. Yossarian screamed a second time and squeezed both hands over his eyes. His teeth were chattering in horror. He forced himself to look again. Here was God's plenty, all right, he thought bitterly as he stared—liver, lungs, kidneys, ribs, stomach, and bits of the stewed tomatoes Snowden had eaten that day for lunch. Yossarian hated stewed tomatoes and turned away dizzily and began to vomit, clutching his burning throat. (449)

He continues to vomit. Snowden wakes up, sees him vomit, faints. Snowden complains. Yossarian comforts. It is no use.

> Yossarian was cold, too, and shivering uncontrollably. He felt goose pimples clacking all over him as he gazed down despondently at the grim secret Snowden had spilled all over the messy floor. It was easy to read the message in his entrails. Man was matter, that was Snowden's secret. Drop him out a window and he'll fall. Set fire to him and he'll burn. The spirit gone, man is garbage. That was Snowden's secret. Ripeness was all. (451)

Here, then, at once grimly encapsulated and casting for lines everywhere from Shakespeare to Eisenhower's secretary of defense, is a novel not only about war but about the whole war-breeding system. It is about war, that is, as Alfred Kazin has observed, exactly as it is about the modern nation-state, now stripped down to its pure function, which is to make war. The system runs on its own power. It is not so much controlled as administered by smiling engineers of destruction: generals like Dreedle, Peckem, and, eventually, Scheisskopf; military bureaucrats like Cargill, Cathcart, Korn, and Danby, all contending for first place on the murder roll; paranoid midlife executives like Major Major Major Major, in when he is out, as he instructs his office sergeant, and not in when he *is* in; ingratiating wheeler-dealers like Milo Minderbinder, Corn Belt capitalist making a killing on killing. There are captains by the score and pilot officers designed as interchangeable parts but survivors, virtually none. As the individual chapters unfold, often named for such individual figures—Dunbar, Clevenger, Orr, Appleby, Havermeyer, Nately, Hungry Joe, McWatt, Dobbs, Aarfy, Kid Sampson—the first thing we have to get used to is that they are usually irrelevant to the story at hand. The chapters are almost invariably *about* someone else. When we do get to the figures named, there is the equally invariable information of their demise. Only later comes the shock of realizing that we have been reading a roll call of the dead.

Amidst all this, rising steadily, are the new mutants: ex-PFC Wintergreen, who controls the mimeograph, terrifies his superiors over the phone by telling them their memos are too prolix, and whispers the dread incantatory name, "T. S. Eliot." He in turn is eventually topped at the top by the ex-lieutenant, Scheisskopf, now promoted to Lieutenant General Sheisskopf, the shithead now become the head shit, because he can make men *march*—and thereby nosing out even Peckem, head of USO tours and other activities deemed "Special Services," who contends that if precision bombing cities into rubble isn't a special service, what is?

At the bottom are the victims: the Soldier in White, Lucianna, Nately's whore, Nately's whore's little sister.

Against such a prospect of disaster, one American captain perseveres, a captain with the very un-American name, Yossarian. *John* Yossarian in fact, we eventually discover, as Cathcart and Korn, increasingly thwarted by his hijinks, try to cajole him on a first name basis. All you have to do is "like us," they plead. That would be "odious," Yossarian replies. And of course that *would* be odious, we see, for from word one he is a lover, not a fighter. John is a man with a redeeming Word. He is also Prometheus the yellow-belly, with a nearly jaundiced eye for nearly everything, and a code that is exactly the opposite of any military code.

So little, indeed, is Yossarian a war-lover that he becomes a walking inventory of offenses against such a code[28]—here, in horrific simplicity, taken down to its one irreducible provision, "Catch-22." Its classic application comes early in the novel when Yossarian asks the squadron surgeon to excuse him from flying on the grounds that he has become insane. The Doc agrees, only to say, however, that, since he has asked, he cannot be excused, since to ask such a thing on the grounds that one is crazy is to reveal a rational concern for one's own welfare. Thus, one is not really crazy. Yossarian tries to interpret:

> There was only one catch, and that was Catch-22, which specified that a concern for one's own safety in the face of dangers that were real and immediate was the process of a rational mind. Orr was crazy and could be grounded. All he had to do was ask; and as soon as he did, he would no longer be crazy and would have to fly more missions. Orr would be crazy to fly more missions and sane if he didn't, but if he was sane he had to fly them. If he flew them he was crazy and didn't have to; but if he didn't want to, he is sane and had to. Yossarian was moved very deeply by the absolute simplicity of this clause of Catch-22 and let out a respectful whistle.
>
> "That's some catch, that Catch-22," he observed.
>
> "It's the best there is," Doc Daneeka agreed. (47)

But Catch-22 is not just there for Yossarian, of course. It is there, as invoked even by a sibylline old Italian woman, for everyone. "Catch-22," the old woman repeated, rocking her head up and down. "Catch-22. Catch-22 says they have a right to do anything we can't stop them from doing" (416).

In response to this, for both his own sake and everyone's, Yossarian can only act so as to have them literally throw the book at him. He is a coward, a slacker, and a malingerer, a drunkard, and a sexual profligate. He is continually insubordinate, shows relentless disrespect for superior officers, and provides false information on military matters whenever possible. In a desperate plot—which naturally backfires—he momentarily avoids action by changing a bomb line on a map, making it look as if a major target, Bologna, has been captured when it has not. He appears for an awards ceremony, where he is to receive a medal for bravery, totally naked. He is, in a phrase, out of uniform. (There is also, of course, the technical problem of finding a place to pin the medal.) On nearly any occasion possible, he is AWOL—and at one point is actually arrested for being so by military police ignoring a cohort, Captain Aardvark, who has just thrown a young woman to her death in a courtyard several stories below.

At the end, like crazy Orr, he even plans the big one: Sweden and desertion. In a war, this is the truly capital crime: refusal to stay and kill or be killed is punishable by execution.

By the mid '60s, the imaging of the war-breeding system in *Catch-22* had found for American youth its newest correlative horror in Vietnam. Indeed, as Kazin especially had predicted, here was realized what had always been the true genius of Heller's text—it was not about the last war so much as the next one. Accordingly, it found new audiences in both print and movie versions and was complemented by new absurdist experiments such as Norman Mailer's *Why Are We In Vietnam?* and Kurt Vonnegut's *Slaughterhouse Five.* In turn, out of Vietnam itself would come texts in brilliant creative extrapolation: John Sack's *M;* William Eastlake's *The Bamboo Bed;* Charles Durden's *No Bugles, No Drums;* Michael Herr's *Dispatches.* Meanwhile, at home, one no longer had to go to Vietnam or anywhere else to find Catch-22. Catch-22 had become a conversational commonplace, a catch phrase for anyone's being in a situation where *they* can do anything *we* cannot stop them from doing. By the mid '70s, it may still have been likely that many Americans had not actually read the book. But they knew the text.

Herr, Michael. Michael Herr's *Dispatches* continues to be regarded both as a major depiction of the experience of the Vietnam War for Americans who went there and as one of the most brilliant analyses of the larger cultural and geopolitical vectors intersecting there to make the resultant tragedy for Americans *and* Vietnamese a defining moment in our history. If Vietnam was America's Nineteenth Nervous Breakdown, it was also, as Herr put it brilliantly, where all the mythic tracks converged. Beyond

fifty-eight thousand American dead and the more than two million Vietnamese likely killed or wounded, what also died in Vietnam was the myth
of American historical innocence.

Dispatches did not appear as a book until 1977. It had its origins, however, in a number of *Esquire* articles that became instant late '60s classics.
Six months after the 1968 Tet Offensive, in the August issue, the first appeared. Its title, "Hell Sucks," taken from a G.I. helmet graffito, was a
giveaway. Sherman may have said that war was hell. A nineteen-year-old
American kid in Vietnam was more likely to say just that it sucks. Somebody had finally found a way of writing about the first rock n' roll war.
The one-liners were song titles: "Born to Lose," "Born to Raise Hell,"
"Time is on My Side." The war stories were cartoons. " 'Hey, Esquire!' "
he remembers a Marine shouting at him in Hue. " 'Hey, you want a story,
man? Write this: I'm up here on 881, this was May. I'm up here walkin'
the ridgeline an' this Zip jumps up smack into me, lays this AK-47 right
into me, only he's so surprised I got my whole clip off 'fore he knew how
to thank me for it. Grease one' " (67).

Here was reporting in Day Glo images and words that no one truly had
ever used to write about war before. The New Journalism had found its
heavy Heart-of-Darkness trip in Vietnam.[29] Perhaps, Herr began, it may
have been possible for *someone* to write something like straight reportage
about Vietnam. But now, as in Conrad, the moral seemed to be about just
the unending darkness, a horror that had become all-enveloping. "Before
Tet," wrote Herr,

> there was some clean touch to jungle encounters, some virtue to their
> brevity, always the promise of quick release from whatever horror there
> was. The war went on in bursts, meeting engagements; and cover-
> ing it—particularly in the Highlands and the Delta, II Corps and IV
> Corps—you were always a tourist, a tripper who could summon up
> helicopters like taxis. You would taxi in, the war would break over you
> suddenly and then go away, and you would taxi out. Enough chances
> were taken to leave you exhilarated, and, except for the hangovers that
> any cheap thrill will give you, it was pleasant enough. (66)

"Now," he goes on, "it is awful, just plain awful, awful without relief."
And it is awful, he concludes, in ways only Americans can make it. "We
are not really a particularly brutal people," he observes, "certainly no more
brutal than we've been in other wars, acquiring it as the war goes on. But
our machine is devastating. And versatile. It can do almost everything but
stop" (66).

This celebrated essay was followed by two others, in the same magazine during September and October 1969, about the Marines and the siege of Khe Sanh. Then, in April 1970, appeared a troubled, meditative reflection entitled "War Correspondent: A Re-Appraisal."

It would take seven more years for the text we now know as *Dispatches* to appear. Yet somehow, then and now, no one and no thing about the Vietnam in the text had seemed to get a day older. Herr had done through journalism what Vonnegut had proposed in fiction: he had frozen something in Time while setting it loose in History. "Somewhere all the mythic tracks intersected," he wrote, "from the lowest John Wayne wetdream to the most aggravated soldier-poet fantasy, and where they did I believe that everyone knew everything about everyone else, every one of us there a true volunteer" (20). As he affirmed at the end of the completed book, as a defining experience of the '60s, what happened to the Americans and the Vietnamese in that unforgettable place had happened to us all. "Vietnam Vietnam Vietnam," he wrote, a dreadful mantra, at once a remembrance and a prayer, "we've all been there" (260).

Hesse, Hermann. Of the three or four fantasy mythicists most widely adopted by '60s readers—Vonnegut, Tolkien, Brautigan, possibly Castaneda—Hermann Hesse remains notable both for the variety and proliferation of his texts at one time or another adopted as '60s youth-scriptures. Only Vonnegut seemed comparably diverse. On the other hand, as the latter himself noted, there was in Hesse a remarkable consistency of general appeal: "seeking and finding," described simply and innocently, could not fail to make one "deeply loved among the American young who are questing" (*Wampeters* 108). Best of all, on a fallen, materialistic, bourgeois landscape of *kultur,* was Hesse's world-embracing spirit of cosmic inquiry. Here, on one hand, in texts such as *Demian* or *Steppenwolf,* was a saintly outlaw-connoisseur of Western postromantic decadence across the range of literature, music, philosophy, and the arts, and, on the other, in texts such as *Siddhartha* or *Journey to the East,* was the voyager toward nonwestern mystic enlightenment. Whatever the passage, Vonnegut noted, the result was always "something satisfying—holiness, wisdom, hope" (108).

Further, the always close, confiding reflections of Hesse's life and thought in individual protagonists and works invited '60s youth to sense in experience *and* art a prophetic inventory of uncanny alignments in attitude. They relentlessly read the master into the texts and vice versa. As the Vietnam War took precedence among national issues, readers found literary solace in Hesse's life as an artist-pacifist among angry patriots in

World War I–era Germany and later as a Swiss exile devoting his life to the quest for a new spiritual individuality. They applauded his lifelong quarrel with middle-class moralism, smugness, dullness, comfort, piety, and mediocrity. They joined in his celebration of the sensual life—food, drink, sexuality, ritual pharmotherapy—and of the body as integral to the quest for spiritual completion. And they followed his probing into alternative theories of consciousness, which often presciently came up looking very like '60s meditation and drug mysticism. Many of them even literally enacted, like Hesse himself and earlier Hesse-pilgrims, a Journey to the East; others, interiorizing the quest, devoted themselves to lives of reading and writing in search of their own eclectic new syntheses of spiritualities and philosophies of consciousness.

The result of such work was a huge body of textual production, widely published and translated, and, from the late '50s through the early '70s, issued and reissued in a bewildering array of editions.[30] Of those in paperback that found favor at some point or another, one should mention in the order of their writing: *Demian, Siddhartha, Steppenwolf, Narcissus and Goldmund, Magister Ludi* (also published as *The Glass Bead Game*), and *Journey to the East.* In all these, Hesse seemed to have written over and over again the Bildungsroman, the old romantic novel of education in a brilliantly prophetic '60s key. And Vonnegut, if playing somewhat for laughs, did not overestimate the romance of the generic Hesse plot (or, as he wisely observed for that matter, among other contemporary favorites, the Salinger or Kerouac plot):

> A man travels a lot, is often alone. Money is not a serious problem. He seeks spiritual comfort, and avoids marriage and boring work. He is more intelligent than his parents and most of the people he meets. Women like him. So do poor people. So do wise old men. He experiments with sex, finds it nice but not tremendous. He encounters many queerly lovely hints that spiritual comfort really can be found. The world is beautiful. There is magic around. (107)

What was unique to Hesse in this regard was the global character of his cultural synthesis. Out of the cultural legacy of the West and the ritual encounter with the East had come the latest version of the old romantic narrative of growth of consciousness. Yearning adolescence met itself coming back around in cosmic hallucination.

Across the range of his works, Hesse, to use his own phrasing from *Steppenwolf,* was "Magic Theater"—perhaps "not for everybody," but among intiates at least offering something for anybody. And nowhere was that more clearly demonstrated than in *Steppenwolf* itself, the master-text in which the figure was contained.[31]

To put this another way, of all Hesse's works, *Steppenwolf* provides the site of entry into the Hesse-world of *Krisis*—itself the title of another intensely lyrical text by the author of the same period. In its ever unfolding intertextual layerings, its endless compoundings of illusion upon illusion, *Steppenwolf* itself becomes the Magic Theater in which Hesse stages the hallucinatory drama of twentieth-century consciousness.

The framing of crisis of instant appeal to '60s readers was, in this case, the familiar one inherited by Hesse and other critics of philosophy in the West from Nietzsche: the dialectic of the Apollonian and the Dionysian, the endless Western estrangement of mind from body by Reason, Science, and Objective Knowledge. Yet beyond this historical politics of consciousness lay more immediate appeals to identification as well.

The tale begins by explicitly connecting the first stages of the titular protagonist's quest after authentic selfhood with his sense of alienation from the mediocre contentments of the middle class and a nostalgia for an older "bourgeois world as something solid and secure" (26). There follows dialectical flirtation with a utopian socialist dream of transcending the traditional, centered, bourgeois historical self (52). But shortly a new synthesis is achieved through further alternative visions of self offered through Eastern modes of consciousness and through the protagonist's accompanying experiences with popular dance, music, sex, and drugs. Along the way, we also find that a primary ground of Harry Haller's estrangement from the world has been his public opposition to his Kaiser's and countrymen's pursuit of what he has seen from the outset as a stupid, unjust, and jingoistic war (116). In this position of making "war against war" (118), he has consequently been adjudged a traitor in his own land.

Further adventures and crises unfold: Harry meets a mysterious dance hall hostess, Hermine, at once a kind of new, mysterious spiritual guide and a simulacrum of his trusted childhood friend, "Hermann." She/He, and new cohorts such as the prostitute Maria and the jazz musician Pablo, lead him further toward full sensual awakening. Harry and Hermine practice a kind of strange polymorphous precoital bundling. Maria introduces him to the mysteries of love. Pablo introduces him to drugs, music, and group sex. Harry Haller, the Steppenwolf, traditional alienated man, the latest candidate for suicide, has now become a living, breathing, counterculture freak. Now he can commit the real suicide, which is the murder of the old alienated self, to find a new integrated self.

Finally comes the Masked Ball, the final entry into the true Magic Theater of consciousness. It is the starburst apotheosis of self, the splintering of self into a prismatic, polyvalent, infinite multiplicity of possible selves. And in the climax to Harry's cruel, hallucinatory passage—the murder, after apparently finding her in the sexual embrace of Pablo, of Hermine—it is also the final dissolution of self. This is the true end of the magical mystery tour, or, as the book phrases it, "HOW ONE KILLS FOR LOVE" (203). At the end, Harry/Hermine is the newest Faust or Don Juan in Hell, which now is simply the core of inner being. Still, there is a resolution to persevere. "One day I would be a better hand at the game," he concludes. "I would learn how to laugh. Pablo was waiting for me, and Mozart too" (218).

Here, then, was the ultimate self-reifying '60s text in the fullest sense. Readers who enter the Magic Theater world of *Steppenwolf,* as Harry himself reveals, know that it is not only the Steppenwolf's story but their own as well:

"Hermine," I said, "an extraordinary thing happened to me the other day. An unknown man gave me a little book, the sort of thing you'd buy at a fair, and inside I found my whole story and everything about me. Rather remarkable, don't you think?"

"What was it called," she asked lightly.

"Treatise on the Steppenwolf."

"Oh, *Steppenwolf* is magnificent! And are you the Steppenwolf? Is that meant for you?"

"Yes, it's me. I am one who is half-wolf and half-man, or thinks himself so at least." (113)

"Yes, it's me." This seems to have been the profound response of a youth-readership who, if given no final answers of identity, could find at least a sensitive and prophetic wonder of identification.

Hoffman, Abbie. Abbie Hoffman is dead, a suicide from booze, pills, and chronic middle-age depression. He had spent much time after the '60s hiding out to avoid imprisonment on a drug charge, surfacing finally as an environmental activist in upstate New York. He had also gotten his face changed. One suspects, though, that twenty years would have done the same thing to the falcon eyes, the fright wig hair, the great beak of a nose, the crazed, glittery smile. Like most of us do, Hoffman had just turned into a gray, nondescript, puffy-looking middle-aged person starting to get old. That is one Abbie Hoffman text.

Some better Abbie Hoffman texts, as far as '60s reading and writing are concerned, will always be titles like *Revolution for the Hell of It* and *Steal*

This Book. To be sure, it is hard, now as then, to assess their circulation and influence. Although widely known and discussed, they always suggested something of the novelty or curio. Especially now, they seem mementoes, relics, pieces of the counterculture action, something different even from dog-eared copies of Heller, Kesey, Norman O. Brown, or R. D. Laing. These were nose-thumbing experiments in every respect, at once passionately political and crassly promoted, the true marketing of the Revolution: part polemic and serious how-to-do-it; part hip comic and graffiti scrawl. In Hoffman's case, if he could have gotten paperbacks to talk, sing, dance, or fly, he would have done it.

Revolution for the Hell of It, for example, claimed an author named "Free." It was also dedicated to "Free." In a prefatory letter from a concerned mother to her children, "Free" was a legendary New York hippie. It was full of pictures of "Free," always somebody different. Free is the one with the mustache, free is black, free is a young woman in a drum major's coat (arm in arm in this case with somebody who looks like Abbie Hoffman). Free is a Hell's Angel. In one last shot, echoed on the back jacket, Free is being busted. *Revolution* contained advice, encouragement, and warning to "Free"; instruction, in a phrase, in how to be "Free." "Free" is anybody. "Free" is everybody.

As to genre or mode, on the other hand, one quickly undergoes a shock of distinctly American recognition. Like his revolutionary twin Jerry Rubin in *Do It!,* Hoffman is also writing his '60s antitext in that great national tradition of the popular mechanics of the American soul as purveyed by Benjamin Franklin, Ralph Waldo Emerson, Dale Carnegie, and Norman Vincent Peale. It is the text as great American do-it-yourself project in which the project is yourself,[32] but the product is Revolution.

"Revolution for the hell of it?" asks the author. "Why not? It's all a bunch of phony words anyway. Once one has experienced LSD, existential revolution, fought the intellectual game-playing of the individual in society, of one's identity, one realizes that action is the only reality; not only reality but morality as well. One learns reality is a subjective experience. It exists in my head. I am the Revolution" (9).

The text that ensues truly can be described best as a homemade autobiography of the Revolution: diaries, letters, reflections, self-interviews, newspaper clippings, inside history, cartoons, posters, slogans, the attempt to construct from the pop detritus at hand, personal and social, something like new Instructions to Youth. When all else fails, there can be citations of acceptable "authority." Marshall McLuhan, for example, taken from, of all places, an interview in the Columbia University yearbook, proves helpful with the idea of Yippie: "Young people are looking for a formula for putting on the universe—*participation mystique*. They do not look for detached patterns—for ways of relating themselves to the world, a la nineteenth century" (103). Abbie Hoffman, however, still has to supply the new active ingredient: "a high element of risk, drama, excitement and bullshit" (103).

As a text of Yippie, *Revolution for the Hell of It* found commercial publication in 1968 with the Dial Press—even as Hoffman tried his best inside and out to make a total mockery of the enterprise. Maybe he is writing this work, he admits up front, "just to see that title on a book jacket." Or, maybe "the book jacket won't have the title on it" but instead "two sleeves, a collar, buttons down the front, and the word BOOK on the back" (62). That, one assumes, would be as close to a confession from the heart as one could get. Or maybe it would be getting something off one's chest? Or perhaps giving the reader the shirt off one's back. Or just a way of saying "Free" on one side and "Book" on the other.

Precisely in his acting out the text as a one-man Yippie-dada show, Hoffman was uproariously reinventing the '60s paperback youth-scripture as a cultural commodity. By being an autobiography of somebody named Free, the book *was* in fact an autobiography of the Revolution, and as such it also offered a fairly substantial inside history of the Revolution. Like Jerry Rubin's *Do It!* two years later, *Revolution for the Hell of It* became the textual equivalent of a happening. Most of the legendary high moments of the Movement get covered: the first great Central Park charge of the Flower Brigade; the driving of the Moneychangers from the Stock Exchange; the levitation of the Pentagon; the founding of the Youth International Party; Chicago 1968; and the ultimate achievement of Yippie, the Perfect Mess ("where everyone," we are told, even Mayor Daley, "gets what he wants" [122]). Advice is rendered on future action along with notes on props; leftover "extra quotes, bits, and pieces"; and assembled insights from Terry Southern, George Sorel, and Albert Camus to Lewis Carroll, Abraham Maslow and Marshall McLuhan. Jesus is there, as is Nicholas von Hoffman, telling us "We are the people our parents warned us against" (183). Finally, there is leftover "Ego Tripping" and something called an Epilogue.

And then, naturally, there is more: "This Part is Absolutely Free" reads the title of a completely new section—the recycling, it turns out, of an older textual project by the author entitled, "Fuck the System." As promised, it is a complete guide to free living in America—food, clothing, shelter, entertainment—something like a Yippie Baedeker. At the end, as at the beginning, *Revolution for the Hell of It* pushed the idea of a totally free book about a totally free country to the literal limit.

Shortly, a newer Hoffman property, *Steal This Book,* pushed the idea over the edge. The manic hilarity now seemed unable to avoid a sense of the new political urgencies. To be sure, the rip-off gag of the title—the text as revolutionary appropriation—was complemented on the back by a photo of the author smirking larcenously near a bookrack with notice of his thanks to the thirty or so major publishers who refused to print his text.[33] ("This book," one editor was happily cited as saying, "will end free speech!")

Yet there on the back as well was the secret subtitle—"A HANDBOOK OF SURVIVAL AND WARFARE FOR THE CITIZENS OF WOODSTOCK NATION"—suggesting that the title meant exactly what it said about matters of language, power, authority, and commodity. Further, as in an increasing number of works late in the decade, the text now began with the author himself actually in prison, the new American "graduate school," he calls it, "of survival." For so, in effect, are, he implies, we all: "Here you learn how to use toothpaste as glue, fashion a shiv out of a spoon and build intricate communication networks. Here too, you learn the only rehabilitation possible—hatred of oppression" (iii). He goes on: "*Steal This Book* is, in a way, a manual of survival in the prison that is Amerika. It preaches jailbreak. It shows you where and exactly how to place the dynamite that will destroy the walls" (iii).

This is what it has come to in America at the end of the counterculture trail. *Steal This Book* is one last anarchic run for daylight, one last attempt either to keep the Revolution afoot or to go down alive and giggling in the crazy chase. In the first sense, *Steal This Book* is truly a kind of last Yippie whole earth catalog or "access to tools"—including lists, diagrams, bibliographies, addresses, and contacts. On the other, it is one last effort at keeping up the old loony vaudeville: the stoned author and friends posing for illustrations of key instructional points; Nancy without Sluggo booming "Right On"; Goofy giving Power to the People; an FBI post office wanted poster of Richard Nixon.

Meanwhile, the last-ditch curriculum unfolds. First comes "SURVIVE," one more guide to the ways the land of the free can really *be* free: free food, clothing and furniture, transportation, medical care, communication (including press conferences, wall painting, use of the flag, radio, free telephones, and pay phones—the last case complete with technical circuitry diagrams for easy access), even free money; but also free dope, complete with free introductory full-page Gilbert Shelton diptych of the

Fabulous Furry Freak Brothers "Before" and "After" dope, and illustrated instructions on how to roll a joint. Next comes "FIGHT," a current counter-culture guerrilla guide, with sections on communications, equipment, tactics, chemical and explosives fabrication, first aid, and legal aid. In addition, there is useful information on theft, as well as good prankster stuff and monkey warfare, and also, if necessary, weaponry and underground intelligence data. Then comes "LIBERATE!," a latest updating of "Fuck the System," with assistance-information now greatly expanded and divided city by city into Fuck (in the following order) New York, Chicago, Los Angeles, and San Francisco.

Finally comes an extensive appendix, arranged carefully according to chapter and section, an annotated bibliography of texts recommended as further resources. It is entitled "Other Books Worth Stealing." After all, the text concludes (just below the picture of Janis Joplin singing at the bottom of the last page), "FREEDOM'S JUST ANOTHER WORD/FOR NOTHIN' LEFT TO LOSE/NOTHIN'/I MEAN NOTHIN' HONEY IF IT AIN'T FREE" (308). In a typical last attempt at connection between words and things in America, such remained the better text of Hoffman's own exemplary life.

Kerouac, Jack. Some readers of this study will have identified the origin of its theme in a quotation from Jack Kerouac's *On the Road* cited in my opening comments. The particular passage reads: "I pictured myself in a Denver bar that night, with all the gang, and in their eyes I would be strange and ragged and like the Prophet who has walked across the land to bring the dark Word, and the only Word I had was 'Wow!'" (37). The sentence captures the spirit of one of the two or three books of the '50s that most fully imaged the sense of generational restlessness and anticipation that would find its expression in '60s youth-culture:[34] the bebop Denver night, the bar, the gang, the strange and ragged pilgrim-Prophet having walked thither out of the Western landscape, the ultimate illumination that would be the Word. Here and at other sites of epiphany, young Americans afoot on the continent would find a common source of identity in the knowledge, described by the work's narrator, Sal Paradise, that "they were like the man with the dungeon stone and the gloom, rising from the underground, the sordid hipsters of America, a new beat generation I was slowly joining" (54).

At the same time, in arguing how important a text *On the Road* turned out to be for '60s youth, it is important to note from the beginning all the other '60s books, often with less happy effects, it turned out *not* to be. It is all quite male, for instance. Women in this book are girls, good ones are chicks, and bad ones are whores. Also, of course, queers are queers. And similarly, for all their romanticizings of the racial other—"the happy, true-hearted, ecstatic Negroes of America" (180), for instance, or "the great, grave Indians" (280)—the White pilgrims of *On the Road* retain a strictly tourist status.

Throughout Kerouac's novel, as in so much '60s thought and writing to come, moral prestige among youth is often built upon comfortable contempt for a material culture that makes many of its countercultural gestures possible. There is an easy hedonism, a romanticization of voluntary poverty, and a glorification of sexual freedom coupled with a strange domestic nostalgia. As to that archdemon, American technology, it should not be lost on anyone that the chief embodiment of freedom in the text, the literal modus operandi of its possibility, is the automobile—and the bigger, faster, more flashy and American, the better. If Dean, the book's hero of action, the Zen-master of the driveshaft (234), is something like the king of time, the manic industry of his schedule-keeping in the quest for Kicks also suggests something like Benjamin Franklin on amphetamines. Similarly, if Sal, his narrative alter ego, seems on a desperate search for authenticity, he often hucksters into makeshift truth his own windy in-articulateness. The narrator's superlatives are relentless. At a finite limit one simply stops counting, for instance, the number of "greatest laughs in the world." As with Holden Caulfield, adolescent rhapsodizing becomes pure bombast: "We lay on our backs, looking at the ceiling," Sal says after a failed lovemaking session with Rita Bettencourt ("a nice little girl," he says characteristically, in one of his bad Hemingway imitations, "simple and true, and tremendously afraid of sex"), "and wondered what God had wrought when he made life so sad. We made vague plans to meet in Frisco." He goes on:

> Boys and girls in America have such a sad time together; sophistication demands that they submit to sex immediately without proper preliminary talk. Not courting talk—real straight talk about souls, for life is holy and every moment is precious. I heard the Denver and Rio Grande locomotive howling off to the mountains. I wanted to pursue my star further. (57)

Yet here at least, for the young, was straight talk of sex and souls that captured the poetry of their collective yearning. Someone, writing directly out of life, in their thoughts and their language, was pushing toward a new discourse of epiphany. As a Jack Kerouac could become a Sal Paradise; a Neal Cassady, a Dean Moriarity; or an Allen Ginsberg, a Carlo Marx (as the trio of leading personae in this book could be readily identified), so every youthful seeker after enlightenment might participate in the excitement of a new creation. Accordingly, *On the Road* and the other writings by Kerouac and the Beats came to comprise a body of cultic reference, complete with commentaries, concordances, glosses, and cross-listings of who was who and what was what. And in a larger cultural domain, these texts also wrote a holy roadmap of the continent, with most of the stations of the pilgrimage fixed at the urban loci of that generation's sacred places: New York (especially the Village), Chicago, New Orleans, Denver, San Francisco, Los Angeles.

As to the language of a post-1945 literature of youth, *On the Road* mapped a crucial opening exploration in a new geography of style. Automatic writing it was called, spontaneous writing, maybe even, as Truman Capote is said to have snorted, not writing at all but just typing. At its most authentic, however, it could seem nothing less than language reified as generational pulse, the heartbeat itself of huge, teeming, ecstatic life. "The only people for me," Sal tells us early in his narrative, "are the mad ones, the ones who are mad to live, mad to talk, mad to be saved, desirous of everything at the same time, the ones who never yawn or say a commonplace thing, but burn, burn, burn like fabulous yellow roman candles exploding like spiders across the stars and in the middle you see the blue centerlight pop and everybody goes 'Awww!'" (8).

And in turn, through such moments, a style of saying and writing actually did seem to render itself into some pure, unmediated style of being. It found a new hero of action in the hipster-madman-saint, Dean Moriarity, Ahab speeding at the wheel (234). It found, Ishmael-like, its corresponding hero of thought in Sal Paradise, the hip grammatologist, the yearning life-amanuensis. It found its new trip in the manic crisscrossing of the continent itself, the teeming rush of freedom and mobility, for one last moment the attempt to elevate American transience into an ecstasy of flight. "The point being," crows Dean in Denver, high at the top of America, "that we know what IT is and we know TIME and we know that everything is really FINE" (194).

It was, of course, the old dream as well, the American dream of the conquest of History. And eventually, in this text, as in all the others, the road runs out and time runs down in a line of exhaustion. At the end, Sal, deserted by Dean in Mexico City, now in turn prepares to leave Dean behind in New York.

Still, important new visions had been charted of America and also of things beyond. As to geopolitical prophecy, for instance, the road eventually led away from the night-hipster cities of America and off the continent itself to the place of history and epiphany that we would eventually learn to call the Third World. This Sal realizes fully toward the end while pushing southward in the Mexican night. It was now no longer, he says, "like driving across Carolina, or Texas, or Arizona, or Illinois; but like driving across the world and into the places where we would finally learn ourselves among the Fellahin Indians of the world, the essential strain of basic primitive." And "these people," he realizes, "were unmistakably Indians and were not at all like the Pedros and Panchos of silly civilized American lore—they had high cheekbones, and slanted eyes, and soft ways; they were not fools, they were not clowns; they were great, grave Indians and they were the source of mankind and the fathers of it. The waves are Chinese, but the earth is an Indian thing" (280–81). Accordingly, he realizes, "when destruction comes to the world of 'history' and the Apocalypse of the Fellahin returns once more as so many times before, people will still stare from the caves of Mexico as well as from the caves of Bali, where it all began and Adam was suckled and taught to know" (281).

But for the moment, the closest impact of this cosmic voyaging, soon to be imitated and extended by countless youth-successors, would be at home. In more immediate geographies of spirit, they would write their own Beat agendas of the hedonistic and the holy, the sociopathic and the sainted. There would be the attempt to be like Dean, in every moment, the "HOLY GOOF" (194), "out of his mind"—as Sal describes him (and thereby dreams for himself)—"with true belief" (120). "Ahem, Harrumph, Egad" (250), he shouts. "Ah! God! Life!" (140). "Oh, man, the things I could tell you!" (162).

On the Road would eventually help set a succeeding generation on the American journey toward enlightenment. Many of them would indite the poetry of its names into a roll call of legend: Sal Paradise, Dean Moriarity, Carlo Marx, Old Bull Lee, Remi Boncoeur, Ed Dunkel, Chad King, Tommy Snark, Marylou, Camille, Jane Lee, Galatea Dunkel, Rita Bettencourt. Some, as the youth-culture of the new era reified itself into fact, would even know it as a literal roadmap. But even more would know it by its existential vibrations, enacting in journeys of self-discovery—often undertaken while staying at home somewhere in the middle of America— the excitement of the Word so long awaited and now brought to them at last in scriptures they could truly call their own.

Kesey, Ken. Ken Kesey's enshrinement as a '60s culture-hero testified both to the manic genius of his own creativity and to his significant gift for self-promotion. In an era defining itself through various reciprocities of reality and imagining, life and art, Kesey became an exemplar of such composite enterprise. He was Ken Kesey, author of major novels: *One Flew Over the Cuckoo's Nest* and *Sometimes a Great Notion*. He was Tom Wolfe's Kesey of the Pranksters, the Acid Tests, the Magic Bus. He was the Kesey of counterculture legend and anecdote: the star college wrestler and Woodrow Wilson Fellow from the tall timber country of the Pacific Northwest; the writing prodigy among the Stanford bohemians of Perry Lane; the part-time orderly in a VA mental hospital paid by the government to experiment with LSD; the high priest of La Honda;[35] the international fugitive from a drug warrant; the aging, self-important, brain-dead party-crasher; and now, along with Timothy Leary perhaps, the nation's longest living counterculture joke.

Whatever the various texts of the Kesey legend, it is virtually impossible to overstate the contribution of one of Kesey's books to '60s legend at least as it was understood at the time. That book, for vast numbers of '60s youth *and* their literary mentors, became pure gospel. Its title was, of course, *One Flew Over the Cuckoo's Nest.*

In design and appeal, it too was, above all a testament to Kesey's composite order of genius, a total performance. A first masterstroke was his focusing of a sensitive youth-genre, the mental illness narrative as depicted in Salinger's *The Catcher in the Rye* or Plath's *The Bell Jar,* through the strange, silent, often hallucinatory refraction of events as seen by the giant Chinook Indian, Chief Broom, the original American, the last of his mighty race. A second was the conflation in Nurse Ratched of the devouring mother of every child's nightmare and the ultimate functionary in a society of adjustment, not so much the main cog in the totalitarian, thoroughly bureaucratized, antiseptic, operational system as the jeweled bearing upon which the whole apparatus depends.

Kesey's crowning creation, however, was of course Randall Patrick McMurphy. Directly in the lineage of the hero-as-revolutionary-sociopath variously depicted by contemporaries such as Kerouac, Heller, Fariña, and Pynchon, he is surely the complete madman-saint: the jailbird who talks his way into the nuthouse, the con artist as self-anointed bull goose loony, the sane lunatic with the true revolutionary method in his madness, and the inmate who ultimately liberates himself and all the other inmates from the asylum and the totalitarian regime of the keepers. "One week," he proclaims, throwing down the gauntlet upon arrival, is all it will take to show the head lady who is in charge. "One week, and if I don't have her to where she don't know whether to shit or go blind, the bet is yours" (68).

The "head lady" so named, Big Nurse as the inmates call her, is surely the toughest customer in the place. Presiding behind her thick glass window in the control room, a walking manual of procedures, protocols, precedents, and regulations, she somehow absorbs all energy and radiates it back outward through her network of cowed and sold-out government shrinks, her indoctrinated staff, her ward boy minions who measure out their bullying and sadism in direct relation to the fear she generates with a word or a look. "But you do understand," we hear her say even now in that calm, soul-shredding voice, "*everyone* . . . must follow the rules" (28).

Brushfire insurrections erupt. Under McMurphy's careful nurture, small rebellions waged over poker games, TV privileges, or the right to watch the World Series, soon flower into the natural inclinations of men quarantined from booze, women, and even fishing. Quickly the atmospherics of the detention hall caper evolve into guerrilla theater with a real program and a real vengeance, truth *and* consequences with an existential shock. By the end, Chief Broom will be redeemed from madness by the example of McMurphy's heroic craziness, empowered to tear up the sinister machine in the equipment room by the roots of its "wires and connections" (271), as McMurphy predicted one day he might, cast it at last out the window and vault through the opening into the moonlight. And so too, in one way or another, emboldened by the power of McMurphy's gorgeous out-crazyings of the crazyhouse's regime, the other assorted broken spirits: Harding, Cheswick, Martini, even for a moment at least, the doomed Billy Bibbitt.

For all its antic topicality, however, from an intellectual standpoint *One Flew Over the Cuckoo's Nest* also seemed to dramatize uncannily the preoccupations of many of the great institutional critiques emerging from the era. A kind of early counterculture comic book, it also seemed, without any particular evidence of direct intellectual derivation, a storehouse of poststructuralist metaphor. It contained much, for instance, of Michel Foucault's *Madness and Civilization:* the project of reclaiming the power of an insurgent unreason, that powerful Other consigned by a Western culture of therapy and adjustment to silence, straitjackets, padded rooms, and asylums, now once again asserting itself against the hegemony of an institutional regime of the Rational, the Scientific, the Objective, and the Technocratic. At a closer range of cultural indictment, it also seemed in direct ways an allegory of the American condition of cultural lobotomization described by Marcuse, in *One Dimensional Man,* as we have seen, as the Happy Consciousness: the culture of conformity, the regime of social adjustment and totalitarian therapy. And by further extension it also seemed to affirm R. D. Laing's characterization in *The Politics of Experience* of the true madman as shaman, as creator of an alternative and even redemptory reality.

Most importantly, as to the text's academic repute, it was all impeccably lit crit as well. Giving students something they could "relate to," as the saying went, it also encouraged them to grow as adepts of the kinds of official exegesis useful in the high school and college classroom. Meanwhile, in its portentous invocations of *kultur,* it proved irresistible to literary academics.

Classroom adoption was instant. Notes, articles, and casebooks proliferated. Mythic resonances crowded each other for interpretive recognition. The great fishing trip near the end became at once the ship of fools *and* the drunken boat. The priapic hero became the latest avatar of the trickster, the confidence man, the existential outlaw. In turn, finally unmanned by the system's and Big Nurse's last resort, a prefrontal lobotomy, McMurphy became a newest version of Eliot's late great Fisher-King, reunited in deep archetype with the slain corn god. For madmen and misfits, there were the shared martyrs' crowns of the shock treatment apparatus, the spread-eagling on the table, the anointment of the palms and temples, then the *power:* how the system shoots the juice over and over into the ones remanded for brain-crucifixion. Billy Bibbitt reenacted the passion of Melville's Billy Budd in his intransigent innocence, his pathological stutter, and his boundness for a death almost cosmic in the vindictiveness of its injustice. And, in final triumph, Chief Broom was seen to rise Samson-like, casting out the infernal machine and bringing down the system and the curtain with an epic crash.

In the ambitious conflations of literary reference and popular culture myth, interpreters found almost too much America to be handled: the Native American, the frontier hero, the tall tale, pranksterism, baseball on TV, basketball on the playground, chewing gum, whores with hearts of gold, Mom.

Mom. Billy Bibbitt's mother, Harding's wife, the Big Nurse. Here, as the '60s evolved, many readers would eventually find a deeply disabling blindness in Kesey's allegorical scheme. Particularly in the late decade, the novel began to come in for increasing disparagement for its constructions of women and gender oppositions as a whole. To some readers, it would have been enough had it seemed merely retrograde. McMurphy, enlisting his train of adoring, compliant, gold-hearted groupies, brings sexual liberation to the repressed institutional masses. Or, as he bellows early on by way of introduction: "Now they tell me a psychopath's a guy fights too much and fucks too much, but they ain't wholly right, do you think? I mean, whoever heard of a man getting too much poozle?" (18). To many others, on the other hand, it seemed downright pathological, a vicious countertheology fashioned from some very old, very familiar tropes of male self-vindication. The cold, impenetrable, deep-breasted bitchery of Nurse Ratched somehow made up for generations of vindictive, ball-busting grammar school teachers, Mrs. Bibbitt for generations of vindictive, ball-busting moms, and Harding's wife for generations of vindictive ball-busting wives. Woman again became, in primordial male nightmares, the avenging Fate, the Fury, the killjoy All-Devourer. *One Flew Over the Cuckoo's Nest* began its popular sojourn among the youth-literature of the early to mid '60s with the reputation of being one of the few books progressive enough to say out loud what the counterculture wanted to say to the world: To Hell with the Combine, Fuck the System. As the decade wore on and the youth-culture evolved, however, the latter, on the basis of new critiques of its own institutional assumptions, discovered how deeply it remained implicated in a larger official narrative that it had secretly been saying to itself: the one that also said, simply, across generations, periods, politics, nationalities, and literature at large—Fuck Women.

Kesey's intransigent male self-caricature would come to dominate assessments of his influence as a '60s figure. The Day Glo adventures with the Hell's Angels at La Honda, the Acid Tests, the Pranksters on the Bus: these elements of the Kesey legend shortly begin to look merely sophomoric in the way that adjective has always seemed exclusively masculine. In '60s reading and writing, Kesey the author would achieve some further success with an ensuing second novel, *Sometimes a Great Notion,* a brawling autobiographical saga of generations wherein he tried unsuccessfully to follow up on the energy of *One Flew Over the Cuckoo's Nest.* Here too, in this second chronicle of Kesey boy-men, the secret irony would be apparent even in the very entitling. The old, lonely, vagabond-male song it came from was "Good Night, Irene." This book, like virtually everything else of his to follow,[36] revealed itself pursuing the cultural dead end that would be reserved for Kesey himself. Like McMurphy, he would live on mainly as a piece of epic nostalgia.

King, Martin Luther, Jr. Martin Luther King Jr.'s books of the late '50s and early '60s enjoyed the public status of texts like John F. Kennedy's *Profiles in Courage:* if not widely read, at least widely purchased and applauded as works of timely political inspiration. With the appearance of increasingly disturbing and angry texts of black America such as *Manchild* *in the Promised Land, The Autobiography of Malcolm X,* and *Soul on Ice,* King's writings, like Kennedy's among radical youth and their revolutionary idols, went increasingly out of fashion with '60s constituencies black *and* white. The pulpit style of *Stride Toward Freedom* or *Why We Can't Wait* seemed out of touch with the bloody stridencies of political drama being played out in Vietnam and in the streets. As to media moments, even King's magnificent 1963 "I Have a Dream" speech before the Lincoln Memorial had been quickly installed, like Kennedy's 1961 inaugural address, as documentary classic, replayed over and over again on directorial command, the rhetorical event neutralized into instant history. Meanwhile, the black media voices the '60s were really hearing became those of Malcolm X, Muhammad Ali, Stokely Carmichael, H. Rap Brown, Bobby Seale, and Huey Newton. By 1968, with a culminating irony, the murder of King by James Earl Ray set the cities of America on fire with a violence of response that he had long ceased to provoke in life.

For nearly any '60s student, however, there would always be the Martin Luther King of the '60s freshman writing essay collection or humanities reader. That, of course, was the Martin Luther King of "Letter from the Birmingham Jail."

As to larger meanings, of chief interest in retrospect is how King and his text were "taught"—for such, as can be said with certainty about few other curricular items of the era, was surely the dominant means of readerly and interpretive dissemination. Did committed graduate teaching assistants show how one could pry from the homiletic cracks a secret discourse on radical method? Did more traditional purveyors of the freshman essay rejoice in the conjunction of political relevance with the virtues of the prose model? How many erstwhile philosophers of consciousness puffed up the genre to conduct a short course as well on Gandhi and Thoreau? Or, at a closer range, how many people even bothered to know—as did King and everyone white *and* black in Alabama at least—that from the title on he was writing but the latest version of a jailhouse blues that comprised the secret history of the South? Today, it is perhaps possible again to read the "Letter" and see more fully what *it* taught: that it was impossible to put historical talking and historical acting in arbitrary discursive categories: that a political text was a form of political action and vice versa. In functioning politically itself in the fullest sense, the "Letter" was thus King's essential contribution to the '60s.

As to clarity of political vision and purpose, in no other exposition of his argument anywhere did King go further to articulate a policy of determined action. At the same time, here was a work of enormous political passion. The "Letter," after all, was the work of the nation's best-known civil rights activist who had just succeeded in getting himself thrown in Bull Conner's Birmingham, Alabama, jail. Its addressees, moreover, are fellow black clergymen who have in turn accused the author of encouraging extreme varieties of political action that they have denounced publicly as "unwise and untimely." Incredibly, they too, echoing their white oppressors, have accused him of "outside" agitation (77–78).

To all this, King begins by replying simply and categorically. "I am in Birmingham," he says, "because injustice is here" (78). As to the "wisdom" of the forms of "direct action" he has encouraged—"sit-ins" and "marches," as opposed to "negotiation"—it is a matter, he argues, of making negotiation *itself* not an idea but a political inevitability by carrying events themselves to a precipitating point of creative crisis. "Indeed, this is the very purpose of direct action," he writes. "Nonviolent direct action seeks to create such a crisis and foster such a tension that a community which has constantly refused to negotiate is forced to confront the issue. It seeks so to dramatize the issue that it can no longer be ignored" (81). As to "timing," he asserts, one steps outside the imperative relation between moral justice and political necessity and again joins the oppressor in even arguing such issues. There likely is never a proper time for liberationist revolution as far as the official timetables of history are concerned. "We know through painful experience," he says, "that freedom is never voluntarily given by the oppressor; it must be demanded by the oppressed" (82). As to the "willingness to break laws," it is the purpose of the true moral revolutionary, in the tradition of Woolman, Thoreau, and Gandhi, to rewrite them, if necessary, as texts through action if that is what will be required to redeem history. "There are two types of laws," he writes:

> just and unjust. I would be the first to advocate obeying just laws. One has not only a legal but a moral responsibility to obey just laws. Conversely, one has a moral responsibility to disobey unjust laws. I would agree with St. Augustine that "an unjust law is no law at all" (84).

Further, distinguishing between the two is a matter of simple, active, moral recognition. "Any law that uplifts human personality is just," he says. "Any law that degrades human personality is unjust" (85).

There remained the whole question of justifying extremism regardless of the cause. The proximate case, as a conjunction of the need for just thinking and just acting, has moved this too, he says, out of the domain of philosophical inquiry and into that of imperative moral response to a world "in dire need of creative extremists" (92). In fact "the question," he says, "is not whether we will be extremists, but what kind of extremists we will be. Will we be extremists for hate or love? Will we be extremists for the preservation of injustice or for the extension of justice?" (92). And just as such questions are no longer philosophical, neither must philosophical approaches be taken to act out the answers. Fellow black clergy, "the white moderate" (93), and "the white church and its leadership" (93): all these thinkers of the moment, he concludes, will likely fail of revolutionary courage. The true political actor, in contrast, the simple engaged person, will know what to do. "One day the South," he predicts, "will recognize its real heroes" (99).

And they would be the James Merediths, for example, with the noble sense of purpose that enabled them to face jeering and hostile mobs and with the agonizing loneliness that characterizes the life of the pioneer. They would be people like Rosa Parks of Montgomery, Alabama, who rose up with a sense of dignity and with her people decided not to yield her seat to a white man, and who responded with ungrammatical profundity to one who inquired about her weariness: "My feets is tired, but my soul is at rest." They would be the young high school and college students, the young ministers of the gospel and a host of their elders, courageously and nonviolently sitting in at lunch counters and willingly going to jail for conscience's sake.

The actual work of change will be the work, King says, of such foot soldiers of liberation, who may yet make an old moral imperative flower into a political fact:

> One day the South will know that when these disinherited children of God sat down at lunch counters, they were in reality standing up for what is best in the American dream and for the most sacred values in our Judaeo-Christian heritage, thereby bringing our nation back to those great wells of democracy which were dug deep by the founding fathers in their formulation of the Constitution and the Declaration of Independence. (91)

One may argue that in returning his call at the end for a people's politics of liberation to the traditional contexts of appeal supplied by Christian and American democratic belief, King at the last sealed his own rhetorical fate, masking a spiritual agenda that came as close as anyone's ever had to being a true political plan for, to use Emerson's stirring phrase, the transformation of pure idea into practical power. In so doing, moreover, he had probably reenacted exactly the mistake of that great, nineteenth-century American preacher: allowing the text as political action to slip back into the oratorical frame whereby it could be rendered safely academic. Much like Emerson, in fact, King would wind up canonized while still alive, still alive but already history. In a way only the '60s liberal academy could have choreographed, King's textual outline for the work of changing the world achieved safe celebration as rhetorical example.

Knowles, John. The publishing history of John Knowles's *A Separate Peace* illustrates its steady rise to the position of established '60s classic. The Macmillan hardcover of 1960 went through eleven printings, and a Dell paperback of that year was noted, along with Paul Goodman's *Growing Up Absurd* and Philip Roth's *Portnoy's Complaint,* as among the most important new offerings in that format. A 1966 Bantam paperback then went through twenty-nine more printings by 1972. (By 1986, sixty-five more had been added to the total.)

The story this tells, I would propose, is not unlike that of William Golding's *Lord of the Flies,* perhaps the text of the era with which *A Separate Peace* most closely compares in theme, appeal, and popularity. It is again the story of the instant curricular hit become young adult classic. In the better kinds of schools identified with the Devon of the text, academics welcomed a novel of serious craft by an acknowledged younger member of the literary establishment on young adult topics—socialization, friendship, loyalty, and confrontation with new adult concerns forced upon them suddenly by a disordered outside world. Students in turn responded enthusiastically to a text that truly did seem to take them seriously and at the same time was taken with great seriousness by their educational role models and mentors.

As to the mentors, much of the appeal of *A Separate Peace* surely had to do with memories of their own relatively recent youth and coming of age during the years of World War II. Carrying an emotional immediacy still part and fabric of their lives, the novel in its studied literariness now also seemed to invest those lives with new cultural authority. The nuanced, elegiac reminiscence of an extraordinary friendship; the cerebral, cautious narrator, Gene; the golden, athletic, charmed Finny; the morally ambiguous incident of Finny's crippling at the jumping place by the stream where Gene either has or has not been responsible for the latter's fall from the tree; the resultant drama of guilt, expiation, and eventual movement toward new self-knowledge: all these features of the text coalesced into a brilliant, almost Jamesian concentration of moral crisis, an emblematic moment of learning life-and-death matters for a whole generation on the verge of the century's second global holocaust.

And, should it have been needed, in the literariness of the title was the key to that generation's desire to affirm for the new one a function of historical continuity, its sense of the degree to which it had reenacted the generational crisis of value and geopolitical upheaval faced by those just preceding. The title phrase, after all, is Hemingway's, the line uttered by that author's young hero, Nick Adams, to his Italian comrade Rinaldi in one of the war vignettes of *In Our Time*. Realizing that he has been crippled by a shot through the spine, Nick now props himself against a wall and says goodbye to war. "Senta Rinaldi," he says. "Senta. You and me we've made a separate peace."

On the other hand, such purported continuities of generational crisis began to take on their own meanings for the students of the early '60s, as Vietnam came to vex traditional notions of duty with images of the troubled forms of separate peace already having to be made by many in a new and, in many persons' eyes, lost generation. Moreover, one suspects that initially at least such an impact must have been most pronounced in the Devons and Devon-like places of America, places called "the better schools," where young people may have been especially tempted by calls to duty from a young president—a Harvard man, a war hero, a wit, even a person of some literary consequence—and his advisors, like himself, the nation's "best and brightest." And this must also have been true for think-ing young people everywhere who read the book in its representation of particular generational crisis. Here for many of them was an important missing piece of history: a revelatory account of the extremely complicated things one's *fathers* and one's fathers before them may have actually felt about their twentieth-century wars—the war that was supposed to end all wars but which was quickly succeeded by the even bigger one that was supposed to be the "good" one. Here too, given the sensitivity with which such feelings and choices were represented, might be founded at least the honest beginning for a critique of the values involved in their own choices concerning a war that was starting to look like the ultimate *bad* one—albeit justified and defended through many of the same arguments.

This, then, is where *A Separate Peace* became truly curricular for its youth-readers: as a new piece of history about to be written. If for the fig-ures of the generation represented in the novel, the refusal of war and what seems a war-breeding system is sympathetically rendered, then, whatever the outcome, as at least *a* choice, that refusal now seemed to more easily present itself to the generation reading the novel as *the* choice. Moreover, upon formal scrutiny, such a choice began to look like one not greatly afield of those more jarring renditions offered by Knowles's generational contemporaries and youth-favorites, Heller and Vonnegut.

If the martyred Finny was to be believed, a young reader might now begin to suspect "they" had been there to be resisted then as much as now. It is a familiar crew, as he describes them, the ones who have "cooked up this war fake" (107). "Who are 'they,' anyway?" responds Gene. "The fat old men," Finny continues, "who don't want us crowding them out of their jobs. They've made it all up. There isn't any real food shortage, for instance. The men have all the best steaks delivered to their clubs now. You've noticed how they've been getting fatter lately, haven't you?" (107).

Gene shakes it off as roommate whimsy. But in the morning, the truth cuts closer. "Phineas, this is all pretty amusing and everything," he offers cheerily, "but I hope you don't play this game too much with yourself. You might start to believe it and then I'd have to make a reservation for you at the Funny Farm." Finny responds: "'In a way,' deep in argument, his eyes never wavered from mine, 'the whole world is on a Funny Farm now. But it's only the fat old men who get the joke.'" "'And you,'" offers the narrator. "'Yes,'" Finny replies, "'and me.'" And now it is time for the real truth. "'What makes you so special?'" Gene shouts. "'Why should you get it and all the rest of us be in the dark?'" The answer duly arrives. "'Because I've suffered'" (108).

In case the lesson is missed, however, the novel also provides a more decidedly conventional example of a classmate who does not "get it" to the point of allowing himself to be taken in and consumed by the hideous swindle. That, of course, is the example of Leper Lepellier, who enlists. The boys jokingly chart Leper's progress, Leper sinking the *Scharnhorst*, Leper in Tunisia, at Stalingrad, on the Burma Road. Then comes a telegram, but perhaps not the one expected. Leper has deserted ("escaped," as he phrases it) the army. He is about to be boarded out, given a Section Eight, a psycho discharge. Gene sees him at his home, where he is hiding. Finny sees him when he appears at Devon. He too has now become living proof that there is a war on.

Soon, in a mock trial called by a student political manipulator named Brinker to clear up finally the "internal" matter of Finny's accident with Gene, the mad, incoherent Leper, back from the horror just outside, is called as a star witness. Finny rushes from the room in disgust, falls down a flight of stairs, and reinjures his shattered leg. Within a few days, he is dead of a blood clot—but not before he has led Gene to the vision of a spiritual magnanimity larger than the madness of any war-breeding system. "Finny," says the latter. "Phineas, you wouldn't be any good in the war, even if nothing had happened to your leg." He continues:

> They'd get you some place at the front and there'd be a lull in the fighting, and the next thing anyone knew you'd be over with the Germans or the Japs, asking if they'd like to field a baseball team against our side. You'd be sitting in one of their command posts, teaching them English. Yes, you'd get confused and borrow one of their uniforms, and you'd lend them one of yours. Sure, that's just what would happen. You'd get things so scrambled up nobody would know who to fight any more. You'd make a mess, a terrible mess, Finny, out of the war. (182)

And suddenly, we see, Gene has gotten it as well, just in time. He has, in the power of Finny's example of absolute incapacity for hatred, committed himself to a choice of peace over war that requires no veteranship or guilt of complicity. One could do it upfront, this book seemed to say, just say no to it without having to qualify for adulthood in the terrible old ways. It was not necessary ever to become like "them" just to find out that remaining one's self was a clearly better choice. It was possible to be right on one's own in one's own time, in spiritual company with all others then or now like Finny who would—and, as the current issue continued to be pressed, actually did—commit themselves in every way to making a terrible mess out of the latest war, letting "them" down for the first time by not becoming "them." Them. "All of them, all except Phineas," the narrator concludes—achieving for himself closure and, more importantly for his '60s audience, newly contemporary authority—"constructed at infinite cost to themselves these Maginot Lines against the enemy they thought they saw across the frontier, this enemy who never attacked that way—if he ever attacked at all; if he was indeed the enemy" (196).

Kunen, James S. Many '60s people will return to James S. Kunen's *The Strawberry Statement,* like nostalgists anywhere, with generous memories of a text they cherished and recoil at the piece of period silliness they are likely to find. From an age that found oracular wisdom in the druggy profundities of the Moody Blues, that actually had musical groups with names like the Strawberry Alarm Clock, the Lemon Pipers, or Moby Grape, one expects a certain amount of retrospective embarrassment in the return to a nineteen-year-old's recording of his impressions from the late-'60s student revolutionary scene at Columbia University. What one gets instead is a sense of generous recollection. Here is a piece of '60s reading and writing that wears well, that still reminds us of the times with a grace and insight beyond its years.

When *The Strawberry Statement* appeared in 1969, the decade was still notably short on counterculture memoir or documentary.[37] To fill the need, Kunen was a lively witness, with a high sense of the exhilaration of the times and in moments a real reverence for their utopian idealism. On the other hand, he possessed a comic appreciation of the portentous humorlessness of much of the fun and of the dour self-importance of many of the figures supposedly whipping it up. Best of all, however, Kunen was a writer, addressing the general scene with a sound sense of observation and an eye for the ridiculous, in a voice that sounded like that of a real young person named James S. Kunen.

Such a voice wins us over immediately through its opening apologies for belonging to a mere nineteen-year-old pontificating about his times. Nineteen-year-olds born in 1920 no doubt had a great deal to say, he speculates. Surely they must have worried, as he now does, simply about turning twenty, let alone thirty—not that he believes a great deal in a current cliché making the rounds of his friends about not trusting anyone older than the latter. "I agree in principle," he says, "but I think they ought to drop the zero" (3). All in all, he confesses, he is probably just your basic gripey college kid with the usual dislikes. On the other hand, he continues, one might also now add "racism, poverty, and war" to the list of worries. "The latter three," he adds, however "I'm trying to do something about" (4).

Thus begins Kunen's progress. Concerned about his country's policy in Vietnam, he tries to call Ambassador Ellsworth Bunker in Saigon to protest. Starting to get politicized, he gets into heavy discussion with a friend. Then "we both go out and kill ourselves trying to row a boat faster than eight students from MIT will be able to" (20). He gets into a first demonstration, is told to forget about the revolutionary crew and jump from a window because the cops are coming but fails to get the message because he's been reading *Lord Jim* (24). Trying to balance the rowing crew and revolution, he finds himself really getting into "the conflicting imperative scene" (25). He thinks that some of the great human imperatives derived from his Contemporary Civilization readings are starting to sink in, but then realizes that his own nineteen-year-old-American "philosophy of law comes not so much from Rousseau as from Fess Parker as Davy Crockett." He continues: "I remember his saying that you should decide what you think is right and then go ahead and do it." "Walt Disney really bagged that one," he speculates; "the old fascist inadvertently created a whole generation of liberals" (30).

Increasingly immersed in the movement, he muses, "I wonder, as I look about me, whether Lenin was as concerned with the breast size of his revolutionary cohorts as I am" (30). He tries to help radicalize neighborhood kids: "I talk to some of them and they are all conversant with the issues and our side. I conduct an informal class in peace graffiti and distribute chalk" (31). Preparing to face the tear gas, he hears a fellow revolutionary complaining "that he can't get busted or he'll miss his shrink again" (33). Kunen himself gets busted. "We are taken to the 24th precinct to be booked," he writes. " 'Up against the wall,' we are told. I can't get over how they really do use the term" (34).

In an unexpected dividend of his self-conscious scribblings, Kunen bemusedly finds himself a revolutionary authority. "As a result of the proliferation of my diary in *New York Magazine,* I am now a qualified spokesman for the Columbia strikers, the international peace movement, and everyone in the world younger than thirty" (41). On the other hand, on the day Robert Kennedy is shot, he looks with a cold eye on the alternative to the official explanation and decides he can at least do better than that. "This is really no novelty, you know," he writes of the latest political murder,

> because people get shot every day, and bombed and burned and blown up. But no one cares about that. I mean they don't really mind, because it's a question of flags and things and anyway, people aren't really shot; fire is directed at their positions. And they're not really people; they're troops. There aren't even dead men; only body counts. (55)

The course of Kunen's progress has turned a good deal more serious; at the same time, with the increase of spiritual passion, it has gotten a good deal less confusing, exactly because even a nineteen-year-old, he affirms, is entitled to realize that he is too old for this shit and that his government ought to be as well. "Little boys fight," he notes, "but by the age of *sixteen,* as irresponsible teens, *they* see that fighting doesn't prove anything. Young men hardly ever fight. Only when their countries do" (59). And there, of course, is the real epiphany in this remarkable text: that the problem with things is not really, in the barest terms, "a generation gap, it's an idea difference and a power gap. You've got the power. You make millions of people suffer. They're hungry and they've got nowhere to go and nothing to do for it. Well cut it out, will you? Just stop it" (60).

Who are "they" thus applauded? Who are the "you" thus admonished? Who are we and who are those not ourselves: Kunen asks these questions of himself in ever deepening awareness. And in response, he sees that the answers lie not inherently in generations but in the relationships of power *always* implied in ideas of political difference. On Monday, July 1, for example, he quotes a friend as saying, "whimsically, 'You know, after we take over and rule the world, we've got to find out who *They* are.'" Kunen records his reply: "'Then,' I said, 'we'll be *They*'" (64).

Writing in 1969, Kunen was addressing primarily an idea of generations. But he was also coming upon that larger conceptualization of critical difference that may be the great intellectual legacy of the era: a sense of self and other that begins in dialectic but must continually recreate its true existence as *relationship:* a truly generative politics of consciousness and being recognizing that the opposition of a "they" and a "we" must always imply as well a substitution of a "we" for a "they" and vice versa.

Laing, R. D. "He seems to me headed for his ideal fate," offers Bull Lee in *On the Road* about the work's shamanistic genius of disorder, Dean Moriarity, "which is compulsive psychosis dashed with a jigger of psychopathic irresponsibility and violence" (147). The pronouncement echoes a line attributed to the original Bull Lee, William Burroughs: "A psychotic is a guy who's just found out what's happening." As noted frequently here, the great theme in much of the youth-literature of the '50s, '60s, and '70s is the idea of someone's going crazy in America. Sixties anatomies of unreason became a set of notes toward diagnosis of an essential cultural malaise.

The youth of the age required a physician of the soul. In the combined realms of what he would call "existential psychology and psychiatry," the young Scottish psychiatric healer-philosopher R. D. Laing would meet the requirement and more. In *The Divided Mind,* he would outline the psychic crisis of an age in general and a generation in particular: a sense of utter dislocation between self and other far beyond civilized discontents; a new schizophrenia he would call it in *The Politics of Experience,* something like an existential broken heart. Moreover, as the latter work would show particularly, such a condition had become political in the largest sense, a direct experiential consequence of any attempt to be fully human in the world.

Sixties talk about madness as somehow the only sane response to an insane world was cheap, of course. Laing may thus be said to have codified for a '60s audience the diagnostic commonplace: schizophrenia became for him the imperial pathology, "an individual's attempt," as it was described in a 1989 obituary of the author, "to opt out of an intolerable world." (*Time,* September 4, 1989). And to this degree, Laing connected movingly as a popular '6os figure with contemporary exponents of a holy madness such as Norman O. Brown, Alan Watts, Timothy Leary, Ken Kesey, and a host of others: the madness as envisioned by this Scots psychiatrist seemed to offer a "gratuitous grace," to borrow Aldous Huxley's phrase about the LSD experience, of mystic self-healing. But what Laing brought new to the discourse was an aura of clinical authority. Here was a revolutionary confabulation, a creative theory of consciousness appropriated out of the citadel of clinical Reason, Science, and Objective Knowledge: a structural explanation of the existential space of schizophrenia that had to be navigated in the search for individual and social self-recuperation.

Accordingly, *The Divided Self* appeared as a quite sober and, in its way, technical volume, announcing itself as "the first of a series of existential psychiatry and psychology, in which it is proposed to present original contributions to this field by a number of authors" (9). It continues with a no-nonsense description of the immediate subject: "The present book is a study of schizoid and schizophrenic persons; its basic purpose is to make madness, and the process of going mad, comprehensible" (9). Thus, "Foundations for a Science of Persons" is followed in part 1 by "Foundations for the Understanding of Psychosis" and then "Ontological Insecurity." Part 2 explores "The Embodied and Unembodied Self," "The Inner Self in the Schizoid System," "The False-Self System," "Self-Consciousness," and concludes with a case study. Part 3 becomes the most adventurous development, an exploration of the pathology from within, concluding lyrically with "The ghost of the weed garden: a study of a chronic schizophrenic."

As one followed the structural evolution of this largely clinical book, one found a distinct movement of clinical discourse out of its own structures. Schizophrenia becomes the opening into something bigger called madness, going mad; it becomes the essential form of madness, a voyage into the self exactly so that one may begin a newly sane relation to the world. A pathology has already started to become in the fullest sense a cultural trope. And that pathology, a diagnosis of a culture, in turn begins to supply the basis of a new, risky, properly *political* cure, a voyage undertaken from the world as we now know it with the resultant discovery at the end of what is called madness of a new freedom to come back and live in the world as we can *truly* know it.

That is the passage of exploration described in Laing's book best known to '6os audiences, *The Politics of Experience,* a text as visionary and terrifying in its voyagings toward epiphany as many of the experiential narratives of madness familiar to the era and as culturally challenging as many of the era's most explicit attempts at revolutionary statement. *The Politics of Experience* was a work of rapturous beauty delving down to inhabit the region of private madness visited upon persons through the public insanities of an era; and thereby it comprised also an agenda for both existential and, in the fullest sense implied by its title, political action. Laing's book cast itself as the imaginative geography of a world waiting to be rewritten from within.

The word imaginative is key here. Laing's philosophy of madness has often been described as romantic. And the adjective is probably appropriate, although mainly as a point of genealogy. A connection with another romantic '60s icon—Blake—is inescapable as is the connection with the extension of the Blakean strain into the hallucinatory twentieth-century dimension of Hesse. Although Laing's connection with apostles of mind-expanding drugs such as mescaline or LSD is not a major feature in his work, there is a distinctly psychedelic quality to the book, reminiscent of the epiphanic strain of Huxley, Alpert, and Leary, or the Alan Watts, for instance, of *The Joyous Cosmology*.[39]

However, the word that remains ultimtely regnant here is surely "politics." For what the text finally aspires to is the divine madness of a new political imagination. To imagine, after all, against the dictates of a world that commands us to *be* strictly on its own unimaginative—and often unimaginable—terms, is madly, Laing exhorts us early on, even miraculously, to self-create. "If there are no meanings, no values, no source of sustenance or help, then man, as creator, must invent, conjure up meanings and values, sustenance and succor out of nothing. He is a magician" (24).

This then was a truly existential psychology, the total reshaping of one's existence out of the psychological fact of one's consciousness into the political fabric of one's being. However, as the world understands politics, such acts of self-creation are now also "bridgeheads into alien territory" (24), with the institutional peril that these brave acts of self will be considered losses of self. In the world of sanity as most of us know it, he says, "there is a conformity to a *presence* that is everywhere *elsewhere*" (56). Thus one must truly lose one's self anew in order to gain one's self.

If this all sounds distinctly religious as well, it should. For the new imaginative politics of self envisioned here must be a matter of faith gained through an experience of *conversion* from our misplaced faith in the totalitarian political regime of the soul as we know it: a revision once and for all of our very institutional notions of "madness" and "return to sanity" in their private and their public dimensions. "The 'cause' of schizophrenia is to be found by the examination not of the prospective diagnosee alone," writes Laing, "but of the whole social context in which the psychiatric ceremony is being conducted." For "it is clear," he asserts, that through the very experience of living in the world as given, "some people come to behave and experience themselves and others in ways that are strange and incomprehensible to most people, including themselves" (71). Schizophrenia, thus by definition, is *"a political event."* Moreover,

> this political event, occurring in the civic order of society, imposes definitions and consequences on the labeled person. It is a social prescription that rationalizes a set of social actions whereby the labeled person is annexed by others, who are legally sanctioned, medically empowered and morally obliged, to become responsible for the person labeled. (83)

Yet what if, Laing proposes, the existential and political process so described could be rewritten imaginatively from the position of the other? What if the terms of outer sociopolitical space could be rewritten by a cartography gained from a new voyaging of inner space? What if a '60s trip in the fullest sense of the term could also be seen as a real magical journey? Perhaps the return would be, as he proposes, "from a cosmic fetalization to an existential rebirth" (90). Perhaps, he speculates, we now write such voyaging as science fiction or fantasy without realizing that it may not be in the least fiction or fantasy.

If so, the future laugh will be on us: "They will see that what we call 'schizophrenia' was one of the forms in which, often through quite ordinary people, the light began to break through the cracks in our all-too-closed minds" (90). But it is not too late. Instead, he proposes, we can write such a future now into a new politics of self that rescues us from the tyranny of what we have called our minds all these years. "Schizophrenia used to be a new name for dementia praecox," he observes, "—a slow, insidious illness that was supposed to overtake young people in particular and to be liable to go on to a terminal dementia" (130–31). Now, he concludes, we can perhaps save ourselves by learning once again what it is to be young in this particular sense. "Perhaps we can still retain the old name, and read into it its etymological meaning: *"Schiz*—'broken'; *Phrenos*—'soul' or 'heart.' "

"If I could turn you on," Laing writes movingly at the end of a final section entitled "The Bird of Paradise," "if I could drive you out of your wretched mind, if I could tell you I would let you know" (138). Here Laing's own discourse imaged the beauty of his synthesis of the clinical with the passionately imagined. A new holy madness could still do it, he exhorted, could still take us back to a region of the soul somewhere before

History as we now crazily enact it—History as thought, dialectic, reason, sanity—and help us each reclaim original status as "a hierophant of the sacred."

For this, as we now see, Laing could have been called a late mystic or something of a rhapsodic postmodern. At the time, he was just called something of a madman. What he probably did best was to remind us that all categories and taxonomies are ways of *constructing* the self and the world and not ways of describing the self and the world, much in the way that schizophrenia and dementia praecox talk about themselves only as their others. In such assertions, and in the texts that were the flower of his passion, Laing left us with a promise, blinding in the terrible beauty of its illumination.

Leary, Timothy. Few wisdom-figures associated with '60s youth-consciousness come to mind more readily than Timothy Leary. What will probably surprise the student of '60s reading and writing—inclined to construct Leary mainly as a media figure—is the volume of print he put into circulation. Although not identified, like Kesey's or Vonnegut's, with some particularly cherished iconic text or texts, Leary's bibliography was considerable. He was a frequent contributor to periodicals, both alternative and mass-distribution. In the book arena, under the sober attribution of Timothy Leary, Ph.D., he identified himself as coauthor, along with his colleague Richard Alpert, of the "Center for Research and Personality, Harvard University," in the 1962 preface to Alan Watts's *The Joyous Cosmology*. From a succeeding pamphlet-monograph of 1963, "The Politics of Consciousness Expansion," in *The Harvard Review,* again coauthored with Richard Alpert, Leary moved to editorship of the *Psychedelic Review,* issued out of his headquarters at New Hyde Park, New York, by the "International Foundation for Internal Freedom," and of a resulting 1965 anthology, *The Psychedelic Reader,* with Gunther M. Weil and Ralph Metzner. Meanwhile, with Metzner and Alpert, he had also published in 1964 *The Psychedelic Experience: A Manual Based on the Tibetan Book of the Dead.* Nineteen sixty-six brought *Psychedelic Prayers after the Tao te ching* and, from a major trade publisher (Putnam) with David Solomon as coauthor, *LSD.*[40] If 1968 was the apotheosis of the '60s, it also brought the textual apotheosis of Timothy Leary, writer. In that year were published *High Priest, The Politics of Ecstasy,* and *Jail Notes,* with an introduction by Allen Ginsberg.

All this, however, is still to work around the fringes of the ultimate Timothy Leary text of the '60s, which was of course himself. There was the visual iconography: the stylish silver hair framing the square jaw, the patrician nose, the brilliant eye, the beatific face, the flowing shirts, the garlands of flowers, and the imperial gestures of blessing visited upon the rapt, adoring crowds. There was the talent for promotional acronym. The pied piper of LSD became the founder of the League for Spiritual Discovery. But most important of all were the pronouncements, the remarkable things he could say. "Get out of your mind and into your senses." "You have to be out of your mind to pray." "Whatever you do is beautiful." "The LSD kick is a spiritual ecstasy." "The LSD trip is a religious pilgrimage." "Laws are made by old people who don't want young people to do exactly those things young people were meant to do—to make love, turn on, and have a good time." "If anything will survive in the whole world, it's going to be Haight-Ashbury, because Haight-Ashbury's got two billion years behind it."

Then, there was the big one: "Turn on, tune in, drop out." It was frequently described as a slogan or motto. It might have been better understood as a protean theology, recasting itself endlessly in new orders, versions, and elaborations. From a pamphlet entitled *Start Your Own Religion:* "DROP OUT—detach yourself from the external social drama which is as dehydrated and ersatz as TV. TURN-ON—find a sacrament which returns you to the Temple of God, your own body. Go out of your mind. Get high. TUNE-IN—be reborn. Drop-back-in to express it. Start a new sequence of behavior that reflects your vision" (O'Brien 57). From an article in the *East Village Other:* " 'Tune in' means arrange your environment so that it reflects your state of consciousness, to harness your internal energy to the flow around you. If you understand this most practical, liberating message, your are free to live a life of beauty" (Haskins 205). Or, from the classic version supposedly uttered first by the master himself: "Turn on to the scene; tune in to what's happening. Drop out—of high school, college, grade school . . . and follow me, the hard way" (Sann 209).

Of all purveyors of the '60s text, Leary probably came furthest in moving beyond print toward the new technologies of self-fashioning made available by mass communications. Leary exploited all the possibilities of the photograph, the film clip, the headline, the TV news spot, the interview, the celebrity comment, and the cameo appearance at the concert or demonstration. On the other hand, if Leary found it easier than even a Ginsberg or Mailer to live by the '60s media revolution, he also failed to see the new ease with which one could die by it through bizarre overexposure: the increasing ease, that is, by which people who create themselves as media texts become instantly self-parodic, going on in nearly exponential comic repetition. Leary, if anything, went further. He ran for Governor of California, allegedly getting John Lennon to write "Come Together" as his campaign song (Haskins 208). Jumping bond on drug charges, he reappeared in Algeria, along with celebrity exile Eldridge Cleaver. Most recently has come a debate tour with G. Gordon Liddy and the promotion of CD-ROM computer technologies. Even as Leary now becomes, in James Haskins and Kathleen Benson's phrase, "the grand old man of the good old days" (208), one can be sure that whatever the promotion at hand, the real product is a new spiritual technology—or, in a word the master has always been fond of, an avatar—named Timothy Leary.

Mailer, Norman. "These have been the years of conformity and depression," wrote Norman Mailer toward the end of the 1950s in "The White Negro." "A stench of fear has come out of every pore of American life, and we suffer from a collective failure of nerve" (300). The time had come for a politics of culture achieved through a new heroism, he proclaimed, the dialectical struggle of the true cultural outrider, "the American existentialist," the "hipster," the apostle of "the rebellious imperatives of the self" (301). One's great "decision" for authentic selfhood would have to lie in a commitment to "the unstated essence of Hip, its psychopathic brilliance," its gift of "the knowledge that new kinds of victories increase one's power for new kinds of perception" (301).

In retrospect, the passage reads brilliantly as prediction and confirmation, an abstract or epitome of '60s consciousness in a central activist mode: the hipster as holy outlaw, the winter soldier, the new American prototype for geopolitical bad weather. And there is no doubt that Mailer as a literary intellectual wished to assume the mantle of '60s youth-illuminatus, at once existential prophet and pied piper. Accordingly, his career across the decade revealed a relentless, almost obsessive wish to be the voice of '60s adversarial culture in its broadest sense: a voice uniting the radical intelligentsia *and* dissenting youth in a new project of revolutionary consciousness spilling over from bohemian lofts and campus enclaves into the streets of the nation at large.

Mailer's own attempt at the quintessential '60s book, *The Armies of the Night,* testified fully to the grandeur of his ambition. It won the Pulitzer Prize and the National Book Award. It continues to appear on countless reading lists for '60s courses. It commands discussion in virtually every scholarly analysis of the era. As a '60s text in the sense that I have defined here—as a certifiable youth-scripture—the only thing it failed to do was *connect.* "The Novel as History; History as a Novel": the problem for Mailer was reflected exactly in his mirror-image subtitle. Existential claims to the contrary, Mailer was a nostalgic modernist, a philosopher even, above all an author. People were looking for the Word, a new relationship of culture and ideology become part and fabric of their lives. What they got instead from Mailer, here and elsewhere in the '6os, was *writing*—ideology, so to speak, as structural conceit. Not for nothing did the title of the work at hand come from Matthew Arnold. Mailer the would-be philosopher-king of the revolution was the last liberal humanist, working not so much, to use Daniel Bell's phrase, at the end of ideology, as in a moment when radical cultural discourse had become increasingly at one *with* ideology. He was the political genius of the age who seemed to know everything except how to speak to it. To be sure, Mailer had updated the paradigm. The high modernist author as artificer of culture had been conflated with the new figure of the writer as media celebrity—the newest model of the American artist as, in Richard Poirier's acute formulation, the performing self. The fact remained that Mailer also held on to a performative concept of authorship increasingly at odds with the desires of an audience seeking to submerge the egocentric political implications of literary authorship and authority into the communitarian experience of the text.[41]

Meanwhile, moreover, the authority principle had become even more deeply complicated for a '6os youth-audience by issues of the subject as well. In an age of increasing unreality, so too in literature the reality principle, as Todd Gitlin astutely notes, had transferred itself away from the crises of existential and literary authority experienced by the individual writer or the dramatic subject to the distancing pleasures of "postmodern weirdness," "the false calm of allegory," or "the eerie simplicities of the saucer's eye abstraction" (243). In this sense as well, Mailer especially could only be supplanted for a '6os youth-audience, Gitlin correctly observes, by Pynchon, Vonnegut, and Hesse. The text itself—with its own essentially self-reifying qualities of both "vision" and "voice"—had become increasingly generic. The character of author and subject as matters of literary production had both increasingly been subsumed—even down to details of publishing and marketing design—by the identification of the text as product.

Thus, in *The Armies of the Night,* Mailer could be brilliant on Hippies: "They would never have looked to blow their minds and destroy some part of the past if the authority had not brainwashed the mood of the present until it smelled like deodorant. (To cover the odor of burning flesh in Vietnam?)" (110). He could be trenchant on Vietnam:

He did not see all wars as bad. He could conceive of wars which might be noble. But the war in Vietnam was bad for America because it was a bad war, as all wars are bad if they consist of rich boys fighting poor boys when the rich boys have an advantage in the weapons. . . . Certainly any war was a bad war which required an inability to reason as the price of retaining one's patriotism; finally any war which offered no prospect for improving itself as a war—so complex and compromised were its roots—was a bad war. (208–9)

If anything, *The Armies of the Night* grows more astonishing in the richness of its structural or analytic insights with every year. On nearly everything, Mailer was right. At the last, very much like Paul Goodman, Norman O. Brown, and R. D. Laing, he could come even

to the saddest conclusion of them all for it went beyond the war in Vietnam. He had come to decide that the center of America might be insane. The country had been living with a controlled, even fiercely controlled, schizophrenia which had been deepening with the years. Perhaps the point had now been passed. Any man or woman who was devoutly Christian and had worked for the American Corporation, had been caught in an unseen vise whose pressure could split their mind from their soul. (211)

In the same moment, however, for Mailer and literary intellectuals like him, the question of a real constituency of '60s reading and writing in America—through audience developments undreamed of by even a Roland Barthes or a Michel Foucault—had passed beyond concerns with *either* and *both* of those poststructuralist favorites, author and subject. The performing self had quite literally become the property of the reified, generic text under unprecedented (and never again to be replicated) conditions of textual commodification and political community. Accordingly, Norman Mailer himself, along with his writing, had become, exactly in the Barthesian or Foucaultian model, something requiring a subtitle or at least a gloss. In the last age of literature as a putative battleground of culture and ideology, Mailer had continued to define the scene of the political action in its very traditional sense: the old agon, as he conceived it, the dialectical self-encounter of the existentially engaged author and the historical subject. Meanwhile, in the '60s youth-scripture, writing so defined had become increasingly, like Norman Mailer himself, the last thing the author of "The White Negro" and *The Armies of the Night* might have dreamed: irrelevant.[42]

Malcolm X. How strange it is, yet somehow unsurprising, all these years after the '6os, to see the "X" everywhere again, on baseball caps, banners, belt buckles, on shirt and pants pockets, across the backs of jackets; to be reminded of that old lost African name, before the slave name or the American name; to see *him* again all over the place—on posters, book jackets, screen-print T-shirts—wearing those Malcolm X glasses, pointing that Malcolm X finger, looking that Malcolm X look.

One does not remotely speculate in saying that three decades after its publication the 1965 *Autobiography of Malcolm X* continues to live. Publishing and curricular data tell us that it has continuously been purchased and read. (Also familiar knowledge now is the career of the work's co-author, Alex Haley, the author of *Roots* and, as a consequence, the progenitor of the first great TV docudrama.) In 1992, the *Autobiography* even became a major motion picture, produced and directed by Spike Lee and starring Denzel Washington in the title role. Publicity for the film generated the concomitant paraphernalia explosion described above, but it also spawned an important new array of Malcolm X texts, memorials, biographies, and scholarly analyses.

Given all this, in a study of '6os reading and writing one struggles uncommonly with *The Autobiography of Malcolm X* to recover the print moment in order to help define its peculiar status as textual icon and as a case study of '6os self-creation amidst the era's other rapidly evolving textual media. It is to see the construction of an autobiographical figure clearly in the tradition of black American spiritual autobiography but also of a strange new hybrid of biographical chronicler and autobiographical subject as media auteur. It is also to see how such a composite text attempted to locate itself politically in a racial agon already couched in varieties of rhetoric and mode extending from Martin Luther King Jr. and James Baldwin to Muhammad Ali, Stokely Carmichael, and H. Rap Brown, not to mention Malcolm X's initial patron and mentor, the powerful Elijah Muhammad. Finally and most recently, of course, it is to see that subject and text newly constructed interpretively through a process initiated over the years by college and university curricula but now extended again into the larger domains of public discourse. It is to see, in sum, a text that somehow knew itself from the outset to be a new kind of writing drawing on past forms of black autobiographical expression but capable of locating itself in rapidly changing conditions of reading.

The book begins, not surprisingly, with that dramatic merging of spiritual autobiography into exacerbated mythic history peculiar to black

American narrative: the opening of consciousness into a primal vision of fear, violence, and pain. It opens, in fact, in a chapter entitled "Nightmare," with the hero unborn, lodged in his mother's womb, as Klan nightriders in Omaha, Nebraska, come in search of his Baptist minister–Garveyite father. The latter dies during the son's childhood, his skull crushed and his body nearly cut in half in a streetcar "accident" in Lansing, Michigan (10). His mother is gradually claimed by madness (18–19). As with so many questing American protagonists white and black, Malcolm X becomes from the outset, in his world and in his text, his own genealogy. As with many questing American protagonists of midcentury embraced by the Generation of Youth, he quickly becomes a jailkid, a hipster, a hustler, an outlaw, and a con.

However, in contrast to all of these—a Dean Moriarity, a Randall McMurphy, or a literary-philosophical concoction of Norman Mailer's called The White Negro—Malcolm Little, soon to become Malcolm X, is also, of course, a nigger. That fate is ineluctably inscribed, not as some trope of unhappiness, alienation, absurdity, or ground of existential rebellion, but as reified cultural-autobiographical *fact*. "Malcolm," cautions an early teacher who has seemed to open the doors of education to an eager boy, "one of life's first needs is for us to be realistic. Don't misunderstand me, now. We all here like you, you know that. But you've got to be realistic about being a nigger. A lawyer—that's no realistic goal for a nigger. You need to think about something you *can* be" (36).

As in much American autobiography, the drama of self-discovery eventually finds its dramatic climax in a conversion experience. Again, however, it is a decidedly black conversion. Huck Finn elects to "go to Hell." In his prison conversion Malcolm X goes him one better by adopting the infidel code of Islam which *is* Hell, is the color of his skin, his race, and his destiny. It is a faith designed precisely to *embrace* the darkness, the mystery, the diabolism, the pure mythic otherness of black Americans in a white America; and it is the attempt to throw that black otherness back up against white America in moral, political, religious, even metaphysical opposition.

Malcolm becomes, in every sense of the term, the other's other, complete with the whole theology of otherness by which it is authorized. In Detroit, a Mr. Wallace D. Fard "had given to" one Elijah Muhammad "Allah's message for the black people who were 'The Lost-Found Nation of Islam here in this wilderness of North America'" (161). This message, anticipating various current Afrocentric theories of history, asserted that the true black builders of civilization had been seduced by "the devil white man" (162) into assuming the position and cultural genealogy of "Negro." Further, "this 'Negro' was taught to worship an alien God having the same blond hair, pale skin, and blue eyes as the slave-master" (163). How did such a Fall occur? That "demonology" was recorded in something called "Yacub's History," where is recounted the rebellion of the titular protagonist against Allah, and while in exile on the Isle of Patmos, his perverse "eugenic" creation of a "bleached-out race of white devils" (165). Thence ensued the hell of recorded history as it is known, culminating in the event "that some of the original black people should be brought as slaves to North America—to learn to better understand, at first hand, the white devil's true nature in modern times" (167). So arose the new race of Islam in which Malcolm Little now found himself "Saved."

Never mind that the theology reads like something out of Vonnegut or Pynchon. That is just the point: a far-out metaphysics of the other that becomes the new Revelation; a new basis of self as liberating fantasy of alternative consciousness and world. The more other, indeed, the better. The mythology that is white history has concocted a master-narrative crazy enough to create black devils. What, therefore, is so crazy about a self-authorized countermythology, an antimythology, really, down even to an anticreation narrative, devised in the image of its equally insane other? A metaphysics of Manichean, cosmic conspiracy in the literary hands of Pynchon, Vonnegut, or others would cause them to be hailed as the patron saints of '60s paranoia. Here, translated into the most intimate terms of everyday fear, anger, inexplicable hatred, and gratuitous suffering and oppression, it is simply autobiographical reality.

In these new terms, the *Autobiography* now proceeds to reconstruct the old story of American self-development. Some of it remains curiously familiar. By way of Benjamin Franklin, updated through Frederick Douglass, Malcolm finds the connection in literacy between language and power, becomes himself a construction of the prison library—words, titles, authors, books—an educational account of his own new self-authorization. Like many romantic predecessors, in his own bold eclecticism and powers of intellectual-imaginative synthesis, he undergoes that passage of spectacular unfolding familiar to us as growth of consciousness.

On the other hand, when epiphany comes, it is a bizarre compounding of the religious and the ideological. Upon his release from prison, he immediately apprentices himself to Elijah Muhammad, "the One to whom the Jews referred as the Messiah, the Christians as the Christ, and the

Muslims as the Mahdi" (208), the complete Savior-Master. He becomes Malcolm X.

And now in turn his story becomes, in every sense of the term, news. There is his political rise, amidst his conflicts with the mainstream civil rights movement. He has nothing but scorn for the "farce on Washington" (281). "The black masses in America were," he exclaims, "—and still are having a nightmare" (281). Sexual scandal and political rivalry bring the Master and the Minister into a struggle for power over the movement. Malcolm X moves further into the rhetorical excesses of a media-generated celebrity. John Kennedy is assassinated, and now it is "the chickens coming home to roost" (301). Publically, he is mythologized as a prophet of hate. Privately, he finds himself drifting into new passages of self-exploration: for example, his eventual journey to Mecca and his late internationalist realizations of new possibilities for human brotherhood, including new ways of seeing "white," even as he becomes the pawn in a larger political drama of Third World programmatics.

Suddenly, in a final chapter, entitled simply, "1965," Malcolm bursts forth in a voice filled with breathtaking new assertions of racial comity. "I have learned that not all white people are racists," he writes. "I am speaking against and my fight is against the white *racists*. I firmly believe that Negroes have the right to fight against these racists, by any means that are necessary" (367). He also prepares, in what he somehow knows to be his own last chapter, to die. And so, as the newspapers would soon inform us, he does.

There follows an epilog by Alex Haley. At once continuing the story in the text and supplementing it with the story the text has become, it uncannily goes on to predict in the last paragraph the new self-reifications the *Autobiography* has wrought before our eyes nearly thirty years later. "After signing the contract for this book," Haley recalls, "Malcolm X looked at me hard. 'A writer is what I want, not an interpreter.' I tried to be a dispassionate chronicler. But he was the most electric personality I have ever met, and I still can't quite conceive him dead. It still feels to me as if he has just gone into some next chapter, to be written by historians" (456).

Or perhaps by actors. The movie was still long in the future. But even at the time the text included comments by the black theatrical figure Ossie Davis showing how Malcolm X's life would continue to reproduce itself in a politics and a poetics of active identification. History can talk, Davis writes, "but in personal judgment, there is no appeal from instinct. I knew the man personally, and however much I disagreed with him, I never doubted that Malcolm X, even when he was wrong, was always that rarest thing in the world among us Negroes: a true man" (459). "And if," he goes on:

> to protect my relations with the many good white folks who make it possible for me to earn a fairly good living in the entertainment industry, I was too chicken, too cautious, to admit that fact when he was alive, I thought at least that now, when all the white folks are safe from him at last, I could be honest with myself enough to lift my hat for one final salute to that brave, black, ironic gallantry, which was his style and hallmark, that shocking *zing* of fire-and-be-damned-to-you, so absolutely absent in every other Negro man I know, which brought him, too soon, to his death. (459–60)

Here then, in the last words of "his" book, as testimony and performance, Malcolm X is translated into something like the living word. It is the *word* his book confirms, even as that word leaps beyond the page into the drama of history.

Marcuse, Herbert. During the period of his elevation into '60s intellectual celebrity, Herbert Marcuse, of all the chosen youth-prophets and elders of the era, remained a solitary, austere eminence. Beyond the theoretical intelligence revealed in such dense, challenging texts of cultural analysis as *Eros and Civilization* and *One-Dimensional Man,* the author's association with continental Marxism injected a certain note of menace.[43] On the other hand, whatever the difficulty of his texts or the formidability of his radical reputation, Marcuse's position as resident left dialectician of the American academy just as surely brought considerable luster to his status in the eyes of revolutionary youth.

Now, more than a quarter century into the poststructuralist revolution in American universities, with its various continental borrowings —semiotics, hermeneutics, phenomenology, Marxism, deconstructionism, the new psychoanalytics, the new historicism—Marcuse can be more easily "placed." First, he can now be seen along with '60s cohorts such as Paul Goodman and Norman O. Brown as offering mass culture-oriented yet theoretically complex and prescient work toward the ongoing revision of Freud that has been at the heart of so much subsequent postmodern cultural critique. Similarly, with that other great object of postmodernist revisionism, Marx himself, Marcuse's studies in mass culture and ideology may now be seen in their affiliations with the Frankfurt School of Walter Benjamin and such now familiar names as Gramsci, Adorno, and Horkheimer. More generally, Marcuse may now be seen as what we have come to call a cultural materialist, a specialist, that is, in the study of individual psychology as part of the material relations of culture: beginning with basic questions of wealth and distribution of goods but extending (especially in advanced capitalism) to what might also be called "the culture industry" at large—the media-manipulation of consumer tastes and attitudes as a function of ideology and often as a means of ideological regimentation.

The single concept Marcuse will most likely be remembered for is contained in a phrase: "repressive tolerance." By this he meant the capacity of a mass production, mass information society, given certain conditions of late capitalist power and affluence, to allow for and at the same time absorb virtually all forms of alternative social understanding.[44] His more permanent contribution, however, will surely lie in the application to '50s and '60s America of a larger conceptual style of ideological critique that made the former insight possible, a style based on the idea of culture itself as material-ideological discourse; an official narrative concentrated increasingly in *information* itself as a product capable of neutralizing voices of dissent, judgment, or other countercultural statement. The result, he suggested, was an already evident ideological stasis: a "pacified existence" (235) literally absorbing all thought and activity into a pattern of operational self-reification. Language itself had become a monolithic vehicle of ideology and the world of culture an essentially closed universe of discourse. Culture had thus reached the ultimate state of industrialization and commercialization and was now capable of buying out all options on consciousness itself.

The first of Marcuse's two great installments in the project just defined was *Eros and Civilization,* which was subtitled "A Philosophical Inquiry into Freud" but which was really, as Morris Dickstein acutely points out, "an attempted synthesis of Marx and Freud in which the word 'Marx' is never mentioned." The cause of such self-censoring was quite possibly, Dickstein goes on, either the "paranoia of the refugee" or the prudent calculation of an author in his "desire to reach an audience inoculated against radicalism" (68). Whatever the strategy, the resultant volume comes out very much in the meditative vein of analogous neo-Freudian texts of the late '50s such as *Life Against Death* and *Growing Up Absurd.*

Indeed, begins Marcuse, agreeing with Brown and Goodman, the problem of the Happy Consciousness so characteristic of mass democratic society in conditions of general material affluence is psychological in a uniquely pernicious and subtle way, namely in the utter "painlessness"

with which it confuses material and spiritual comfort, thereby equating
individual freedom with the acceptance of something called happiness as a
means of monolithic social control. "Mass democracy" especially, he writes,
"provides the political paraphernalia for effectuating" such a delusive

> introjection of the Reality Principle; it not only permits the people (up
> to a point) to choose their own masters and participate (up to a point) in
> the government which controls them—it also allows the masters to dis-
> appear behind the technological veil of the productive and destructive
> apparatus which they control, and it conceals the human (and material)
> costs of the benefits and comforts which it bestows upon those who col-
> laborate. The people, efficiently manipulated and organized, are free;
> ignorance and impotence, introjected heteronomy is the price of their
> freedom. (xiii)

As with Brown in relation to Freud, so now with Marcuse and Marx.
Or better, to *Freud* within a *Marxian* frame of analysis specially devised for
democratic, mass-media, late-capitalist society. The result is the logic of
relation imaged in the title and subtitle of Marcuse's great '60s book, *One-
Dimensional Man: Studies in the Ideology of Advanced Industrial Society*. The
"philosophical" part of the "philosophical inquiry into Freud" in *Eros and
Civilization* has now become "industrial" as well, with issues of identity
themselves now considered *as ideology* in the sense of a total socioeconomic
production. Here a simultaneously neo-Freudian *and* neo-Marxian synthesis becomes a total, mass-cultural wake-up call. It has become the social
project and the great liberating social theme. It has become, in a word, a
revolutionary discourse.

Only a total revolution in consciousness, says Marcuse, can make possible the new act of historical will that he calls The Great Refusal—an imperative response to the predicament described in the title to an introductory section as "The Paralysis of Criticism: Society Without Opposition."
Dialectic, once the promise of Western consciousness, has now become
totally institutionalized and materialized into Western production-logic,
the triumph of Reason, Science, and Objective Knowledge in a reign of
quantity. Western consciousness now drowns in an inundation of its own
material fruits. "We submit to the peaceful production of the means of destruction," writes Marcuse, "to the perfection of waste, to being educated
for a defense which deforms the defenders and that which they defend."
He continues: "If we attempt to relate the causes of the danger to the way in
which society is organized and organizes its members, we are immediately
confronted with the fact that advanced industrial society becomes richer,

bigger, and better as it perpetuates the danger" (ix). To invoke Thoreau, we have become the tools of our tools; but according to Marcuse, we have now done so in an age when the most advanced of those tools are productions, both materially and spiritually, of a logic of mass destruction. What is needed now, Marcuse asserts, is "qualitative change" (xiii).

This will take some doing, but, according to a kind of double hypothesis, Marcuse proposes a still workable plan. It may be, Marcuse writes, "that advanced industrial society is capable of containing qualitative change for the foreseeable future"; on the other hand, it is not inconceivable now "that forces and tendencies exist which may break this containment and explode the society" (xv).

And chief among these forces is the power of a revolution that may yet reopen the gap between words and things, a revolution of ideological discourse itself as a form of social production. The source of that power? In the broadest terms, art, but art in its largest sense as the expression of The Great Refusal, "the rationality of negation," "the protest against that which is" (63). Art is the site of the new dialectical consciousness that would refuse the identification with the traditions of Reason, Science, and Objective Knowledge precisely in order to keep open the spaces of possible difference. Indeed, art is now more than ever the enemy of institutional thought exactly because of the "essential gap between the arts and the order of the day, kept open in the artistic alienation," but "progressively closed by the advancing technological society" (64). At the maximum point of such closure, "the works are themselves incorporated into this society and circulate as part and parcel of the equipment which adorns and psychoanalyzes the prevailing state of affairs. Thus they become commercials— they sell, comfort, or excite" (64).

At such nodes of discourse we must begin to exercise the new art of The Great Refusal: the resistance of consciousness in its various forms of symbolic expression to what Marcuse now calls the Closing of the Universe of Discourse, a regime of language production that replicates the established culture in the totalitarian quality of its own capacity for something like material self-reification. It is a realm of production in which "the concept tends to be absorbed by the word" into a discourse of the totally "operational." Language becomes, in all of its forms, essentially the medium of advertising or merchandising, "the hypnotic formula," the production of some "image" of an essentially image-less reality.

"North Atlantic Treaty Organization," "Luxury fallout shelter," these are two such phrasings noted by Marcuse. "Your AT&T Representative," "Friendly Fire," "Servicing the Target" would be some recent equivalents.

The aim of such discourse-formations according to Marcuse will continue to be "the blocked development of content, the acceptance of that which is offered in the form in which it is offered" (90)—a conceptualization proscriptive of all thought as we know it, precluding critical questioning, and proposing an operation that at once precedes and constitutes any reality.

This, Marcuse concludes, is the Universe of One-Dimensional Man, a Discourse World of nothing but closed opportunities for what must become new critical openings. "Abridgement of the concept in fixed images; arrested development in self-validating, hypnotic formulas; immunity against contradiction; identification of the thing (and of the person) with its function—these tendencies reveal the one-dimensional mind in the language it speaks" (96–97). And this accordingly is what The Great Refusal must refuse. The dimension that must be invited back into discourse is the dimension of History in its fullest sense, the space of critique of the present. To put it more technically, the reinvention of the world must come through the reinvention of discourse itself as a form of social production that acknowledges History in the form of a distinction between history and historicity (or perhaps the rhetoricity of history), a distinction now lost. History must be rewritten through art and its capacity for "naming the 'things' that are absent, . . . breaking the spell of the things that are, . . . the ingression of a different order of things into the established one—'le commencement d'un monde' " (68). But this also must be done in the largest sense of History as Art, of History itself as a new politics of discourse. It must be insisted that "the philosophic universe thus continues to contain 'ghosts,' 'fictions,' and 'illusions' which may be more rational than their denial insomuch as they are concepts that recognized the limits and the deceptions of the prevailing rationality" (186). The great universals—beauty, justice, freedom, and the like—must in turn be newly seen as "conceptual instruments for understanding the particular condition of things in the light of their potentialities. They are historical and suprahistorical; they conceptualize the stuff of which the experience of the world consists, and they conceptualize it with a view of its possibilities, in the light of their actual limitation, suppression, and denial" (215).

This must be the properly revolutionary and utopian goal of The Great Refusal, Marcuse concludes, echoing his own source for a new dialectics of inspiration, Walter Benjamin. "It is only for the sake of those without hope," he says, "that hope is given us." In the means of oppression must be found the means of liberation. And so with the liberation of discourse will come the liberation of life as we know it in the world. From "the primary subjective prerequisite for qualitative change—namely, the *redefi-*

nition of needs"—will come a new politics of human personality, a revolution spearheaded by a rewriting of consciousness through language into a new discourse of culture. In sum, from the "redefinition of needs" will come a redefinition of the quality of our wants, and not the least of these will be the quality of our new capacity for spiritual belief.

Millett, Kate. The '60s antiwar movement grew out of the older pacifist and antinuclear movements; the '60s student left grew out of a marriage of the Old Left with the liberal intelligentsia; '60s black radicalism grew out of the civil rights movement. In these contexts, the '60s women's movement may claim uniqueness in having had to grow largely out of *itself* by reinventing feminism in America as a cultural discourse. For feminist readers early in the decade, Simone de Beauvoir in *The Second Sex* supplied a history of identification, and Betty Friedan in *The Feminine Mystique* went far toward giving a middle-class American definition of the predicament she called "the problem that has no name." On the other hand, within the New Left women such as Mary King and Casey Hayden found it necessary to draft a critique, published under the title "Sex and Caste," of the institutional oppression practiced by major revolutionary elements of the counterculture such as SNCC and SDS. Similarly, in underground media such as the New York *Rat* and the Berkeley *Barb,* figures such as Robin Morgan and Valerie Solanis lashed out even more vehemently against betrayals of women by the revolution: Morgan achieving fame as the author of the groundbreaking essay, "Good-Bye To All That," and Solanis issuing the legendary "S.C.U.M. Manifesto" and crowning the deed with the near fatal shooting of Andy Warhol.

Where the most rapid progress was made by women in '60s reading and writing was ironically in more conventional arenas of discourse production. In publication media of women's own devising, marginalized figures from all realms of both the dominant and the alternative culture— students, activists, journalists, academics, intellectuals, black women and other women of color, Third World women, professional women, lesbians, wives and mothers, elderly women—began to speak out and write out. Accordingly, such media themselves often became expressive of women's new ideas of discourse: revised conceptions of the status of texts, authorship, copyright, literary authority, and the politics and economics of literary production at large. The New York Women's League published collections such as *Notes from the First Year* and *Notes from the Second Year,* and anthologies appeared including the classic *Sisterhood Is Powerful* and the ensuing *Radical Feminism.* Texts appeared increasingly under collective authorship and as cooperative projects such as *Our Bodies, Ourselves*. Periodicals such as *Ms.* emerged as productions of women's authorship, editorship, managership, promotion, and entrepreneurship.

Albeit coming relatively late to the '60s scene, women's texts of the era nonetheless seemed often to seize most effectively on reading and writing as forms of social action, thus producing numerous and visible changes in the conditions of public discourse itself. In 1970 appeared a prodigious ideological summation of the project: Kate Millett's *Sexual Politics*. At once describing an old set of historical conditions and a new set of rhetorical possibilities, it envisioned a stylistics that could only be a politics, a criticism that could only be a moral agenda. It was an attempt, as Millett concisely put it in the preface, to conflate analysis of "the role which concepts of power and domination play in some contemporary literary descriptions of sexual activity itself" into the formulation of "a systematic overview of patriarchy as a political institution" (xi). The result, she proposes, "composed of equal parts of literary and cultural criticism, is something of an anomaly, a hybrid, possibly a new mutation altogether" (xii).[45]

As to the need for a new politics of criticism in America, Millett was surely correct, and, as the poststructuralist revolution was beginning to be wrought in America by the importations of continental thought, she provided an important American voice. Moreover, she did so not simply for the sake of a women's cultural criticism but for the sake of other emergent discourses of political criticism at large. "I have operated," she went on, "on the premise that there is room for a criticism which takes into account the larger cultural context in which literature is conceived and produced. Criticism which originates from literary history is too limited in scope to do this; criticism which originates in aesthetic considerations, 'New Criticism,' never wished to do so" (xii). The object of a genuinely "new" criticism, she went on, should thus be the invention of a political method at last calling into question the hierarchical structures and absolutist truth-claims of traditional modes of critical investigation. For women's discourse in particular, she asserted, the inscription of such relationships of power had long been a singular case in point of the general conditions of patriarchal or hegemonic discourse. To borrow the great feminist commonplace for women operating in the world of language, Millett insisted that the personal is always the political, and a culture's assumptions of cultural discourse must be constantly read and reread as the expression of that relationship.

A titular phrase, then, became at once a naming and an enactment. If *Sexual Politics* supplied American feminist criticism with a theoretical matrix, it also resulted in a textual model, a critical discourse that was itself a merging and rearranging of texts, genres, and discourses. The book begins memorably with three brief commentaries on sexually explicit passages from Henry Miller, Norman Mailer, and Jean Genet, "instances" of sexual description each "remarkable," Millett writes, "for the large part which notions of ascendancy and power played within them" (23). The procedure, demurely entitled "Instances of Sexual Politics," is what criticism at the time would have called an "interpretive" reading. What follows, however, in an ensuing section entitled "Theory of Sexual Politics," turns out to be not just a theory of interpretation supporting such readings, but rather a theory of interpretations constructing such texts *and* such readings in their inherently ideological relationship. To put it more directly, we encounter a politics of interpretation asserting that the conditions of reading and writing themselves are in fact always political constructions of gender and power. This theory is in turn given its intellectual provenance in a history of modern feminism, 1830–1930, as well as a counterhistory centered on the reactionary regimes of Hitlerian Germany and Soviet Russia and on twentieth-century revisions of Freud.

History merges back into literary study as Millet attempts new readings of the authoritarian sexual politics/poetics of D. H. Lawrence, Henry Miller, and Norman Mailer but also the explorations of homosexuality of Jean Genet.

Here the text completes itself as literary critique. At the same time, it also proposes a movement of literary thought beyond traditional history and criticism into a new vision of political futurity. With the end of "literature" must come the beginning of the world. "Genet's homosexual analysis of sexual politics was chosen," she concludes in a postscript,

> not only for the insights it affords into the arbitrary status of sexual role, but because it was against the taboo of homosexuality that Mailer's counterrevolutionary ardor has hurled its last force. Yet there is evidence in the last few years that the reactionary sexual ethic we have traced, beginning with Lawrence's cunning sabotage of the feminist argument and Miller's flamboyant contempt for it, has nearly spent itself. (362)

An old politics of writing, she suggests, is already displacing itself. But the process must now be abetted by a new politics of reading, in which the idea of the text is extended from the sacrosanct precincts of literature to the ideological constructions of politics that are imposed on us every day as the master-narratives of history and culture. Interpretation must be, as here, an unwriting, but it must also begin to find ways toward what might become a new writing of the very categories of human relationship. Accordingly, the aim facilitated by a new politics of criticism would be "realizing not only sexual revolution but a gathering impetus toward freedom from rank or prescriptive role, sexual or otherwise" (363). "For to actually change the quality of life," she goes on in a utopian diction now speaking to much of the hope of the decade, "is to transform personality, and this cannot be done without freeing humanity from the tyranny of sexual-social category and conformity to sexual stereotype—as well as abolishing racial caste and economic class" (363). This, then, would be the ultimate politics of criticism, a rereading of all the texts of culture that are the constructions of power relationships in that culture, and as a consequence the rewriting of nothing less than ourselves into a new being.

Mills, C. Wright. C. Wright Mills claims importance as an exemplary elder in the realm of social theory of the 1950s and early 1960s because he supplied '6os reading and writing with a structure of analysis and, as indicated by the titles below, a taxonomy that often supplied the very categories for that analysis. Other "elders" included such generally known figures as John Kenneth Galbraith (*The Affluent Society*), William Whyte Jr. (*The Organization Man*), David Riesman (*The Lonely Crowd*), Daniel Bell (*The End of Ideology*), Paul Goodman (*Growing Up Absurd*), and Michael Harrington (*The Other America*); and cultish authorities adopted by a youth-audience such as Norman O. Brown (*Life Against Death*), Herbert Marcuse (*Eros and Civilization, One-Dimensional Man*), Frantz Fanon (*The Wretched of the Earth*), or R. D. Laing (*The Divided Self, The Politics of Experience*).

Mills's major contributions to the store of new phrases and texts were mainly two, contained in the titles of his major works.[46] In 1951 he published *White Collar*. Then, in 1957, he followed with *The Power Elite*. The former took a major category of work relations in twentieth-century America and projected it forward into the precincts of organizational dread charted out by fictional texts such as Vonnegut's *Player Piano* and Joseph Heller's *Something Happened*. The latter investigated increasingly totalitarian hierarchies of position, wealth, and power at the level of national government and beyond.

Mills's title, *The Power Elite*, said it all, in a key of midcentury national self-recognition. In the United States, Mills posited, a traditional social elite and a new American elite of wealth—made possible, he noted astutely, by the absence of an aristocracy to prevent an increasingly affluent bourgeoisie from becoming, in a phrase, incredibly rich—had now overleapt their conventional differentiations to form a *power* elite radiating throughout the major spheres of national decision-making. A suggestion of the problem, he went on, had been contained in Dwight Eisenhower's somewhat surprising admonitions against the growing power of "the military-industrial complex." A more accurate identification, according to Mills, would now involve a tripartite complicity: "By the power elite," he wrote, we should actually include "those political, economic, and military circles which as an intricate set of overlapping cliques share decisions having at least national consequences. In so far as national events are decided, the power elite are those who decide them" (18). The result of this power distribution, he went on, is a conception of "classic democracy" in America that must increasingly be seen as comprised of "a set of images out of a fairy tale" (300). The chief effect in actual power relationships was already in progress. "The classic community of publics," he asserted, "is being transformed into a society of masses" (300). Or:

> The top of modern American society is increasingly unified, and often seems willfully co-ordinated: at the top there has emerged an elite of power. The middle levels are a drifting set of stalemated, balancing forces: the middle does not link the bottom with the top. The bottom of this society is politically fragmented, and even as a passive fact, increasingly powerless: at the bottom there is emerging a mass society. (324)

The American masses, Mills predicted, would eventually have to rise against mass production forms of cultural control never envisioned by theorists of the masses stretching from Marx to Ortega y Gasset and beyond, and rise thus against racism, militarism, sexism, exploitation, and repression. And so by the height of the '60s, with its operations increasingly made visible in the terms identified by Mills's conspiracy theory, the power elite had on its hands just the battle it had contrived for so long to disguise and avoid. Moreover, by enlisting the new power configurations of law enforcement and domestic intelligence-gathering ranging from the FBI and CIA to prosecutorial activities by the Attorney General's Office and the Selective Service, the system had made obvious its real contempt for individual citizens. In matters of power-relation *reified* in ways undreamed of by '50s prophets, "paranoia," that favorite '60s word, had become the only legitimate response to an actual power elite from anyone who, to borrow William Burroughs's memorable phrase, had "just found out what's happening."

Morgan, Robin, ed. *Sisterhood Is Powerful.* Women of the '60s youth-culture went into the decade, I would propose, largely undifferentiated from their male counterparts with respect to anything we would now call feminist awareness. Certain cognoscenti had claimed Simone de Beauvoir's *The Second Sex*. They might have read Betty Friedan, along with Mary McCarthy or Doris Lessing; begun to rediscover Gertrude Stein, Virginia Woolf, Anaïs Nin; found awakening to classic documents such as The Seneca Falls Declaration and the works of Margaret Fuller or Mary Wollstonecraft.

For the moment, however, many women in search of '60s scriptures likely underwent what Judith Fetterley has described as the process of "immasculation" so long required of female readers in an essentially male tradition: of adopting, that is, literary reading strategies whereby they were assumed capable of identifying with fictional youth-heroes such as Holden Caulfield, Sal Paradise, or Dean Moriarity, and then coming back out into the world with insights supposedly as applicable to their lives as to those of their male cohorts. Progress on all textual fronts was complicated and slow. The 1963 appearance of Friedan's *The Feminine Mystique* coincided with the English publication of Sylvia Plath's *The Bell Jar*. After 1964, a high school age constituency found a new mirror of identification in Joanne Greenburg's extremely popular *I Never Promised You a Rose Garden*. Through the later '60s, the literary status of Plath the poet as feminist youth-icon continued to grow, especially after the posthumous publication of *Ariel*. Gloria Steinem began *Ms.* magazine. On the West Coast, Joan Didion emerged as the laureate of exhaustion in the Land of the Golden Dream. In 1970, *Sexual Politics* defined for the first time a feminist poetics of literary *and* cultural critique.

Then, in 1971, finding an appropriate mode of statement in the collective possibilities of the anthology, the movement got a great, eclectic Scripture: *Sisterhood Is Powerful*. From the title onward, it proved a text truly worthy of being called revolutionary. To begin with, there was even the title itself. In keeping with the book it represents—a book announcing itself straightforwardly in its earliest pages as an *action*—it does not symbolize, suggest, or imply some master encoding of something else but makes its own meaning as simple predication. It does not even make a statement; it just *is* a statement. It predicates a relationship between something concrete called sisterhood—as opposed, say, to a historical abstraction such as "brotherhood"—and something equally concrete called power, forged through the utterly unambiguous verb "is." The title may have sounded like a slogan, a formula, a political motto declaimed as rallying cry, or, as it often turned out to be, a confession of political faith. It was also, however, quite simply true—a statement of political fact.

The text that followed likewise became a concrete, revolutionary exercise in collaborative discourse as a powerful new means of textual production. The result of countless testimonies of belief and experience, continually multiplying possibilities of genre, subject, perspective, and mode, it compounds itself into a true politics of polyphony. Throughout, there are voices, names, and identities, but there is no author. There turns out to be an editor, Robin Morgan. She, too, turns out to be the contributor of an introduction. Unlike most introductions, however, it does not authorially lay out a textual architecture, surveying the work anthologized within some centered structure of summary, argument, or explanation. Rather, it is the attempt of a single person trying personally to describe the purposes of the book, the way it came to be the way it is, the work that went into it, and the set of goals it hopes to help women achieve. It ends, moreover, in an equally personal connection, an address to someone else very particular, another woman described as "a sister underground," an actual person who has just made a radical choice. The final message is a letter. It is also a poem. It is signed, "Robin."

An essay then follows on "historical perspectives." It, too, is something of an introduction, but also something of a history. It has the decidedly unstudied title, "You've come a long way baby." It has not one author but two. It proposes an account of the rise of historical feminism, they tell us, that still needs, even as *they* write, to get written. They offer a set of notes toward that history. In the process, we realize, they have now actually begun to construct that history, a scrupulous history by anyone's definition complete with names, places, dates, and documents. It is also, we now see, exactly that new history proposed, one that would be an account of its own ideological self-discovery.

By now, we have plunged into the anthology proper. The opening entry in the first section headed "THE OPPRESSED MAJORITY: THE WAY IT IS" turns out to be "Know Your Enemy: A Sampling of Sexist Quotes." It has no author or editor. Its first part is a historical anthology of sexist pronouncements from celebrated sources and people accounted part of cultural "tradition." The end is a prose poem, punctuated by slashes, built entirely out of sexist commonplace and cliché, beginning with "A woman's place is in the home" and ending with "Some of my best friends are women" (38–39). Next, in stark, empirical juxtaposition, comes "The 51 Percent Minority

Group: A Statistical Essay," by a person named "Jorene," comprising the hard facts of woman's position in a man's world; percentages, degrees, salaries—the utterly numbing, leaden quantification of reality.

New openings of difference unfold. An essay follows on traditional marriage and motherhood. It is succeeded, in a new section on "Women in the Professions" (subtitled "Five Personal Testimonies") by others on women in medicine, publishing, television, the military, and journalism. Following are related discussions entitled "The Secretarial Proletariat," "The Halls of Academe," "Women and the Welfare System," "Two Jobs: Women Who Work in Factories," "Women and the Catholic Church," and "Does the Law Oppress Women?" Topics of psychosexual inquiry ensue: aging, orgasm, birth control, prostitution, radical lesbianism, and a feminist poetics.

As the text enlarges and the topics evolve, innumerable voices join in the discourse, black women, high-school women, Mexican-American women, ideological theoreticians, protest poets. In some cases we have the names of an author or authors. In others, we hear from women's caucuses, groups, collectives, committees. The text also invokes the testimony of "Historical Documents," everything from the NOW Bill of Rights to excerpts from the S.C.U.M. Manifesto, the Redstockings Manifesto, WITCH documents, "songs," and finally something called "Verbal Karate: Statistical and Aphoristic Ammunition" (625).

At the very end comes an appendix, with brief "Reference Notes" on sources of further information and a section entitled "Notes on Sister Contributors." As the text's beginning and middle have turned out to be anything but a standard beginning and middle, so this ending, a convention of most anthologies, turns out to be anything but conventional. What we learn of these women is the story of their lives as each chooses to tell it in a short testimony; in some cases what they have done, in some cases where they are and what they are doing now, in many cases what they are planning to do. Notable in nearly every case is the degree to which they define their lives only as they relate to collaborative relationships with other persons engaged in the work of liberation. Personal histories extend themselves forward into possible political histories, new communitarian contributions to a history that will continue to grow out of each woman's story and other stories.

The feminist assertion that "the personal is the political" has been realized in its fully operative political sense. Here at the end, as in the beginning of this remarkable text, the personal has wound up being inextricably political, exactly as the political has remained unapologetically personal. To put this another way, a text has enacted a shared politics of personhood. Moreover, if we look back, we now see that this has been the point of the text from word one on. "The collectivity, cooperation, and lack of competition," reads the first sentence of the book,

> (even from sisters who were also putting together collections on women's liberation) that marked the process of creating this book are proof of how radically different the women's movement is from male-dominated movements. Sisters, all over the country, some of whom I have not yet met in person, were of invaluable help in acting as regional contacts, and as sources of information, material, encouragement, and editorial suggestions. (n.p.)

And by the end, we see that the politics of personhood so envisioned has now revised accordingly our notion of the politics of the text. What is an author? we now ask in a truly revolutionary political way. What is a text, a subject, an audience, and a source?; what is a contribution, an organization, and a document?; a biography, a history, or a community?

Such was the real achievement of this remarkable work and of other major texts to follow, such as Annie Koedt's anthology *Radical Feminism* and the Boston Women's Health Collective's at once inspiriting *and* best-selling *Our Bodies, Ourselves:* a new politics of the text that would also be a new politics of consciousness and community even down to new notions of what a community could do with massive book royalties. Of all the scriptures emerging from the Generation of Youth to appropriate most fully the bracing challenge of theoretical postmodernism and to execute a vision of its possibilities for discourse and politics, *Sisterhood Is Powerful* earned the status of the true original. In its conflated visions of language and power, it is faithful to a new politics of authority, language, representation, textual production and distribution exactly to the degree that it is in the same moment the enactment of a new politics of personhood. It rewrites the popular, mass-production, printed text for the sake of something called liberation that would no longer be just a word.

Pirsig, Robert. Although not published until 1974, Robert Pirsig's *Zen and the Art of Motorcycle Maintenance* stands for many readers as a kind of '60s *summa theologica*. Certainly it incorporated the true spirit of the paperback scripture of that era: the how-to-do-it book for the rewriting of Western consciousness. Moreover, like comparable texts such as those by

Vonnegut especially, it took no pains to disguise a distinctly lunatic connection—in this case searingly autobiographical—between its claims of cosmic significance and its status as a self-contained fable of origin.

The structure of the narrative, summoning up the older visionary tradition of Melville, Thoreau, and Whitman, is itself a model of the fabulous quest of consciousness it enacts. It becomes the itinerary of a voyage toward sane living in America born out of the attempt to reconstruct the personal history of a madman. As a deeply private fable, it also attempts to make public that eccentric history as a possible source of transfiguration for American consciousness at large.

Appropriately, like Melville's, Thoreau's, or Whitman's, this text too, on its way toward becoming a popular classic, had its own quite literally mad history. It was first submitted for publication in the mid-to-late '60s and, as noted earlier, by the author's own count was rejected by 120 publishers. Its conceptual genesis belonged to the narrator's graduate study of more than a decade before—or, to be more precise, the study begun by some lost other person the narrator seems to have been known as, here named "Phaedrus." This study had been conducted with the prestigious University of Chicago Committee on the Analysis of Ideas and Study of Methods. The latter was itself a radically eccentric curriculum that in turn had arisen, the narrator tells us, from "that famous revolt against empirical education that had taken place in the early thirties" (336).

It was through such a complicated and bizarre transmission of consciousness, we eventually discover, that the narrator—or again, Phaedrus—had found it possible to conceive of something called Quality as a potential new topic of theoretical philosophy. This construct he proposed to his shocked mentors as a countertheology sufficient to bring down the Church of Reason that had come to be the grand edifice of philosophy in the West. Through Quality he proposed a final unworking of the crisis of consciousness provoked by the traditional dialectical character of that philosophy—its relentless patterns of binary categorization and opposition—such as, spirit and matter, mind and body, imagination and reason, art and technology. The result, he confidently predicted, might be a new sense of whole relation to the world that would also restore to that relation a lost ground of predialectical origin.

This Quality, then, Phaedrus set for himself as his thesis, both as a structure of inquiry and as a textual project. Not surprisingly, the whole business was rejected by his mentors—the newest priests, it turned out, of the Church of Reason—as impossible, perhaps even mad. Still, Phaedrus continued to pursue the idea, as an itinerant journeyman academic, a freshman writing teacher, a faculty gadfly and irritant, and an increasingly distracted and incoherent husband and father. Shortly, he plunged into madness—pathological, certifiable, absolute.

Eventually Phaedrus vanished. Pirsig again became his name. The latter devoted himself as far as he could to coming back to a reconstituted, newly integral way of living in the world. Yet somehow, that other—Phaedrus—remained hauntingly and ubiquitously out there. Even in places where he is about to travel, Pirsig/Phaedrus, in a present tense of becoming, recognizes them as places where he has already been.

The quest takes over the new life. His thesis also gets written, finally, and approved, but not by the Church of Reason. Rather, it finds its public approval as an enormously popular paperback text, something of an alternative scripture for a new generation of students, and then a steady seller for other students to whom they recommend it or for whom it increasingly appears on college or university syllabuses in courses in English, History, American Studies, Sociology, Psychology, Anthropology, and—perhaps, if the topic is postmodernism—even Philosophy. That thesis is called *Zen and the Art of Motorcycle Maintenance.*

It is still about Quality. What has made it finally possible to write and publish is that Pirsig has once again found Phaedrus, or perhaps Phaedrus has once again found Pirsig. Accordingly, the thesis has recovered the discourse of epiphany that can now make possible its articulation. Quality has actually found its meaning.

But now, like many a quintessential youth-text of the era, such a synthesis of holy wisdom and existential discovery in its title had also found for itself appropriate terms of promotion. Especially in paperback, from the cover onward, *Zen and the Art of Motorcycle Maintenance* seemed the ultimate extension of the '60s text. The title sounded like a combination of the *I Ching* and *Easy Rider.* The same composite spirit was projected by the brilliant cover logo (available on backgrounds of popsicle green, yellow, pink, and purple): the monkey wrench in the lotus. It heralded the history of Phaedrus-Pirsig the crank-philosopher arising out of the beautiful blossom of Zen. On the back was the portrait of a man and a boy in a meadow, standing beside a motorcycle, and looking toward a mountain peak. This would be an exact visualization of the end of the text, at once dramatic scene and mystic reprise.

To be sure, the narrator is at pains to open with a Vonnegut-like disclaimer of technical seriousness. The account of experience depicted, he says, "should in no way be associated with that great body of factual information relating to orthodox Zen Buddhist practice." Further, he adds, "It's not very factual on motorcycles, either." On the other hand, as we begin the odyssey toward Quality, from the first page on that same text is often quite wise and good about both of those things and usually best when it uses one to speak of the other. For exactly this new spirit of homemade dialectic has already set in motion what might be more properly called here, in Bakhtin's sense, the dialogics of the text. "And what is good, Phaedrus," asks an ensuing epigraph, "And what is not good—Need we ask anyone to tell us these things?" Out of an old discipline of reverent wisdom framed in a new key of wise irreverence, we begin the journey.

A narrator and his son are crossing the Central Plains on a motorcycle. In every sense of the term, the motorcycle is an important vehicle for the narrator: "On a cycle the frame is gone," he tells us. "You're completely in contact with it all. You're *in* the scene, not just watching it anymore, and the sense of presence is overwhelming" (5). The choice of roads, like William Least Heat Moon's blue highways, is important also. They are state roads, routes on which to make "good time," but also roads on which a spiritual emphasis is possible on " 'good' rather than 'time.' " "And when you make that shift in emphasis," the narrator adds obliquely, "the whole approach changes" (5).

For the reader with the title in mind, this ordinary book is already making its extraordinary journey toward new meanings. As to subject, it is a motorcycle book; it is also, clearly, a Zen book. As to the method of rendition, the narrator tells us, it is likewise two books, a riding book and a thinking book. He calls it an ongoing Chautauqua, the account of a physical journey that is also the account of a metaphysical journey and vice versa. It is a narrative account always paired, so to speak, with the discourse of its spiritual supplement (8). As in the grand traditions of American physical/metaphysical journeying, whether those of Thoreau or Whitman (which Pirsig's odyssey often actively resembles) or those of Melville and Dickinson (which it often recapitulates in style), the text becomes at once metonymy and metaphor, in Roman Jakobsen's useful formulation, metaphor and metonymy. To use a simpler and more available '60s word, the trip becomes a "trip."

Pirsig himself effects this translation. The object of the trip is the old thesis, and the old thesis is again the object: Quality. But it may also be stated in a decidedly contemporary way. It does truly have something to do now, the narrator asserts, with what he calls his musician friend John's capacity for "a groovy dimension." Although related to "beat" or "hip," he insists, however, "this dimension isn't a fad that's going to go away next year or the year after. It's here to stay because it's a very serious and important way of looking at things that *looks* incompatible with reason and order and responsibility but actually is not" (53). Similarly, this "dimension" is also a view that often assumes *itself* incompatible with "scientific explanation" when in fact it often most clearly constructs science's "underlying form" (65) in its most pure and perhaps original relation to "reason and order and responsibility" (54). "You might say there's a little problem here," he concludes modestly (54). And somehow "it" is always there, truly physical and metaphysical, presence and ghost, same and other. It becomes a trip where one describes the breeze on one's face and itemizes the practical necessities for the complete motorcyclist as one pulls into a new town, perhaps the long-awaited place of epiphany and where, at the same time, one also knows strangely that someone called Phaedrus has been there already.

Laid out in part 1, this is the structure of the thesis, dialectical in the full Hegelian sense, and at the same time the projection of the newly possible vision of synthesis that will ultimately be achieved through its articulation as text. As mentor and guide, the narrator moves us through a myriad of oppositional pairings, cherished by the West, beginning with the titular one: we locate the space of the discourse between the compression of the incomprehensible Zen on one hand and the oxymoronic latitude of the "art" of motorcycle maintenance on the other. We learn of the oppositional categories of the Romantic and the Classic (64), of art and technology (161), of phenomenal appearance and underlying form, discourses of "structure" that are themselves paired structural discourses requiring each other for their own definitions. As the categories of philosophy are newly reshaped in endless proliferation by the metaphorical "Phaedrus' knife"—here conceived as the exact other of Occam's razor—philosophy itself turns back to a final contemplation of some "other" or prior ground of its structure of categorical assumption in the West, which is dialectic. And here we witness the final application of Phaedrus's knife, which suddenly turns out to be the knife of an actual other Phaedrus in an actual other time as well: that of the figure of pre-Socratic wisdom, someone called Phaedrus, the wolf, long consigned to the status of misguided "other" voice in one of Plato's dramatic renditions of the triumph of the Socratic. With one final sweep that last oppositional structure of all oppositional structures, pure dialectic, is cut apart revealing categorical logic to be itself but a category among categories in endless supplementation. We find again the phenomenological origin of Quality then and now, at once before and beyond dialectic, somewhere back with Phaedrus in Plato's text and somewhere ahead with Phaedrus in Pirsig's text. Quality, we see, was never in the first place a subject or an object and can never again be thought of as a subject or an object. "It is the point at which subject and object meet." It is "not a *thing*" at all. "It is an *event*" (233).[47] "The sun of quality," shrieks a passage from an old text by someone called "Phaedrus" just as he emerges on a motorcycle out of a storm into blue sky as a man named Pirsig with a son named Chris, "does not revolve around the subjects and objects of our existence. It does not just passively illuminate them. It is not subordinate to them in any way. It has *created* them. They are subordinate to *it!*" (234).

What we are presented with, then, in *Zen and the Art of Motorcycle Maintenance,* is a homemade American pre-Socratic and poststructuralist odyssey of consciousness for the weather of our times. Somewhere back before the West, a Sophist named Phaedrus made a lonely attempt to keep philosophy from the darkness that would ensue should it disconnect living consciousness from something called Quality constituting its ground of origin. Somewhere at the far end of the West, a man named Pirsig and his son named Chris arrive for the moment at least at that same vision of Quality as a new prospect of illumination. Back there, in the East, somewhere before dialectic in the West, was Quality, as there was also the Tao; in the West there was *Arete,* as in the East there was *Dharma*. Here, before time as we know it, was the liberation from time, the sense of whole relation to the world. Now it is newly recoverable, carrying us at last beyond the postmodernist quandary. Now, at the last, for Phaedrus-Pirsig, with the road opening up, it is all present tense again:

> He crosses a lonesome valley, out of the mythos, and emerges as if from a dream, seeing that his whole consciousness, the mythos, has been a dream and no one's dream but his own, a dream he must now sustain of his own efforts. Then even 'he' disappears and only the dream of himself remains with himself in it.
>
> And the Quality, the *aretê* he has fought so hard for, has sacrificed for, has *never* betrayed, but in all that time has never once understood, now makes itself clear to him and his soul is at rest. (390–91)

Plath, Sylvia. The history of Sylvia Plath as a '60s youth-icon is a case study in the era's strangely interlocking vectors of literary and mythic celebrity: a total textual phenomenon, the combination of publishing event and cultural legend. To an early coterie of readers, she was Sylvia Plath, new American poet, author of *The Colossus* (1961), wife of the English poet Ted Hughes, and also author of the autobiographical *The Bell Jar,* published in England in 1963 under the pseudonym Victoria Lucas. Shortly in that same year, she became Sylvia Plath, suicide and literary-feminist martyr; and then, after 1965, she was apotheosized into Sylvia Plath, tragic genius and haunting poet-presence of the posthumous collection, *Ariel.* Such accretions of celebrity then once again turned interest back on her as Sylvia Plath, author of *The Bell Jar,* finally published in America as a youth bestseller and an instant feminist classic of 1971.

By 1967, Plath had also gained uncommonly swift canonization in the *Norton Anthology of American Literature* (at the time the standard text of the college survey) with three poems, "Black Rook in Rainy Weather," "Morning Song," and "The Rival." In 1974, added to "Morning Song" and "The Rival" were the more vociferously militant "The Applicant," "Death and Company," and "Daddy." Later editions also reprinted the celebrated "Lady Lazarus." A certain kind of Sylvia Plath had thus been produced as a cultural text for which selected works came to be slotted into particular mythic assignments. This proved especially the case with *The Bell Jar,* the narrative text, ironically, along with perhaps just a few poems— "Ariel," "Daddy" and "Lady Lazarus"—for which Plath continues to be popularly known.

The novel's predominance over the poetry as the essential Plath text for '60's youth-culture is curious but not particularly difficult to understand given the context of its publishing. From its appearance in the American market first as a cult favorite and later as a bestselling paperback, it was widely promoted among general readers and quickly made a staple of the college and university syllabus, capitalizing on a contemporary genre of autobiographical narrative—albeit to date monopolized by male protagonists—already of considerable appeal to youth readership, male and female: the story of the young person most likely to succeed going crazy in the land of opportunity. Indeed, the brilliant, erratic history of Esther Greenwood—English prodigy at a well-known women's college whose descent into madness during a sojourn as student editor for a well-known women's magazine results in her confinement in a mental hospital—was instantly recognized in its parallel to an immediate male literary predecessor, Holden Caulfield. As one reviewer put it, "the hand of Salinger lay heavy upon her" (34).

If that judgment was often rendered in a tiresome key of masculinist construction—as the roughly contemporary Scout Finch in *To Kill a Mockingbird* was invariably accounted a female Huckleberry Finn—it stemmed from a structural parallel that it surely invited. Opening on the memory of a youthful sojourn in New York, the text quickly casts the episode as the beginning of a troubled psychic passage that has not yet ceased.

On the third page or so—as we go along with details about a writing contest, twelve college women taken to the city as summer interns by a fashion magazine, and their residence at a Barbizon-like women's hotel called, brilliantly, the Amazon—we see it and know: "but later, when I was all right again."

Yet from the first sentences on, there was also a distinctly political voice investing this new protagonist's retrospective account of her own experience of going crazy in America with a contemporary feminist immediacy. "It was a queer, sultry summer, the summer they electrocuted the Rosenbergs," the narrator begins, "and I didn't know what I was doing in New York." It may sound like Holden Caulfield, perhaps, or Sal Paradise, this location of the narrative in a "current event," but the response is somehow political *and* personal in ways that neither would dare. Esther Greenwood is interested in "what it would be like, being burned alive all along your nerves." She goes on: "I thought it must be the worst thing in the world" (1).

The point for Esther Greenwood, returnee from the land of burned nerves, is that the personal is from the outset merged with the political and the political merged with the personal in ways that women have learned Being a bright, sensitive, disturbed, and genuinely misunderstood young person who happens to be a woman works here as a seamless merging of the metaphorical and the existential. Esther Greenwood is a brilliant student at a prestigious northeastern women's college who wishes to be a poet but who must content herself with the literary thrill of having a senior thesis professor become "very excited" about a project she has proposed on *Finnegan's Wake* and who has "promised to give" her "some leads on images about twins" (28). As a scholarship student, she has a patron, Philomena Guinea (33), a well-known women's novelist.[48] She has been given the opportunity by *Ladies' Day* magazine to spend the summer in New York. In that capacity, she has a mentor and career role model, the hard-driving albeit admirable and sympathetic Jay Cee. She is not only sexually inexperienced and socially maladroit but she does not understand, as she looks about at her peers, what makes her so different.

Soon, in Esther's own sexual explorations, the crisis of difference culminates explicitly. Her more or less intended, med student Buddy Willard, whom she met at a Yale prom, is a patronizing male traditionalist of an order of doltishness that approaches real genius. A chief measure of his development is a mother to whom most of the women he goes out with refer simply as "Buddy Willard's Mother." He has tried to help Esther learn the facts of life by taking her to witness a hospital childbirth. This is followed by a private tutorial in male anatomy, involving a sober, clinical display of his own gear, which Esther commits to memory by noting something like a "turkey neck and turkey gizzards" (55). These units of instruction have been reinforced by the laboratory examination of various fetuses preserved in jars, looking not unlike—a connection Esther eventually seems to make—the "Eisenhower faced" infants she later sees while looking through a nuthouse copy of *Baby Talk* (181).

In a series of grotesque, dispiriting encounters elsewhere, Esther tries to lose her virginity. She engineers a surrender to a cosmopolitan UN interpreter (the introduction supplied by Buddy Willard's Mother), which proves so labored that in the process they both fall asleep. A subsequent encounter with a misogynist playboy results in a near rape.

Esther returns home hoping to write but is instead hounded by her mother into receiving a set of maternal lessons in shorthand. She becomes solitary, introverted, sleepless, apathetic. She is taken to her family physician, by chance a woman, who turns her over to a male psychiatrist. Medication fails. She is taken for therapy. There are shock treatments. "I wondered what terrible thing it was I had done" (118). The destroying madness begins to gather. She tries to kill herself with pills. She is hospitalized. Dr. Nolan, another psychiatrist—this time a woman—attempts to bring her back. But there are more shock treatments. Dr. Nolan says she cannot stop them.

Eventually Esther stabilizes, develops a friendship with an earlier acquaintance named Joan, also a patient and also, coincidentally, another Buddy Willard woman. Joan goes into outpatient placement and eventually so does Esther. Finally, as they both try to make it on the outside in Cambridge, Esther achieves her deflowering in the apartment of a young math professor named Irwin who picks her up on the steps of Widener Library.

" 'It hurts,' I said. 'Is it supposed to hurt?' "

Irwin does not say anything, but then he offers, "sometimes it hurts" (184). As it turns out, Esther must call Joan, who takes her to the emergency room to stop the hemorrhaging. "You're one in a million," the doctor whistles (190), making like Heller's Doc Daneeka. "But can you fix it?" she asks, taking the role of Yossarian. "The doctor laughed. 'Oh, I can fix it all right' " (190), he said, *Catch-22*–like.

Esther is returned to the hospital. Shortly she is told that Joan is dead, a suicide. Buddy returns, visits, seeks comfort for his fear that *he* has been the one responsible for making Esther and Joan crazy. Esther goes to Joan's grave, stands there listening, and hears, she says, "the old brag of my heart.

I am, I am, I am" (199). As the novel concludes she prepares to face the medical board, to work the catechism whereby she will be declared mad or sane, or, more likely, still "sick" or perhaps "well" again.

Even in so simple a description, one senses in Plath's quiet masterpiece the true existential authority of the feminist original. It *is Catch-22:* Doc Daneeka explains how anybody who is crazy has a right to ask to be removed from combat status but how anybody who asks is revealing a rational concern for his own safety that makes him not crazy; Snowden lies there in the moment of the primal wounding and keeps asking why it hurts so much, and all Yossarian can say is "There, there. There, there." Or Yossarian lies etherized on the table and keeps hearing the mocking, clinical voices saying "We've got your pals." And here it is again, Catch-22 as a *fact of life:* take a brilliant, creative young woman, it says, encourage her brilliance and creativity through the best education a culture can provide, promise her the world professionally, perhaps even literarily, and then tell her to go out into the world and learn to be Buddy Willard's wife: Buddy Willard's mother, Jay Cee, the professional woman and wife: Esther Greenwood's mother, the widowed shorthand expert: or Dodo Hathaway, the blooming fount of Catholic fecundity. Marry someone, anyhow, but just forget that you were once led to believe that you were a person full of brilliance and creativity with a real life. Accept that it is their right to take it away any time they want, because they can do anything we cannot stop them from doing.

The difference here, as in so much women's writing to come, is that the "catch" is no existential conceit. The long road beckoning toward the end makes itself clear for Esther Greenwood in particular. *Catch-22* becomes *No Exit.* The short passage is better. Here is true madness. Here is an insane world full of only insane choices for the living. Here is *No Exit* without the existential conceit. Here is no separate peace, not even limping by on a survivor's code. Esther, we simply understand, at a certain point is going to have to "deal" with her problem herself.

And she does, Esther does, eventually, when Sylvia does, when Ariel takes the final flight. The space between sanity, normal life, and reason is one that cannot be crossed except by an act of imagination that for certain persons in the world can only be embodied by suicide. Robert Lowell, writing toward the end of his own madness in a brief introduction to the *Ariel* volume, must have understood that fact for both of them. "In these poems," he wrote, "Sylvia Plath becomes herself, becomes something imaginary, newly, madly, and subtly created— . . . one of those super-real, hypnotic great classical heroines" (vii). She did, and her name turned out to be Ariel, the text of a consummated life. These are the last lines of the poem "Ariel":

> White
> Godiva, I unpeel—
> Dead hands, dead stringencies.
>
> And now I
> Foam to wheat, a glitter of seas.
> The child's cry
>
> Melts in the wall.
> And I
> Am the arrow
>
> The dew that flies
> Suicidal, at one with the drive
> Into the red
> Eye, the cauldron of morning. (26–27)

Sylvia–Esther–Ariel was as good and as brave as her word.

Portola Institute, *The Last Whole Earth Catalog.* With the 1971 publication of *The Last Whole Earth Catalog,* '60s reading and writing made its final step into alternative publishing as total design. In one sense, the text is pure content, information, communicative function, an *omnium gatherum* of counterculture lore: as its subtitle demurely announces, it provides "access to tools"; or as popular phrasemakers elaborated, it was the Sears Roebuck of the Hippies. On the other hand, it is pure performance, or, rather, a vast, collaborative compilation of individual performances. Authorship is attributed, by a small notation on the spine and a copyright notice buried at the bottom of the opening page of text, to an agency calling itself "The Portola Institute." Descriptive entries on particular products or items by particular contributors are often accompanied with commentary by others. Sometimes these are general editors identifying themselves with their initials. Sometimes they are just interested parties with other useful opinions. Often the person suggesting the entry in the first place will be identified. At times the suggestion will come from a letter to the editor. The response may often involve a letter from someone else with a related invention or particular expertise on the problem at hand.

The shape, size, and heft also testify to the mix of promotions. Huge and imposing, bearing on its cover the image of a whole earth silhouetted against the blackness of space, the *Catalog* suggests itself to be in its way the ultimate planetary paperback, perhaps even the last one, as the title claims, a person will ever need. At closer range, it also seems like the ultimate counterculture version of the coffee-table book, total information as cosmic decor item all for five dollars.

Meanwhile, we ponder the title. Why the *Last* Whole Earth Catalog? Why the Last *Whole Earth* Catalog? Why the Last Whole Earth *Catalog*? One finds a fairly simple answer to the first question. There had been a previous *Whole Earth Catalog* and a *Supplement*. "The CATALOG," as noted by the editors, "was formal and responsible; the Supplement wasn't. In this LAST CATALOG they are mixed" (2). As we proceed to the second point, however, larger textual and political implications begin to unfold. Also on the cover, we will have noticed, beneath the aforementioned photo of the whole earth, is a small legend. "Evening," it says. "Thanks again." This may be, we see, the last whole earth catalog in relation to the one before; but it may also be the last one, we suddenly see, in relation to the earth itself. Simultaneously, we now come to understand the term "catalog" as at once encyclopedia and curriculum, a total course of education.

The Last Whole Earth Catalog was everything its title and cover billed it to be, the counterculture apotheosis of a long national tradition of do-it-yourself *kultur:* "access to tools" on a grand scale, American bounty, everything from parkas to children's playthings, sourdough starter to insanity cures. It was at once a guide to life on the planet and the door-to-door salesman's dream of the total family almanac-encyclopedia: a compendium of description, commentary, review, digest, and test report; an anthology of editorial, essay, humorous anecdote, and opinion; an inventory of technologies; a reference guide to further resources; an enormous mail-order address book; and for the reader's continuing information *and* entertainment, a running novel attributed to one Gurney Norman, entitled *Divine Right's Trip,* filling portions of the right-hand column on most odd-numbered pages. From start to finish, it was a cottage industry version of the ultimate alternative text.

So too, in organization, it somehow managed a characteristic American blending of the practical and the cosmic, arraying itself impressively according to major subjects, disciplines, areas of study, and listings of primary and supplementary readings. "Whole Systems" is the heading for the first section. Then follow major divisions of text according to such topics as "Land Use," "Shelter," "Industry," "Craft," "Community," "Nomadics," "Communications," and "Learning." These in turn have subdivisions within. A sample of headings under "Land Use," for instance, includes

"Pests"; "Soil"; "Seeds, Vegetables, and Fruit"; "Trees and Flowers"; "Farm Stuff"; "Wildlife"; "Wells"; "Mining"; "Trees and Saws"; and "Mushrooms." Under "Nomadics" one finds, among others, "Buses & Campers," "Car Repair," "Bicycles," "Mountains," "Horses," "Moccasins," "Survival," and "Boats." If an entry is itself about a text or other information source, it will have a review as well as representative extracts. The reviewer is identified, as is the person suggesting the item for inclusion. If the entry concerns material objects, consumer items of one kind or another, it will be accompanied by full technical data, often including diagrams. All entries also provided full cost and supplier information.

The page layout is a collage of text, picture, diagram, and illustration. Under "Whole Systems," one quickly samples advertisements for a small library of texts by R. Buckminster Fuller, a wall poster of Andromeda, Loren Eisley's *The Unexpected Universe,* two obscure science fiction novels by someone named Olaf Stapledon, *The Hubble Atlas of Galaxies,* and five recent NASA earth photo books. Shortly begins as well the novel, a story of the long search for happiness by a freak named Divine Rights and a '63 Volkswagen named Urge. Meanwhile, new entries move along to the *Tao Teh King,* Norbert Wiener's *Cybernetics,* Aldo Leopold's *Sand County Almanac,* and a long-playing record personally produced by John Cage. In the midst of all this suddenly appears Wendell Berry's famous essay, "Think Little." (Later, a similar cameo will involve some papers of Ken Kesey's found in a box by one of the editors.) Meanwhile, *Divine Right's Trip* propels itself "Westward, Westward."

For nearly 400 pages more, entries unfold on macramé; communes; aerobics; geodesic domes; Euell Gibbons; *Be Here Now, Remember;* Frank Herbert's *Dune;* Carlos Castaneda's *The Teachings of Don Juan* and *A Separate Reality* (the only two works then published); *Women and Their Bodies* (eventually to become *Our Bodies, Ourselves*); and nearly anything by Joseph Campbell. Strunk and White's *The Elements of Style* and the L. L. Bean Catalog mix with Dr. Spock, *Black Elk Speaks,* Ken Kesey's *Sometimes a Great Notion,* Robert Townsend's *Up the Organization,* and (under recommended educational readings for children) Richard Bach's *Jonathan Livingston Seagull.* Under the large final category of "Learning," "Science" meets "Myth," and "Psychology" finds a connection with "Calisthenics." Appropriately, the section is closed with a short page on "Serendipity." The key text recommended is the *I Ching.*

An afterword provides detailed, technical instructions and words of encouragement on "How To Do a Whole Earth Catalog" and an index of sorts. The back cover reprises the whole earth picture from the front, this time without shadow, together with an inscription reading, "We can't put it together. It is together."

The performance of the task of enlightenment set forth for itself by the text is complete. It is a total curriculum. It has delivered as promised according to function. More importantly, as to consciousness of ourselves and our relation to the earth, it has also made the world look different in the sense described in one of its myriad intertexts, a passage from Thomas S. Kuhn's *The Structure of Scientific Revolutions:*

> Lavoisier, we said, saw oxygen where Priestley had seen dephlogisticated air and where others had seen nothing at all. In learning to see oxygen, however, Lavoisier also had to change his view of many more familiar substances. He had, for example, to see a compound ore where Priestley and his contemporaries had seen an elementary earth, and there were other such changes besides. At the very least, as a result of discovering oxygen, Lavoisier saw nature differently. And in the absence of some recourse to that hypothetical fixed nature that he "saw differently," the principle of economy will urge us to say that after discovering oxygen Lavoisier worked in a different world. (393)

Pynchon, Thomas. There remains now something so quintessentially '60s about Thomas Pynchon's *The Crying of Lot 49* as to make one feel it was made for the decade. And one feels that way, I would suggest, with good reason. While the cult reputation of *V,* Pynchon's dense, challenging, hermetic first novel had proved gratifying, sales figures had not.[49] *The Crying of Lot 49* called for less readerly exertion. In a relatively brief and seemingly less formidable book, he nonetheless achieved again the sense of paranoiac self-reflexiveness that inhabited the earlier text. At the same time, he had also managed to project this set of metafictional congruencies into a saturnalia of '60s plastic schlock: a free spirit heroine from California named Oedipa Maas, pursuing her discovery of an eight-hundred-year-old antipostal service and people's conspiracy against the System called Tristero; her disc jockey, ex-car–salesman husband, Wendell ("Mucho") Maas; a psychiatrist who does LSD experiments named Dr. Hilarius; and a mop-topped local singing group affecting lower-class British accents named "The Paranoids," modeled along the lines of a popular British band called "Sick Dick and the Volkswagens" with a signature tune entitled "I Want to Kiss Your Feet." The setting is a Southern California hallucination: places with names like Kinneret Among the Pines, San Narciso, Yoyodyne Aerospace, and Fangoso Lagoons, not to mention Los Angeles, San Francisco, Berkeley, and Oakland. It is a world awash in acronyms. The call sign of Mucho's station is KCUF. He has worked in the car lots under the sign (one so real, in fact, it seems as if it could only be made up) of "N.A.D.A."—National Automobile Dealers Association. Often placed on or near cans, baskets, and other convenient receptacles is "W.A.S.T.E."—eventually revealed to be the sinister motto, "We Await Silent Tristero's Empire." The drama unfolds through a labyrinthine pattern of involvement implicating a host of strange California types: Metzger, once a child-actor named Baby Igor, now a lawyer, assigned with Oedipa as coexecutor of the estate of her hi-tech industrialist tycoon ex-lover, Pierce Inverarity; Manny Di Presso, a lawyer turned actor; Mike Fallopian, a lounge lizard in a local cocktail hangout; Randolph Driblette, an impresario in the local Little Theater; Stanley Koteks, an employee at Inverarity's aerospace company, Yoyodyne; John Nefastis, inventor of a perpetual motion machine linking energy and information transfer through a principle called Maxwell's Demon; and Genghis Cohen, a professional philatelist, called to examine a collection of stamps that forms part of the estate and that suddenly looms into cosmic importance. For the '60s Pynchonian, the novel seemed to have everything: sophomore humor, senior erudition, cosmic irreverence, and heavy paranoia—something like the party scene from *Laugh-In* filtered through a hard-boiled Southern California detective story.

As a textual conundrum, the novel telegraphed its clues using everything from recondite allusion to an ever enlarging communications network of graffiti. Having chanced first upon the Tristero story through a set of coincidences involving the development of an Inverarity real estate project with the plot of an obscure seventeenth-century revenge tragedy by one Richard Wharfinger, Oedipa is plunged into a mystery of competing versions and editions, plot revelations, probable and spurious readings, textual cruxes and new textual leads and relations—curious footnotes, as it were, somehow bound up with corresponding mysteries of real events themselves. The mystery literally recapitulates itself through a set of parallel texts unfolding in the present. A strange trail of Tristero iconography—heraldic symbols such as hieroglyphic post-horns and acronymic slogans like W.A.S.T.E.—reveals itself blazoned on walls and underpasses. These are revealed through philatelic inquiry to be repeated in corresponding textual variations and watermarks discovered amid the Inverarity collection. Such variants turn out, in fact, to be so curious a collection of such interesting counterfeits that they are finally separated out from the rest and labeled "Lot 49." These are to be sold—or as the argot of the auction trade puts it "cried"—by themselves. In the last sentence of the novel, we continue, along with Oedipa, searching for the next clue in the conspiracy and wait for some new development to emerge. We Await Silent Tristero's Empire, as we suddenly see we have been doing from the title page on, in something—a fiction, a story, a text perhaps—called *The Crying of Lot 49.*

As suggested by this brief summary, for all the pop culture horseplay, the book also offers plenty of serious, cosmic-conspiracy Pynchon as well. At the beginning of all this, Oedipa Maas crawls into bed with the wrong techno-industrialist developer/one-man cartel. Has the whole business, she wonders, been something contained in a single word, *"Bought?"* (170). The personage, Pierce Inverarity, who has given us all this—Yoyodyne, Fungoso Lagoons, Lot 49, San Narciso—has become a national problem. Oedipa "had dedicated herself, weeks ago," she realizes, to making sense of what Inverarity had left behind, never suspecting that "the legacy was America" (178). It now seems to have been something at least that old. The Tristero, for instance, seems to have arrived in the New World just at the time when the European revolutions of the 1840s coincided with the reforms of the U.S. Postal Service, the development of the Pony Express, and the opening of the West. But there are other connections that also predate the nation itself. One crucial text of the sinister Wharfinger play, for instance, *The Courier's Tragedy,* turns out to have been a pornographic parody circulated by an utterly joyless, Manichean, and literalistic sect of Puritans called "Scurvhamites," fanatics of The Word attempting by textual sabotage to ensure the death of the Theater. And this somehow has been connected with a conspiracy back in the Middle Ages to break the postal monopoly of the houses of Thurn and Taxis. Meanwhile, this all appears to be connected with independent discoveries in physics brought to light by Oedipa's Yoyodyne inquiries. Specifically, one John Nefastis, a disgruntled employee fired over some patent or copyright dispute, seems to be working on a principle of entropy discovered by an earlier eccentric named Clerk Maxwell that is at once a principle of energy and a principle of information. It is all now enclosed in the principle of Maxwell's Demon, an invention that somehow connects the world of thermodynamics with information flow, things conceived of in the world and things conceived of as the word (106).

Given this combination of appeals to the youth-reader and the scholarly exegete, *The Crying of Lot 49* became the curricular Pynchon in every sense of the term. One need look only at nearly any reading list for a course on American fiction since 1945 to see how thoroughly it remains the Pynchon text for the syllabus—now increasingly assigned, one might suspect, by '60s people who, realizing it was the one Pynchon they themselves were able to get through at the time, pitch it to their students in the same hope. It also continues to generate commentary—notes, journal articles, chapters in books. Of all Pynchon's books, it is the one that the widest audience will know as '60s Pynchon. It is how we are helped by Pynchon to remember the '60s. It is how we are helped by the '60s and our retrospective constructions of the era to remember Pynchon. One suspects in fact that *The Crying of Lot 49* may have been Pynchon's great serious joke on the '60s in the fullness of the cosmic sophomorism that has always been at the heart of his work. As a recent text on the author by Dwight Eddins reminds us, "A hoax set up to resemble an elaborate conspiracy is," after all, "in itself an elaborate conspiracy" (93). *The Crying of Lot 49* is Pynchon's historical exegesis on the conspiracy theory of the '60s. It is (with *Vineland* now to offer us perspective) Pynchon's prophecy of '60s nostalgia. It is Pynchon's great '60s trip.

Reich, Charles. At the turn of the decade, Charles Reich, author of *The Greening of America* and inventor of Consciousness III—or, in his own deft formulation, "consciousness consciousness"—became the last of the great popular '60s youth-oracles. As campus guru and bestselling hip explainer, he readily conjured up the figure of *Doonesbury*'s Professor Charlie Green, linen-shirted and love-beaded, floating along in his own aura of good vibes. "The most beautiful course around," Megaphone Mark Slackmeyer calls the Professor's "Consciousness 10-A," albeit "a little unstructured." "My friends, there is little in the consciousness II mentality which I find alluring," the eminence himself intones from the lectern. "It is based on a false love of achievement, of wanting to appear successful in one's neighbor's eyes! Success, glory, gratifications, and hero-worship are the barbaric remains of an archaic society!!" The accolades filter up from the rapt audience. "Heavy! Wow! Clap! Clap! Yea! Clap! Clap!" "Oh Wow!" (*Doonesbury Chronicles*, n.p.).

Such with-it posings and profundities on the part of a magisterial figure culminated a '60s procession. Timothy Leary had early in the decade cornered the role of philosopher-apostle to the young, sharing it eventually with other figures as various as Dr. Benjamin Spock, the Reverend William Sloane Coffin, and Kurt Vonnegut. The line of transmission was also traced backward. With great ardor, historians of the movement identified the first hippie as Socrates, with Jesus Christ and Saint Francis as clear inheritors.

Reich certainly cast himself avidly as counselor and youth-apologist in something like a quasi-religious order of succession. Here is his gloss, for instance, on that great '60s word, "together": "The peasants of a medieval manor, or the anonymous craftsmen who worked on a great cathedral, must have had a feeling akin to 'together'" (387). Here he is on communal drug experience followed by communal eating and drinking—a ritual practice more commonly recorded in most people's memories, no doubt, as getting stoned and having the munchies: "It is no accident that marijuana joints are always passed around from hand to hand and mouth to mouth, and never smoked separately when people are in the same room; or that a single pizza or a single Coke is passed from person to person in the same room; the group is sharing its bread and wine" (387).

At the same time we have fun with Trudeau's Reich-like Professor Charlie Green, we should also insist on the essential accuracy of Professor Charles Reich's structural insights into the relation of '60s youth-culture to earlier forms of American consciousness. Like more prestigious thinkers such as Paul Goodman, Norman O. Brown, Herbert Marcuse, and R. D. Laing, Reich pinpoints from the outset the crucial role played by counter-culture thought in effecting something very like a postmodern critique of institutional reason. "The rationality" of the youth-revolution, he begins, "must be measured against the insanity of existing 'reason'—reason that makes impoverishment, dehumanization, and even war appear to be logical and necessary" (4). Moreover, in the contexts of twentieth-century American social thought and behavior, by positing the replacement of a condition of political innocence called Consciousness I with an "organizational" mentality called Consciousness II, Reich, like Goodman, Brown, Marcuse and such cohorts as C. Wright Mills or William Whyte, also identifies the specific state of affairs against which the critique is directed: the institutionally lobotomizing effects of the "administrative" state as opposed to a properly "political" state that would allow for creative pluralism, dialectic, and generative conflict. The "administrative" state wants things "adjusted," "settled"; it figures out what is "best" and pursues it. "It is a therapeutic model of society, in which variety is compromised and smoothed over in an effort to make everything conform to the public interest" (98).

Just as importantly, Reich now also yokes the psychologically disabling effects of such "impoverishment by substitution" (187) together with the need to resist what he identifies as the two newest and most immediate perils facing young Americans in their larger attempts to live as citizens of the earth—first, the domestic destruction of the environment and, second, the geopolitical disaster being allowed to run its course in Vietnam. In the case of the natural universe, there now looms the prospect of a completely artificial life, an AstroTurf world, in which nothing is really real: "To a young person, the Corporate State beckons with a skeleton grin: 'Step right in, you'll love it—it's just like living' " (187). At the same time, however, it is in the latter neatly arranged trap that the dominant culture has also overstepped itself. "The Vietnam War," Reich claims, "is the Corporate State's one unsalable product." Accordingly, "the war did what almost nothing else could have: it forced a major breach in consciousness" (215).

The result is a new capacity for ideological critique tapping into other psychological potentialities just beginning to be reckoned. "The new consciousness is the product of two interacting forces: the promise of life that is made to young Americans by all of our affluence, technology, liberation, and ideals, and the threat to that promise posed by everything from neon ugliness and boring jobs to the Vietnam War and the shadow of nuclear holocaust" (218). Thus empowered, it now opens into what Reich calls a new "radical subjectivity," not an "egocentricity" in the traditional sense, "but honesty, wholeness, genuineness in all things. It starts from self because human life is found as individual units, not as corporations and institutions; its intent is to start from life" (226).

Here, at the crucial moment, we seem to have come to it: beyond mere rewritings of Freud or Marx, a homegrown redefinition of historical subjectivity; an original counterculture theology displacing the old Western Post-Enlightenment Bourgeois Centered Self. In this, however, we will be disappointed. Reich's title is, after all, *The Greening of America*. It is a market-friendly book, and Professor Charles Reich has a promotional interest in being Professor Charlie Green as well. The progress of a good idea is mainly downhill from here, with structural insight yielding to hip glossolalia. Illustrative argument strains after adoring analogies drawn between the Grateful Dead's *Live Dead* album and the complexities of classical music. Bob Dylan is proclaimed "a true prophet of the new consciousness."

Thus, at the last, Reich's text makes a late-'60s turn toward a newest metaphysics of the groovy. Meanwhile, a contemporary, Theodore Roszak, would be thinking through to many of the same conclusions—but through far less flashy forms of intellectual and documentary analysis—in *The Making of a Counter-Culture*. And a decade later, Morris Dickstein in *The Gates of Eden* would also carry ideological critique back into the arena of '60s pop culture in ways that avoided the fatuities into which Reich allowed himself to be propelled. Still, Reich's basic insights proved correct and consonant not only with those of Roszak and Dickstein but also with what many individual members of the generation actually would remember as a hope for the redefinition of systematic rationality itself. Further, as to the capacity for belief so devised, whether or not Professor Charles Reich finally did slip over into being Professor Charlie Green, the inventor of Consciousness III turned out to have captured acutely that feature of the times as well. The generation of the counterculture did believe in magic and practiced it to substantial effect and brought about a radical and incredibly rapid transformation of American society at large. It did appreciably help change our ways of thinking about reason, science, and knowledge; about gender, class, and race; about neocolonialist war; and about the ravaging of the global environment. And it did so through a belief in something very like the shamanism implied in the work of Consciousness III—by putting on, that is, a " 'new head' " (5).

Rubin, Jerry. Nearly a quarter century after he told us not to trust anyone over forty,[50] we now wonder how we could have trusted Jerry Rubin at any age. By enlisting in the service of the higher greed—as investment counselor, corporate marketer, and freelance entrepreneur—Jerry Rubin, the gonzo Paul Revere of the '60s, has become the ultimate '80s and '90s networker.[51]

Once upon a time, however, there was a book by Jerry Rubin entitled *Do It!* It was a true expression of anarchic genius—in its way, perhaps, the genuine '60s text as testament of cultural resistance and new cultural production. Beyond Marshall McLuhan even, it seemed the happy conflation of the medium and the message, or, more properly perhaps, the message *become* the medium. *Do It!,* the title, said what it meant and vice versa: you do it, do it yourself, and do it now. *Do It!,* the text, showed *how* to do it. *Do It!* was all at once the rallying cry, spiritual manifesto, and practical handbook of Yippie.

In concept, design, and content, *Do It!* attempted to extend the potentialities of the popular counterculture text into something like mass-media assault. In print, it became anything and everything: autobiography, alternative history, cultural essay, poem, play, comic book, group cheer, and graffito. This grab bag was combined with outrageous visual overload, cartoon art from R. Crumb and Gilbert Shelton, and news photos and family snapshots from the Revolution. On page 14, one encountered a totally naked young woman walking down the aisle of an auditorium filled with well-dressed people who looked like Republicans. She is carrying a slimy, slick, somehow grinning, just-skinned pig's head on a silver platter. The shock on the woman's face second from the left reminds you of your Aunt Mary. Spread across pages 53 and 54 is a group portrait: everybody naked again except for motorcycle helmets, a London bobby hat, cameras, canteens, tennis rackets, sneakers, a pot plant in a coffee can, and those funny little black-framed plastic glasses favored by nerds with slide rules on their belts and ballpoints in their pocket protectors. What one mainly sees, however, is pubic hair and breasts of all sizes and shapes, hairy chests and chests as bald as a baby's butt, and—my god—dicks.

This, then, was the total '60s text, revolution made easy in every sense of the term. It was the counterculture's multimedia epic, defining itself by immediately severing all possible connections. "The New Left sprang, a predestined pissed-off child," the author announces peremptorily, "from Elvis' gyrating pelvis" (17). The car was the vehicle. The threat of being deprived of its use on Saturday night was the opening skirmish in the power-property war. "It was a cruel weapon, attacking our gonads and our means of getting together" (19). "Holden Caulfield," he goes on to proclaim for the sake of reading types, "is a yippie" (86). "The Old Nixon," he adds for political clarification, "was a yippie; the New Nixon is not" (86). Eventually, we will also find that "Sirhan Sirhan is a Yippie" (161) just after we have been told that "George Wallace is Bobby Kennedy in disguise" (144). And slightly before that we will have just been told, in enormous cartoon letters with a cartoon exclamation point for emphasis that "God is a Yippie" (112).

That being the case, one understands that one can actually say, if one wishes, "Fuck God" (109) just as one can say "Fuck War" (110), or, for that matter, just "fuck"—as many times as one wants. Thus, we discover, down a long single-spaced half-page, one fuck after another after another.

As composite sermon and sell, the text rewrites the revolution as pure advertising. "*Straights of the world, drop out!*" exclaims the new Karl Marx. "*You have nothing to lose but your starched shirts!*" So another page pronounces, with maximum verbal *and* visual effect. "The revolution will come when everybody is a"—in psychedelic poster-cartoon letters—"Yippie!" (86).

In the deeper political dimension of the text as media experiment, there is frequently astute media analysis. "Walter Cronkite is SDS's best organizer," the narrator proclaims. "Uncle Walter brings out the map of the U.S. with circles around the campuses that blew up today. The battle reports" (106).

Every kid is out there thinking, "Wow! I wanna see *my* campus on that map!"

Television proves the domino theory: one campus falls and they all fall.

TV is raising generations of kids who want to grow up and become demonstrators.

Have you ever seen a boring demonstration on TV? Just being on TV makes it exciting. Even picket lines look breathtaking. Television creates myths bigger than reality.

Demonstrations last hours, and most of that time nothing happens. After the demonstration we rush home for the six o'clock news. The drama review. TV packs all the action into two minutes—a commercial for the revolution. (106)

Equally bold, and much in the vein of what heavy intellectuals elsewhere were writing dense, involuted, philosophical reams about, is a critique of the politics of youth-education, which makes such disturbances on the part of the young inevitable and necessary:

Babies are zen masters, curious about everything.
Adults are serious and bored.
What happened?
Brain surgery by the schools. (212)

"Dig the environment of a university!" the author writes. "The buildings look like factories, airports, army barracks, IBM cards in the air, hospitals, jails. They are designed to wipe out all individuality, dull one's senses, make you feel small" (212).

The scene depicted by Rubin is something like educator Ivan Illych's worst fears of intellectual discipline transported into an actual regime of Foucaultian punishment. Further, in the spirit of Foucault, R. D. Laing, Robert Pirsig, and others, Rubin identifies the totalitarian presence in the scene that makes it possible: the benign imperviousness to critique of the underlying idea of the "critical" that empowers it.

" 'Critical' or 'abstract thinking,' " he pronounces, "is a trap in school."

Criticize, criticize, criticize.
Look at both sides of the argument, take no action, take no stands, commit yourself to nothing, because you're always looking for more arguments, more information, always examining, criticizing.
Abstract thinking turns the mind into a prison.
Abstract thinking is the way professors avoid facing their own social impotence.

Our generation is in rebellion against abstract intellectualism and critical thinking. (213)

And this new spirit of the critique of institutional reason, of course, is also the spirit of the Revolution. "We admire the Viet Kong guerrilla," he says, in conclusion and credo, "the Black Panther, the stoned hippie, not the abstract intellectual vegetable" (213).

One may recognize in such epiphanic hot-wirings the often caricatured textual strategies of many of the youth-scriptures of the era. Still, with a kind of dazzling facility, such Romancing of the Revolution here does become a way of serious political truth-telling. The opening blurb may trumpet the author as "the P. T. Barnum of the Revolution." But it also details an enviable combat record and list of notable prosecutions. The table of contents may read like an assemblage of counterculture shibboleths. As the text unfolds, however, one also discovers it providing a series of frequently acute aphoristic openings. "Child of Amerika" constructs a boyhood. "Elvis Presley Killed Ike Eisenhower" defines an adolescence. Young adulthood is caught in a simple imperative: "It's Gotta Be More Fun to Be In the Revolution Than Out of It." In exuberant, shouting cacophony, topics of awareness jostle and crowd themselves onto the agenda: "We Are All Human Be-ins"; "Ho Chi Minh is a Yippie Agent"; "Every Revolutionary Needs a Color TV"; "Ideology is a Brain Disease"; "Money is Shit—Burning Money, Looting and Shoplifting Can Get You High"; "Revolution is Theater-in-the-Streets" (132). Interspersed are important Revolutionary Commandments: "Don't Trust Anyone Over 40"; "Fuck God"; "Burn Down the Schools." Meanwhile, an ongoing documentary-line records holy events of movement history—starring, as often as possible, of course, the faithful author: "FSM: Shut the Motherfucker Down!"; "HUAC Creates Subpoenas Envy and Meets Thomas Jefferson"; "The Battle of Czechago"; "The Nomination and Election of Pigasus, the Pig, as President of the United States"; "My 'Bodyguard' Turns Out to Be a Czechago Pig"; "How American Airlines, Richard Nixon, Spiro Agnew, Strom Thurmond, John Mitchell, Walter Cronkite, CBS, NBC, ABC, Uncle Ho and a Million Spirits Conspired to Burn Czechago Down."

The photo opportunities multiply as well, writing their own version of the text and the times. The text has early on given us a clean-cut, well-soaped, necktied, most-likely-to-succeed-looking Jerry Rubin beaming at us in the requisite high school senior picture. Later we get an inauguration day photo of George Wallace Sr. and George Wallace Jr., in top hat and cutaway, with the latter looking like some malevolent freak-miniature of the former. Eldridge Cleaver eats watermelon. With glaucous eye and lacerated neck, Christ-faced Che Guevara looks out from the page in the famous death portrait.

As the book concludes, the chapters become increasingly hortatory. "We Cannot Be Co-opted Because We Want Everything," reads one. "We Are All Eldridge Cleaver," reads the next. "The Viet Cong Are Everywhere," reads the last. What has begun as the Education of the Child of Amerika spins itself off into endlessly multiple demands and agendas.

That, of course, would turn out to be just the problem with the Revolution itself. Along with its myriad co-options came its equally myriad splinterings into endless constituencies and voices, everyone wanting something, or everything, all at once. Accordingly, the text of Revolution so devised here would seal its own prophetic fate by being reduced to the status of '60s curio. Meanwhile, Jerry Rubin, '60s author, would ironically become Jerry Rubin, '80s and '90s personality, by turning into the biggest '60s curio of them all: the boy in the senior class picture, obviously the class clown but also the one most likely to succeed.

Salinger, J. D. Sixties reading and writing for American youth may be said to have entered the decade acknowledging the established reputation of at least one certified literary eminence. That eminence was the J. D. Salinger of *Nine Stories,* and, most especially, of *The Catcher in the Rye.* "A disturbed adolescent" is what the '50s chose to call Holden Caulfield, linking him perhaps to the good-school, white-collar, cocktail dissatisfactions of the harrowed suburbanites of Cheever and Updike or the gabby existential environs of Bellow but emphasizing a note of passing aberration, a "phase." Late '50s and early '60s readers would call him, as they increasingly called themselves, alienated youth and find in his book a trenchant identification of the spiritual impoverishment that for growing numbers of them seemed the direct correlative of the material plenitude of their lives. In Holden's response to his quintessentially midcentury American predicament, moreover, they also found him increasingly the paradigm, soon to be joined by a host of cohorts, literary and actual, of the young person of sensitivity, intelligence, and good will who opts to go crazy *in* America as the only self-respecting way *out.*

As to voice, surely Holden's most important contribution to the '60s was his yearning inarticulateness. For all his bravado, irreverence, and slangy profanity, he is not so much a voice of the young as the voice of a young person searching for some empowerment *of* voice. Not only does this privileged character—as '60s parents were wont to call such young-adult off-spring—agonizingly not know what he wants most of the time; even more desperately and heart-wrenchingly, he reveals in his greatest moments of loneliness that even if he did know he would possess no adequate discourse to communicate it, even to himself. "I don't know exactly what I mean by that," he tells us in one of his most signal utterances, "but I mean it" (75).

Indeed, from the first sentence on, a good subtitle for the performance rendered would be something like "Holden qualifies himself." "If you really want to hear about it," he begins, noting the assumption that we will no doubt expect to hear the Holden Caulfield story via the conventions of the customary "David Copperfield kind of crap," he protests his lack of interest (itself an untruth, of course) in such formulas, adding at the end "if you want to know the truth" (3). "That stuff"; "anything like that"; "and all"; "or something"; "or anything"—such vague formulas of quali-fication (these alone gathered from the first few sentences of the opening paragraph) continue to litter his syntax throughout. He is a master of prissy euphemism, especially on matters of the body. "Crap," "stuff," and "junk" is what we have in place of "shit." Holden imagines Stradlater giving Jane Gallagher "the time" in the back seat of Ed Banky's car. He questions Ackley's account of a girl he "almost had sexual intercourse with." When the word *fuck* actually appears in the book, scrawled on a schoolhouse wall, Holden is utterly paralyzed by it, rendered impotent even unto death. Some creep will always be able to write it somewhere, he realizes, where your little sister can see it. Holden himself will be prevented from trying to wipe it off for fear of getting caught in the act and being accused of putting it there in the first place. When they write his epitaph, someone will probably scrawl it on his tombstone too.

To adopt Holden's own idiom, he tells lousy lies; his histrionic, assumed names are phony; the lines he uses on women are corny as hell. He horses around with any version of reality that comes his way until it meets a Holden-style standard of goofy authenticity. He even gets the title of his own book wrong. The song goes, "if a body meet a body, comin' thro' the rye." He must rewrite it to serve an alternative fantasy of himself, standing by a dangerous cliff as children cross a field, preventing them from falling off, so becoming the catcher in the rye.

Yet the issue remains holy sincerity rather than evasiveness or escapism. Holden's predicament is not some latter-day Prufrockian conceit. Holden frequently may not say what he means, but it's not because he is not *try-ing* to mean what he says. As his language persistently searches for that something else, it maps out his sincere spiritual search as a young American in the middle of the twentieth century for that something else that might still actually *be* something else. It is not that he lacks courage, he says of his failure to confront another student he knows has stolen his gloves. "Maybe I'm not *all* yellow," he says, again falling back on the formulas. But then, he continues: "I don't know, I think maybe I'm just partly yellow and partly the type that doesn't give much of a damn if they lose their gloves" (82).

Somewhere between principle and property, things get tangled up. So it would be for many other Holdens in America at the beginning of the last half of the twentieth century. Their search for an appropriate discourse of connection increasingly became in gesture and language alike a "style" that often lamented its inability to achieve spiritual mediation across a host of divides, beginning in generations but quickly spreading into the total politics of national life. Nonetheless, the appeal of such a style of inarticulate epiphany would continue to reproduce itself in the late '50s and early '60s in an increasingly pervasive youth-style in literature *and* in life. In a 1957 Beat sensation somewhat in the Salinger manner, Sal Paradise and his would-be partner Rita Bettencourt would, as we have seen, lie back after a bungled holy consecration in a Denver apartment and wonder "what God had wrought when he made life so sad" (57). So, too, in dormitories and crash pads across the country, sentences would begin and end, "I mean, like, man, you know. . . ." Meanwhile, new literary voyagers would struggle onward in search of goofy beatitude. Like Holden or Sal, Joseph Heller's Yossarian and Kurt Vonnegut's Billy Pilgrim would opt to be lovers rather than fighters. Charles Webb's Benjamin Braddock and Sylvia Plath's Esther Greenwood would set the adult world on edge through a studied, perverse, moody avoidance of the practical or gainful.

Where Holden hears phony, '60s young people would hear "plastic." Where Holden describes his parents and other elders as "touchy," '60s young people would say "uptight." And the latter would delight in their versions of Holden's fondness for the outlandish, faintly irritating fashion statement: a deerstalker cap worn backwards or pride of possession in an obscure blues record—somehow made even more precious when it gets broken. They would also understand a sexual style that attempts to reinstate—with Jane Gallagher, with a classmate's mother, with the teenage prostitute Sunny, with Sally Hayes, with his kid sister Phoebe— a love that must have been possible in an unfallen world: exactly the style that Leslie Fiedler, in an essay on '60s young people entitled "The New Mutants," would see as the reification of Norman O. Brown's "polymorphous perverse" and which Fiedler himself would call a kind of "subcoital bundling" (258).

Above all, when Holden talks about the place in California where he has had to come because of some "madman stuff that happened to me around last Christmas just before I got pretty run-down and had to come out here and take it easy" (3), everyone would know, as they say, "where he was coming from," and why he had to go there—or more likely had to be "admitted" there, perhaps "suffering from exhaustion"—or why he casually mentions "almost-TB" among his inventory of possible ills so as to stir up confusion over the current euphemism: sanitarium versus sanitorium. And they would also rejoice over and over again at his good fortune, under literary license, at finally getting to say "fuck" out loud in an adult book and then turn it around to make a kind of holy moral. In these ways, and in all the others, Holden would truly prove The Prophet, or something, sort of.

But the '60s that still embraced Holden Caulfield would lose J. D. Salinger as the latter made his own adult retreat into new works such as *Franny and Zooey, Raise High the Roof-Beam, Carpenters; and Seymour: An Introduction.* Students would vanish to country nooks in New Hampshire or Vermont to make craft objects, watch the food grow, and find themselves; Salinger would go there to cultivate literary mannerism and, eventually, just silence. If there was a true '60s J. D. Salinger cult-text, it would probably have been his unlisted phone number. Failing that, there would still always be, of course, his first great novel.[52]

Skinner, B. F. In a leaden joke of entitling, B. F. Skinner's *Walden Two,* first published in 1948, may be said to have drifted in and out of the '60s curriculum mainly as a piece of false advertising. True, as a political fantasy, it does posit some idea of a vague, monastic, natural utopianism, a totally "organic" society in which humans are totally reconciled with the world of external nature, where they are no longer the tools of their tools and where in fact technology itself has now been made a natural servant rather than an unnatural master. The Thoreau original, moreover, also makes an actual cameo appearance near the end through the narrator's somewhat gratuitous coming upon a vagrant paperback from which he, reflecting on the experience of Walden Two he has just shared, quotes its inspirational last lines: "There is more day to dawn. The sun is but a morning star."

That, however, would seem to be just about where all other connections

begin *and* end. Thoreau's *Walden* (or, presumably, by Skinner's logic of entitling, *Walden One*) is after all about building one's own world through a
radical—and, most often in social terms, distinctly nonconformist—individuality. As far as attitudes toward individuality as a function of social
organization are concerned *Walden Two* would seem to be virtually the
obverse.

There is, to be sure, no official law at Walden Two but rather a kind of
organic Walden Code, a set of rules of conduct, some of them "rather fundamental," an official explains, "like the Ten Commandments," some even
perhaps "trivial" but with the code itself "changed from time to time as experience suggests" (162). Likewise, the emotional foundation of individual
attitude and behavior involves a common sense economy of benevolent appreciation for the basic gifts of life. "We overflow with gratitude," says the
same explainer, "—but to no one in particular. We are grateful to all and
to none. We feel a sort of generalized gratitude toward the whole community—very much as one give thanks to God for blessings which are
more immediately due to a next-door neighbor or even the sweat of one's
brow" (170).

But the general work of such an economy of benevolence suggests a
distinctly inside-out Thoreauvianism. Here one does not lose one's self to
a traditional social world so as to gain a better self in harmony with the
natural world. Here one loses one's self so as to gain a better self in harmony with a better *social* world that might also preserve one against the
perils of the natural world, thus navigating between the Scylla of artificial, restrictive government and the Charybdis of natural anarchy. In this
way, one avoids, says a spokesman (Frazier, who often acts as the place's
philosopher-king), that feature of life that comes closest to something like
"our original sin": "Each of us has interests which conflict with the interests of everybody else," he says. "Now, everybody else, we call 'society.' It
is a powerful opponent and it always wins. Oh, here and there an individual prevails for a while and gets what he wants. Sometimes he storms
the culture of a society and changes it slightly to his own advantage. But
society wins in the long run, for it has the advantage of numbers and of
age" (104).

Hence, there can only temporarily be something even resembling com-
promise: there can never be such a thing as organic unity. The only answer
possible is a new alternative synthesis of needs and power devised through
"adequate behavioral engineering" (162). And what makes a behavioral
engineering "adequate" is a new behavioral and cultural technology that
does not make the old mistake of fighting original sin with original sin—

using punishment, or negative behavior, so to speak, as a means of re-
ducing the likelihood of negative behavior. Adequate behavioral engineering instead ensures the inevitability of positive behavior "based on positive
reinforcement alone" (260).

So that, the narrator speculates, was why it was called *Walden Two*.
"The possibility of working out a satisfying life of one's own," he says,

> making the least possible contact with the government, was the bright-
> est spot in Frazier's argument. I thought of the millions of young people
> who were at that moment choosing places in a social and economic
> structure in which they had no faith. What a discrepancy between ideal
> and actuality—between their good will toward men and the competi-
> tive struggle in which they must somehow find a place! Why should
> they not work out a world of their own? (308)

He goes on:

> That was the Thoreauvian side of Frazier, and I liked it. Why fight
> the government? Why try to change it? Why not let it alone? Unlike
> Thoreau, Frazier would pay his taxes and compromise wherever neces-
> sary. But he had found a way to build a world to his taste without trying
> to change the world of others, and I was sure he could carry on in peace
> unless the government took some monstrously despotic turn. (308)

Far more sinister images of behavioral engineering would shortly become the '60s norm in the works of figures as diverse as Vonnegut and
Marcuse, Laing and Ginsberg. In virtually every case, the *Walden Two* so
portrayed would not be an invention, but rather the actual world of post–
World War II American life as already a kind of institutional duplicate of
such a fatal utopia. Indeed, in light of an enlarging body of critique about a
general culture of administration and adjustment—"the happy consciousness," Marcuse called it, as we have seen, "the belief that the real is rational
and that the system delivers the goods" (84)—Skinner's world seemed, if
anything, to wear a beguilingly fascist smile. He was, after all, the father
of behaviorism. Indeed, in one note of Thoreauvian protest, cited on the
jacket of the standard paperback, a *Life* reviewer called *Walden Two* "a
slur upon a name, a corruption of an impulse . . . such a triumph of mort-
main, or the dead hand, has not been envisaged since the days of Sparta."
Even a more measured response still caught the '60s chill: "Alluring in a
sinister way, and appalling too" (book jacket).

On the other hand, as the '60s slid onward from years of hope into
days of rage and the manifold confusions beyond, various New Age fas-

cinations reintroduced exactly such utopian ideas of adjustment. TM, est, the Human Potential Movement, Hare Krishna, the Unification Church, all shared a new emphasis on achieving states of beatific regimentation undreamed of by Skinner or any behaviorist. The Happy Consciousness, victorious over the forces of radical critique, performed its own beautiful adjustment. It assimilated the last '60s true believers into the newest totalitarian metaphysics of euphoria.

Spock, Benjamin. By the 1957 second edition of his 1946 *Common Sense Book of Baby and Child Care,* Dr. Benjamin Spock had become so identified with "permissive" theories of parenting and child rearing as to feel obliged, so to speak, to balance the books. In a new preface, he described a turn toward significant "flexibility" of "attitude." Indeed, he went on, "nowadays there seems to be more chance of a conscientious parent's getting into trouble with permissiveness than with strictness" (2). He also added, among introductory sections, a new discussion entitled "Strictness or Permissiveness?" addressing suggestions that the earlier text had promoted a developmental liberalism (45–49). There, he insisted pointedly—and with a noteworthy choice of authoritarian diction—"the real issue is what spirit the parent puts into managing the child and what attitude is engendered in the child as a result" (46).

By 1968 and a third edition, Spock had become a celebrated radical activist and a champion of the '60s youth movement, with an anti-Vietnam War book, numerous arrests, and a host of well-publicized courtroom appearances to his credit. Yet, in another new preface to his famous Baby Book, he seemed, if anything, to acquit himself even further of the myth of a "permissive" agenda for the generation supposedly of his own making who had now returned the favor by embracing him as an exemplary elder. In particular, he noted "the principal change that has occurred in my own outlook on child rearing." That he summarized as "the realization that what is making the parent's job most difficult is today's child-centered viewpoint." By this, he continued, "I mean the tendency of many conscientious parents to keep their eyes exclusively focused on their child, thinking about what he needs from them and from the community, instead of thinking about what the world, the neighborhood, the family will be needing from the child and then making sure that he will grow up to meet such obligations" (xvi).

Moreover, he found the point worth repeating in a new section, now following "Strictness or Permissiveness?," entitled "What Are Your Aims in Raising a Child?" There, he wrote, "in America very few children are raised to believe that their principal destiny is to serve their family, their country or God. Generally we've given them the feeling that they are free to set their own aims and occupations in life according to their inclinations" (11). Further, such child-centeredness, he went on, had also brought about a total reshaping of generational politics with immense consequences for American social ideology as a whole:

> The tendency is for American parents to consider the child at least as important as themselves—perhaps potentially more important. An English anthropologist said that whereas in other countries children are taught to look up to their parents as rather distinguished superior people, whatever their actual place in the society, the remarkable thing about America is that a father will say to his son, "Son, if you don't do better than I've done, I won't think much of you." This is an upside-down respect. This is why America has often been called child-centered. (11)

Spock had isolated the larger crisis of generational relationship and moral community in which his culture now found itself engaged; and, as to his own alleged historical participation, he had also identified the crisis for which his own book had now been assigned a major causative role. To be sure, one senses in the '60s Spock especially an activist politics reflecting the author's concern with issues of larger human obligation. On the other hand, this hardly sounds like the kiddie-coddler portrayed in the contemporary media. But by now it was too late. For the parents of the post-1945 Generation of Youth, Spock had been the Baby Book. Rightly or wrongly, it had come to be known as the book, more than any other, that wrote the '60s.

And in its homegrown pragmatic genius, its characteristically American blending of practicality *and* idealism, it of course was. On one hand, as may be seen by perusal of any edition, it was and continues to be a fairly innocuous, mainly technical book, with proportionally little interest in issues of social change beyond their acknowledgment as factors in the developmental process.[53] On the other, the unprecedented dissemination of such confident guidance in mass print suggested something of a new, utopian technology of human development firmly within every parent's grasp. The newest texts of post–World War II American possibility would be America's young.[54]

To put this another way, questions of "permissiveness" versus "non-permissiveness" notwithstanding, the "problem" with Spock and with the children of Spock truly did lie in the promise of the social technologies of parenting created within the body of his celebrated text. Yet it was also, one might propose, not so much a problem of Spock's writing as a problem of his audience's reading: a problem, indeed, on the part of the parental generation, of one of the greatest culturally orchestrated exercises in reader-response criticism in history. For, in a line of vision conditioned by Cotton Mather, Benjamin Franklin, Horatio Alger, Dale Carnegie, and others—in which self-help had often merged with instructions to youth— the '60s generation now found the culminating (not to mention the most widely sold, distributed, and read) how-to-do-it manual for human improvement in American history with the *promise* of improvement now translated literally to the issue of posterity. It took, in short, a national idea of happiness—or felicity, as it was often called by the founders of the Republic—and translated it into a home technology productive of off-spring worthy of living in what the nation itself now saw as unprecedented conditions of material and spiritual plenitude. It attempted to write the final installment, to borrow in letter and spirit from Gertrude Stein, in the making of Americans. Conflating the textual and the ideological, it attempted to complete the project of American self-fashioning for posterity by putting it *in* posterity.

So, by 1968, Spock himself had realized that in the generational politics of the project lay the problem. The so-called psychological narcissism of the child really mirrored the *political* narcissism of the parent. Indeed, as sympathetic social scientists began to note (see Miller and Nowak 250–51; compare Slater 57, 69), the crisis of relationship lay not at all in a problem of permissiveness but rather in, if anywhere, a curious parental totalitarianism vested in a "mission to create a near-perfect being" (Millar and Nowak 271; Slater 69). This was exactly the point of Spock's own 1968 epiphany: encouraged to be different, the youth of the '60s in turn perplexed and infuriated their parents for not being the same. The Spock children were the results of following the instructions, parental investments in the socio-textual enterprise. And to this degree, the parents got what they wanted. They narcissistically engineered their own bright and comely inheritors as the fulfillment of their grandest cultural desires. At the same time, they had confused a technology—devoted to the replication of sameness— with a creative human project, in which the key is *always* difference. In turn, it would be inevitable that the parents would hate the children who really tried to be different according to the instructions they received. The parental generation of '60s Americans had invested in a technology of improved administration, adjustment, uniformity, and control; the new and improved Americans resulting from the investment came to hate all that was increasingly administered, adjusted, uniform, and controlled. Locked into an inevitable conflict of goals and outcomes, they took out their frustration on each other and the world.

A moral of the fate of Spock's text might be drawn from a rough contemporary of Spock's, usually thought of as embodying the antithesis of post–World War II democratic American values. That would be Stalin—with his menacing definition of the writer as engineer of human souls. Here in Spock's text was a similar warning, even in the supposedly freest society in the world, to both the writer and the reader as liberal-technolog.

Thompson, Hunter S. Of all the New Journalists, none save Tom Wolfe and, perhaps later, Michael Herr, tapped more fully into the high-energy vibrations of '60s cultural upheaval than Hunter S. Thompson. In the first part of the decade, through his reporting for the *National Observer, The Nation,* and *Esquire,* he gained attention for articles on South American politics; logging championships; Hemingway's Ketchum, Idaho; topless dancing in San Francisco's North Beach; the Berkeley Free Speech Movement; Richard Nixon; Jean-Claude Killy; and the Kentucky Derby. In 1966, with the publication of *Hell's Angels,* an account of his sojourn with the titular gang of sociopathic outriders haunting the freeways and folkways of America, he enthroned himself as the gonzo chronicler of the whole crazed, lurid scene. With succeeding work in *Scanlan's Monthly* and *Rolling Stone,* as well as in increasingly manic and bizarre book-length texts such as *Fear and Loathing in Las Vegas* and *Fear and Loathing on the Campaign Trail,* he dragged the spirit of outlaw journalism of the '60s shrieking and clawing into the '70s; and with it he carried an audience who saw in his increasingly outrageous persona—the depraved, drunken, drug-addled, handgun-crazy, pilgrim-burnout (variously known as Raoul Duke, Dr. Hunter S. Thompson, Dr. Gonzo)—the excitement of their own adrenaline-amphetamine–rush '60s selves somehow still in full cry.

To invoke Thompson's persona or his writing is to wish to remember him as one of the meteors of the '60s, the instant dark star in the New Journalism sky. As it turns out, with rather few exceptions up until the end of the decade, it is fairly hard to distinguish his writing from much else in the contemporary argot. The style, for instance, of *Hell's Angels,* reads now like a ritual formula, a vintage echo that might as easily be vintage Wolfe, vintage Terry Southern, or vintage Joe Esterhas: an attempt, that is, at a kind of hopped-up, go-go, pile-it-on energy that was itself increasingly generic to the form. Here, for instance, is a portion of the opening paragraph:

California, Labor Day weekend . . . early, with ocean fog still in the streets, outlaw motorcyclists wearing chains, shades and greasy Levis roll out from damp garages, all-night diners and cast-off one-night pads in Frisco, Hollywood, Berdoo and East Oakland, heading for the Monterey peninsula, north of Big Sur . . . The Menace is loose again, the Hell's Angels, the hundred-carat headline, running fast and loud on the early morning freeway, low in the saddle, nobody smiles, jamming crazy through traffic and ninety miles an hour down the center stripe, missing by inches. (11)

Several hundred pages and one gratuitous stomping later—the latter at the hands of five of the author's subjects—the existential-journalistic adventure ends. Traveling back to San Francisco, Thompson tries, he tells us, "to compose a fitting epitaph" but is reduced to using someone else's words. "I wanted something original, but there was no escaping the echo of Mistah Kurtz' final words from the heart of darkness: 'The horror! The horror! . . . Exterminate all the brutes!'" (348).

Thompson's real achievement for '60s reading and writing, at least as seen in retrospect, was to preserve the energy of the '60s style in the increasingly numbed, lonely, and confusing years of the early to mid '70s. His was a voice of anarchic excess continuing to sound its solitary howl amidst a psychosocial wilderness of retreats, retrenchments, compromises, co-options, and acceptances. His increasingly outrageous prose became nothing but vintage Thompson, the vehicle of a crazed, nonstop torrent of pure outrage against American awfulness in all its forms.

In an important sense, the saga of the gonzo journalist seemed to preserve the '60s ride: the scenes themselves, often a function of mixed-media collaboration with the cartoonist Ralph Steadman, somehow so quintessentially at the burnt-out end of it all—beyond Guernica, beyond the Grateful Dead—became a last celebration of rebellious excess, elegy and requiem for the era in the form of a howl much like the one with which it began. And if that was a howl of outrage, it was also a howl of pure delirium. It was a chance to rail in Las Vegas—the author and his three-hundred-pound Samoan "attorney" sent to cover the motorcycle races (and instead winding up at a national meeting of district attorneys); blazing their way there in a rented red Chevrolet convertible with a trunk "like a mobile police narcotics lab"; the narrator swatting away at what he takes to be bats; and "a tape recorder turned all the way up on 'Sympathy for the Devil'" (4). It would be an occasion to worship at the shrine itself—

the city as instant cathedral and mausoleum of American garishness and hype—at "the brutish realities of this foul year of our Lord 1971" (23).

In an ensuing adventure, on the equally garish campaign trail during an American presidential election, we already know what we are in for as the harried journalist, faced with last-minute deadlines from unreasonable editors, greets us from a hotel room where he is surrounded by his writing supplies: "two cases of Mexican beer, four quarts of gin, a dozen grape-fruits, and enough speed to alter the outcome of six Super Bowls" (16). We find it all, however, more than justified as we follow along with him on the campaign trail toward a mutual dread recognition: unbelievably, with everything gone under the bridge for a hideous decade and more, American politics has been grinding along as usual and the electorate has once more found itself locked in a room with, of all people, Nixon, *again* Nixon. He *is* Nixon still, exactly as he was in 1968: a man with

> his very existence as a monument to all the rancid genes and broken chromosomes that corrupt the possibilities of the American Dream; he was a foul caricature of himself, a man with no soul, no inner con-victions, with the integrity of a hyena and the style of a poison toad. The Nixon I remembered was absolutely humorless; I couldn't imag-ine him laughing at anything except maybe a paraplegic who wanted to vote Democratic but couldn't quite reach the lever on the voting machine. (213)

But, as is his habit, he is now also something even beyond the old Nixon; he is also, appallingly, the latest new Nixon:

> Nixon himself who represented that dark, venal, and incurably violent side of the American character almost every other country in the world has learned to fear and despise. Our Barbie doll President, with his Barbie doll wife and his box-full of Barbie doll children who is also America's answer to the monstrous Mr. Hyde. He speaks for the Were-wolf in us; the bully, the predatory shyster who turns into something unspeakable, full of claws and bleeding string-warts when the moon comes too close. (416–17)

To the horror of a Nixon redivivus is matched that of the Demo-crats: Muskie, Wallace, and McCarthy, about to pass the banner of idiot-quixotism to McGovern; but especially Humphrey. Humphrey again: "with the possible exception of Nixon, . . . the purest and most disgusting example of a Political Animal in American politics today" (205); "a treacherous, gutless old ward-heeler who should be put in a goddamn bottle and sent out with the Japanese current" (135).

We read this through the '80s and now the '90s as it was written in the '70s. The '60s having been declared officially dead, we recapture it as the ghastly rerun of the old nightmare faces of the '50s that it actually was. We recover, in sum, *what it was like*. And Thompson was right. Something had truly come and gone with the '60s. One simply had to choose one's primal scene. Many would eventually concur in this. "When the Great Scorer comes to list the main downers of our time," he speculates, "the Nixon Inauguration will have to be ranked Number One. Altamont was a nightmare, Chicago was worse, Kent State was so bad that it's still hard to find the right words for it . . . but there was at least a brief flash of hope in those scenes, a momentary high, before the shroud came down" (87).

As for many of us, the years since have not been good for Hunter S. Thompson. If he managed to avoid the big sellout, a la Tom Hayden, Jane Fonda, Jerry Rubin, Rennie Davis, Bob Dylan, or Timothy Leary, he still caught the alternative fate of counterculture self-caricature. He is as memorable in his way now, perhaps, as a Ken Kesey or a Patty Hearst. Gonzo has seemed to become mostly loony and maybe just irrelevant.[55]

It is different, however, for the texts by Hunter S. Thompson that may well have been some of the last great '60s scriptures. Somewhere in them it will still always be hallucination-hour out on the desert at a national DA's convention or aboard the Muskie campaign special. "How would Horatio Alger handle this situation?" the narrator asks. The answer will always be there: *"One toke over the line, sweet Jesus . . . one toke over the line"* (70).

Thoreau, Henry. Although one of the senior authorities most freely invoked by '60s youth, the Henry Thoreau actually known to '60s youth-readers, was, one suspects, a standard curricular Thoreau. From a freshman or sophomore English reader, he was the multipurpose Thoreau of "Civil Disobedience"—or, as originally titled, "On the Necessity of Resistance to Civil Government": an item of contemporary "relevance" for class discussion, a distinguished prose model, an access to the long American "tradition" of principled individual nonconformity, and a connection to philosophies of nonviolent resistance practiced by Gandhi and Martin Luther King Jr. (not to mention—if more political pizzazz was required —Dr. Spock, an adult pacifist willing to go to jail over the draft, or Joan Baez, refusing to pay whatever portion of her taxes might be deemed to support the Vietnam War).

The latter was also Thoreau's specific subject in "Civil Disobedience": his own refusal to pay taxes to support something he deemed an illegitimate exercise of military power by his government outside its borders. This was the dubiously justified, overtly expansionist military conflict of the mid 1840s glorified under the name of the Mexican War. Yet the essay also opened the great domestic issue of individual freedom *to resist* that seemed equally at stake in the Vietnam era as well: the peculiar tyranny of democratic governments in repressing individuals, often in the name of "democracy," who call attention to such governments' betrayals of their own democratic ideals of conscience and right. Indeed, for '60s youth the issue could not have been more simply joined: "I heartily accept the motto,—" Thoreau begins

'That government is best which governs least;' and I should like to see it acted up to more rapidly and systematically. Carried out, it finally amounts to this, which I also believe,—'That government is best which governs not at all;' and when men are prepared for it, that will be the kind of government which they will have. Government is at best but an expedient; but most governments are usually, and all governments are sometimes, inexpedient. (22)

Such is the present case, he concludes: "The government itself, which is only the mode which the people have chosen to execute their will, is equally liable to be abused and perverted before the people can act through it. Witness the present Mexican war, the work of comparatively a few individuals using the standing government as their tool; for, in the outset, the people would have not consented to this measure" (22).

As people used to say in the '60s, "there it was": from the Geneva Accords (or nonaccords) through the Gulf of Tonkin incident (or nonincident) into the hideous bloody morass. The anti-Vietnam parallel could not have been more explicit; nor, eventually, the antidraft parallel; nor, finally, the anticomplicity parallels with the war-breeding system and institutional authority. Thoreau was the philosophical father of Gandhi and King, but he was also in lifestyle, as they used to call it, the original Mr. Natural.

Accordingly, at other points in the curriculum—in American literature surveys perhaps, or in special topics courses arranged on one or another contemporary social themes—the Thoreau of "Civil Disobedience" might also be broadened to connect with the author of *Walden*. Emphasis might have been placed on selections linking his example of radical individuality to critiques of American careerism, materialism, militarism, runaway technology, and despoilation of the natural environment; or a more systematic study might have been undertaken of his existential style of plain living and high thinking as an access to epiphany and purified transcendental consciousness.[56]

To be sure, a cult Thoreau also flourished. At the literal level (and in contravention of an explicit warning contained within *Walden* itself), new '60s agrarians retired to the country to experience nature and watch the food grow—although much less often in the vein of Thoreauvian solitude than in some new communitarianism.[57] In the philosophical and spiritual dimensions, further exploration often involved study of the *Journals* or paperback republications of lesser-known works such as *A Week on the Concord and Merrimack Rivers* and *Cape Cod.*

Best of all was Thoreau the oracle, a storehouse of quotable wisdom at once organic—precisely in the new sense favored by the counterculture and the popular media—and unfailingly heavy, deep, "far-out." On life, for example, within the system: "The mass of men lead lives of quiet desperation. What is called resignation is confirmed desperation" (10). On the price of living there: "the cost of a thing is the amount of what I call life which is required to be exchanged for it, immediately or in the long run" (25–26). On the possibility of cultivating instead a private economy of spiritual exchange: "Simplicity, simplicity, simplicity! I say, let your affairs be as two or three, and not a hundred or a thousand; instead of a million count half a dozen, and keep your accounts on your thumb-nail" (66). And of course the great one, on the virtue of militant, principled nonconformity: "If a man does not keep pace with his companions, perhaps it is because he hears a different drummer" (216).

Thoreau gained a holy relevance among '60s youth in ways that must have surely been the envy of even the most clever of contemporary imitators: he was quotable yet enigmatic—and as an added attraction, with his special fondness for the Hindu scriptures, often deeply "oriental" in his mastery of paradox and obscure-sounding epigram. On the other hand, he was the original no-bullshit American: pungent, dense, nutlike; profound but uncannily sensible on a host of matters ranging from personal meditative practice to collective political action.

In all these respects, Thoreau, among '60s wisdom-figures thought of as *being* old, never really *got* old. His was a voice that never lost its spiritual youth or its political decency.[58] He was a wise, eccentric, admired older brother who had been there and had never left.

Tolkien, J. R. R. The great mythic cycle of story and symbol contained in the body of J. R. R. Tolkien's major texts—*The Hobbit* and *The Lord of the Rings*[59]—also comprises one of the great textual histories of '60s reading and writing in America. Familiar items on student bookshelves everywhere and with a popularity documented by astonishing sales, they laid out the dark, ancient, magical architecture of a fantasy world called Middle Earth. And in the same moment, for vast numbers of American youth they also created, in their timeless exploration of what seemed eternally "relevant" human issues of moral and ideological conflict, something close to a whole alternative cosmology. As with analogous works by Hesse, Heinlein, Herbert, Vonnegut, and Castaneda, they fulfilled the insatiable appetite of '60s readers for a shelfful of happily competing theologies: separate worlds, alternative structures of reality as defined by whole new architectures of consciousness.

In such a curriculum, Tolkien's works made special claims as core texts. Combining fantasy, fairy tale, ancient legend, marvelous adventure, and escape into a vivid, teeming precinct of faraway time and place with the atmospherics of charm, portent, omen, and spell, they also kept an insistent moral focus on the Manichean struggle of the forces of light and darkness and the ultimate triumph of the Good, the True, and the Right. Accordingly, not unlike the mystagogies proffered by contemporary radical politics or by a host of competing meditational and spiritualistic systems, they were something to "get into" for the long run: a textual geography and an argot, a whole universe complete with strange, exotic vocabulary and refulgent with highly technical, obscure, recondite secrets and encodings available only to initiates and shared by such illuminati as proof of mystic solidarity. On the other hand, in spite of such obscurity and technicality, Tolkien's texts—particularly in their narrative informality and the relative simplicity of their moral problematics—proved immensely attractive and accessible for those who were utopian enough for fantasy or stoned enough for easy epiphanies requiring only rudimentary tying-in to the story line or the moral issue at hand.

For a youth-culture, a fantasy-culture, a drug-culture, or an alternative-reality culture of any sort, Tolkien's books were, in a phrase, relentlessly reader-friendly. One was as good as the next. The next was as good as the last. When the last was finished—no small enterprise itself given their length and the riches of attendant apparatus such as maps, glossaries, and source documents—it would be time in any event to start all over again.

A British interpreter summarized with peculiar acuteness the phenomenon of young Americans' embracing of the Tolkien gospel:

like the popular artifacts of psychedelia, it was the product of a strong visual imagination and encompassed the mundane and the mythic. It was readily assimilable through a clearly etched plot and, most importantly, dealt with an ethnic, primitive other-world: it was read by millions in eschewal of the artificiality of modern industrial society and in pursuit of atavism. (Walmsley in Giddings 75–76)

Its chief attractions for such readers included "its blandness of style, its reassuring adherence to narrative expectations nurtured in childhood, its lack of moral ambiguity, its placing of evil and violence in an otherworldly context rather than next door, its safety, its essentially benevolent, anodyne tone" (80). Thus, "it was not so much its drift from reality that made Tolkien's work so popular" but rather "its highly marketable combination of imaginative originality and psychological anaesthetic. As an experience it was neither radical nor disruptive and so provided a secure path for dissenting youth in search of a safe alternative to their own environment" (80).

In response, such youth—as noted above, quite literally by the millions—avidly learned all there was to know about Hobbits such as the elder Bilbo and his nephew Frodo Baggins: their diminutive stature; their hairy feet; their nutritional and smoking preferences; their especial fondness for party food and drink, celebrations, and happenings; their housing (or, more properly, burrowing) arrangements; their homely modes of gaiety; their differences from elves, dwarves, and men; and their tendency to be at once very old and very young, somewhat androgynous, basically innocent, good, and nonviolent yet when threatened fierce and brave, spontaneous but principled, loyal but slightly loopy—in sum, their comfortable reliability as an inventory of the traits and attitudes ascribed to the youth-culture.

As the cycle unfolds from the opening volume into the master-narrative, youth-readers learned the story of the Ring of Power: the visitation of the wizard Gandalf and his legend of The Ring with its dreadful burden of wisdom and might; the Ring's capture by the unlikely hero Bilbo from the wily, terrible Gollum; the risings, forays, and incursions, of the Enemy; the depredations of the Black Riders, minions of the evil Sauron, Lord of the dark land of Mordor; the quest to achieve the Return; the saga of mortal warfare whereby the Return is accomplished by brave Hobbits and a host of allies recruited from the ranks of elves, dwarves, and men; and how, in the face of cosmic evil, they hewed in their happier moments to the distinctly unwarlike Hobbit virtues—antimaterialism, conciliation— all as "attempts" as the lead text puts it, "to buy peace and quiet" (283).

However impossibly, here, then, it seemed that the little people of the world, precisely because of their very militancy as exemplars of the gentle, the homely, and the happy, might still become the vanguard of a quest for nothing less than the envisioning and creating of a new world: "Knowledge, Rule, Order," as the wise Saruman describes them to Gandalf—the great goals of the humble, the true, and the good, now in the hands of the evil Enemy—"all the things that we have so far striven in vain to accomplish, hindered rather than helped by our weak or idle friends. There need not be, there would not be, any real change in our designs, only in our means" (Fellowship 340). Thus spoke the oracular voice of a new fellowship of the humble and meek with the noble and exalted against the dominion of "Power" (Fellowship 340), a fellowship devoted at once to the reappropriation of Power and to the further end of renunciation of Power as an earthly instrumentality.

As if to affirm such reappropriations of power through language especially, by the mid-to-late '6os Tolkien-discourse was everywhere. Edition after edition came into mass-market circulation, and in the youth-culture at large pop exegesis became something of a freak cottage industry. As devotees of Frank Herbert's *Dune* books would nod knowingly about addictive melange or "spice" or those of Robert Heinlein's *Stranger in a Strange Land* about "Grokking," so Hobbit fanciers would delight in complex explanations—origins, customs, technologies, social benefits—of the queer albeit surely harmless cultural pleasure of their habitual smoking of something called "Pipe-Weed." In nearly every commune, as a consequence, at least one member assumed the name Frodo. Similarly, music fans left over from the decade understood why a contemporary, in forming a new '70s and '80s megagroup called the Police, would christen himself "Sting" (Fellowship 363).

Given Tolkien's acknowledged status, on the other hand, as a senior British academic—in fact an Oxford don and eminent scholar in Old and Middle English—the works also continued to carry the cachet of a certain kind of intellectual "seriousness." Tolkien may have been a genial literary hobbyist, but he was also deemed an ingenious and erudite one. His was at once a private and a cultural system, profound, mystical, and endlessly complex and entrancing in its elaborations. Moreover, as was retold in accounts of how the series came to be—the story of the stories, so to speak—it seemed important to know that the work had been done for its own quite serious political reasons as a response to the earlier totalitarian world-convulsions of the century.[60]

Each volume scrupulously constructed itself as a complete textual apparatus, at once authorizing itself and establishing its bibliographic connections to the others. Texts styled themselves in complicatedly self-referential patterns: "Foreword," began some; "Prologue," others. Sequential volumes of the trilogy proceeded from Synopsis to Text. And included in all were extremely detailed maps. At the conclusion appeared a bewildering collocation of technical appendices on source history, numerical chronology, genealogy, and etymology (including, in fact, a complete grammar of "Westron" or "Common Speech" that formed the basis of the texts). There was also A Guide to Poems and Songs. A Glossary-Index divided itself into headings of "Persons, Beasts, and Monsters"; "Places"; and "Things" with a brief "Supplement" devoted, presumably in the interests of unfailing completeness, to "Persons, Places and Things appearing only in Songs or Poems."

Here, then, was not only the mythic legacy of a genial, learned elder smiling down on a new generation of radiant inheritors but the complete packaging of a whole textual evolution. From their relentlessly restyled cover art (Peter Max Day Glo fantasy supplanted by Howard Pyle/ N. C. Wyeth antiquarian hyperrealism) through their exotic typefaces and cartographies, and finally through their endless compoundings of narrative complication—the books carried readers by the millions deeper and deeper into Tolkien-land and toward the ultimate triumph of the humble, the nonviolent, the idealistic, the innocent, and the good. And on the way, '60s reading and writing also made a serious generic adventure. Utopian political fantasy projected itself forward through a simultaneous projection backward into an alternative fantasy of history. To put this another way, Tolkien undertook a visionary postmodernism through an atavistic premodernism with the resulting effect of a simultaneous deconstruction and reconstitution of the present. The style of Middle Earth became the style of the current Middle Ages of man on earth. Accordingly, such a new vision of the truly "medieval" became an index of the discovery often made intuitively by '60s youth and soon to be elaborated upon by '60s, '70s, and '80s philosophers and archaeologists of culture: the idea of the modern itself and of our whole belief in the unholy trinity of reason, science, and nature had itself been a kind of fantastic hallucination. Like Hobbits and others, we do our best simply to live here in the late Middle Ages.

In ways both prophetic in their wisdom and bewildering in their obscure, quaint mystifications, Tolkien's books on the Hobbits and the great War of the Rings wrote for many people the whole '60s scene. He wrote a world, so to speak, that could always provide a certain kind of present peace in the contemplation of its own eccentric genealogy. People, it seemed, no less than "Hobbits . . . delighted in such things, if they were accurate: they liked to have books filled with things that they already knew, set out fair and square with no contradictions" (Fellowship 28).

Vonnegut, Kurt. The career of Kurt Vonnegut, as much as that of any contemporary, comprises the essential story of '60s writing in America. The title, in fact, of any appropriate account might read, "Paperback Writer: Kurt Vonnegut and the Generation of Youth." Vintage Vonnegut, arising out of magazine publication, took shape in works such as *Player Piano* (1952 hardbound; 1954 paperback as *Utopia 14*), *The Sirens of Titan* (1959 paperback original), *Mother Night* (1962 paperback original), and *Cat's Cradle* (1963 hardbound original). Especially as the result of the latter, by the mid '60s, a turned-on youth-audience, discoursing religiously on Hobbits or Beatles lyrics, included in their cherished lore *karasses,* Ice-Nine, and the finer points of Bokononism. *God Bless You, Mr. Rosewater* (1965) achieved both cult and literary status as an antic, coruscating indictment of the American Dream. The same reception awaited a collection of short stories, *Welcome to the Monkey-House* (1968).

Then came the acknowledged '60s classic, *Slaughterhouse Five* (1969). The voyagings of the hero, Billy Pilgrim, were projected forward into the utopian world of love and peace on the planet Tralfamadore exactly as they traced his World War II odyssey backward through the Battle of the Bulge, capture by the Germans, and culminating moment in the firebombing of Dresden. Meanwhile, the reader kept present company with the hero while looking out across the benumbed quotidianness of '60s American life, with middle-class discontents mounting into impotent guilt over the new historical horrors being perpetrated in Vietnam.

Then began the long march of the '70s and '80s. It was initiated with *Breakfast of Champions* (1973), in which an author named Vonnegut seemed to sign off a bitter valedictory on behalf of both his throwaway characters and their throwaway culture. There followed a series of more or less throwaway fictions: *Slapstick; or, Lonesome no More* (1976); *Jailbird* (1979); and *Deadeye Dick* (1982). In between came a play and heavily promoted Kurt Vonnegut paperback editions of the collected works of Mark Twain. Autobiographical "collages" included *Wampeters, Foma, and Granfalloons* (1974) and *Palm Sunday* (1981). Like Twain, Vonnegut became that which his work most surely told him to despise: a "personality." In a new paperback avalanche, this time in a Dell "standard" edition, Vonnegut had once again become a writer too popular to be serious.[61]

Vonnegut has been called nearly everything—a science fictionist, a humorist, a black-comedian, a cosmic ironist, a minimal realist, a magical realist, a brand-name realist, a K-Mart realist. To that litany one should surely add, as far as much post–World War II thought and writing in the West is concerned: philosophical and literary prophet. A wrecked Cadillac in *Slaughterhouse Five*—that of Billy Pilgrim's wife, actually, after it has been backended by a Mercedes—is described as "a body-and-fender man's wet dream" (182). One could now say much the same thing about Vonnegut's writing, I would propose, for the postmodernist. It is not too far-fetched a figure to suggest that in Vonnegut's most important works the text seems to arise out of some attempt to impersonate simultaneously Karl Barth, John Barth, and Roland Barthes. Works especially such as *Cat's Cradle; God Bless You, Mr. Rosewater; Slaughterhouse Five; Breakfast of Champions;* and the recent *Hocus Pocus* all seem written across some strange particle wave continuum linking the hoked-up and the holy, a hypertext always just on the verge of semiotic overload, with vast circuitries of relation hot-wiring themselves off toward some manic indeterminacy.

As for the Vonnegut of '60s reading and writing in America, in all these respects the centerpiece text must surely be *Slaughterhouse Five*. Here is the most topical of all Vonnegut's novels, the one in which he makes his most profound cultural statement about the relationship of personal and national History; and here also is his ultimate wisdom-text, his great science fiction. It is itself, as a Tralfamadorian voice intimates to the protagonist Billy Pilgrim during his sojourn on that distant planet, very much a Tralfamadorian novel. Although it is a "message," that is, linear in print, with a syntax and other familiar textual characteristics, it is not one as we conventionally know it: "There are no telegrams on Tralfamadore," the voice says,

> But you're right: each clump of symbols is a brief, urgent message—describing a situation, a scene. We Tralfamadorians read them all at once, not one after the other. There isn't any particular relationship between all the messages, except that the author has chosen them carefully, so that, when seen all at once, they produce an image of life that is beautiful and surprising and deep. There is no beginning, no middle, no end, no suspense, no moral, no causes, no effects. What we love in our books are the depths of many marvelous movements seen all at one time. (88)

For Americans especially, as might be reckoned, such Tralfamadorian versatility turns out to be of special consequence: it allows one to go forward in time, as all good science fiction must; and it also allows one to go backward in time, as all good American fiction should but generally does not. Indeed, its subject is not simply time, but also History, and the crazy Children's Crusade, as the subtitle names it, that now seems to play itself out over and over again as America's special mission in history. And Billy Pilgrim is in this sense fully present for History. He is like a once-young narrator, presumably named "Vonnegut," and his then-youthful comrade, Bernard V. O'Hare, going off to World War II; and with a son in "the famous Green Berets," he is also like a now-older narrator, also named Vonnegut, watching a lot of young people either going off or trying to avoid going off to Vietnam. He is present, that is, on both the last and the latest American versions of "the Children's Crusade." And as is the case with children's crusades in the name of truth, meaning, and goodness, each one turns out to be a kind of crazed parodic image of every other: noble, ingenuous, deadly, catastrophic. Billy and his fellow prisoners, during the last good war, look out for a moment on all that will not remain of Dresden, "the loveliest city that most of the Americans had ever seen," the narrator tells us. "The skyline was intricate and voluptuous and enchanted and absurd. It looked like a Sunday school picture of Heaven to Billy Pilgrim." He goes on: "Somebody behind him in the boxcar said 'Oz.' That was I. That was me. The only other city I'd ever seen was Indianapolis, Indiana" (148). Billy is there; Vonnegut is there; and if we can answer to "I," "me," or someone from the middle of America, we are there.

Ironically, Billy and those with him, confined to an old animal processing factory, the Slaughterhouse Five of the title, will be among the very few to survive the British and American firebombing version of the Holocaust that will shortly ensue. Billy will come home to live on. By the time of the book, he will find himself in the middle of the latest bad war, even as he seems to live happily ever after in the plastic landscape of the American '60s: shopping centers, freeways, motels, cars with names like Cadillac El Dorado Coupe de Ville bearing bumper stickers that say "Visit Ausable Chasm," "Support Your Police Department," "Impeach Earl Warren" (57), and (no doubt intended in 1969 as black humor) "Reagan for President!" (183). Billy has become an optometrist, grown rich after being brought into his father-in-law's business, the opportunity secured by his union with the adoring, lumpish Valencia Merble.

In an airplane crash, Billy is lobotomized. Or he suffers a mind-altering head injury. Or he has a vision. Or something like that. "Billy Pilgrim," the narrator tells us, "has come unstuck in time" (23). He used to measure eyes. Now his work is to make people see. He becomes a visionary with a message, as has his textual idol within the novel, the science fiction writer

Kilgore Trout, with *his* novel-within-a-novel, *The Gospel from Outer Space* (108). Apace, *this* novel finally undertakes the cosmic project so portended by *that* novel, to rewrite History in Time and to rewrite History out of Time. A formula for such a possibility has been contained all along in the book through a kind of mantra adopted by the narrator to comprehend the deaths of individual persons—and thereby of the global death that somehow marks Billy's and America's fall into History: "So it goes." At the last, however, Vonnegut's Tralfamadorian novel, true to form, passes even beyond verbal formulas of comprehension and acceptance. This occurs when the birds come out again, even after a Dresden, probably as they would even after a Vietnam, but with a song with a question mark—the tentative, halting, but still-forming music of life: "*Po-tee-weet?*" So it goes; and so ends, on a note and a lyric, one of the truly complete '60s novels by a '60s writer who, in the urgent imperative of his narrator, asked us to "Listen," and who more clearly than any other, in the final vision of the lobotomized Christ optometrist of this, his masterpiece, made us see.

Watts, Alan. One of the most magical, incantatory names of the celebrity counterculture continues to be that of Alan Watts. His life story was popular legend: British-born early devotee of Zen; student and popularizer of the classic work of D. T. Suzuki; retro-convert in midlife to the Episcopal priesthood; and self-elevant to the role of '60s guru-high priest officiating at the American group marriage, so to speak, of Beat, oriental mysticism, the cult of LSD, New Age meditation, and pop psychology. His name occurs endlessly in accounts of the era, as do citations of popular Watts classics such as *The Way of Zen* (1957)—itself a popular updating and clarification, as Watts noted, of his own *The Spirit of Zen* (1936, 1955, 1958)—*Psychotherapy East and West* (1961); *The Joyous Cosmology,* with a foreword by Timothy Leary and Richard Alpert (1962); and *This is It* (1967), containing the much cited "Beat Zen, Square Zen, and Zen."

Watts's golden moment in the youth-culture surely must have come, as it did for a number of other legendary figures of the era, at the celebrated San Francisco Be-In of January 1967. The day began with Watts in the company of Gary Snyder and Allen Ginsberg performing a purifying Hindu circumambulation at the site. According to accounts, Timothy Leary wore a wreath of flowers and pronounced blessings upon the crowd, saying "Whatever you do is beautiful." Supposedly, on the same day the phrase "Love Generation" entered the language courtesy of a befuddled police chief (Furlong 162).

By the late 1960s and early 1970s, in the years just before his death, Watts had become, in Theodore Roszak's acute phrase, "The Norman Vincent Peale of Zen" (156). At the same time, if a biographer, Monica Furlong, is correct, Watts's search for satori had been replaced these many years by the dementia and despairing bonhommie of late-stage chronic alcoholism.

To remember Watts merely through the filter of his counterculture persona, however, is to do him major intellectual injustice, particularly in his role as the chief American explainer and popularizer of Zen. In this respect, *The Way of Zen* is exemplary. The first half, "Background and History," includes an exposition of the concept of the Tao, the origins of Buddhism in a confluence with an earlier Hinduism, the development of the Mahayana sect, and the rise of Zen. The second half provides a guide to "Principles and Practice," beginning in personal inculcation and concluding with extensions of Zen in the arts.

To be sure, the subject being Zen, the text throughout confesses frequently to the degree to which the subject outdistances and eludes the discourse. On the other hand, Watts insists, the subject being Zen, one must still extend language to do its chancy work, *even* if its work is to be "about" that which by its very nature cannot be spoken or written, let alone as he puts it "organized" or "institutionalized" (xiv). One cannot presume to name the discipline, he says, for that would be "like trying to wrap up and label the sky" (xiv). Just as surely, one likewise does not subject Zen to fixed categories of analysis, for that would be "like studying bird song in a collection of stuffed nightingales" (xiv). One does as one can and must, Watts asserts, realizing the limits of what one must settle for in "conventional" language and then pushing beyond in spite. "How arbitrary such conventions may be can be seen from the question, 'What happens to my fist [noun-object] when I open my hand?' The object miraculously vanishes because an action was disguised by a part of speech usually assigned to a thing!" (5).

This new semiotic sense of understanding and event, familiar to the Zen disciple, of at once existing in language and moving beyond it at the phenomenological intersection of words and things, once again represented a major Eastern answer provided by '60s American thought to a larger contemporary crisis unfolding in Western philosophy. To the jangle of infinite indeterminacies that we have now come to call the style of postmodernism, it proposed then and now a kind of salutary, ancient, whole-souled and calm alternative. Portending further connections to be elaborated by other figures of '60s reading and writing such as R. D. Laing and Robert Pirsig, Zen here could summon up a seamless magic of premodern thought, working through the cracks of modern dialectical and analytic reason, and carrying us perhaps even beyond the postmodern abyss. Beyond, indeed, the very categories of thought and feeling, self and world, Zen might offer, for instance, the *hsin,* something at times like "mind," at others more like "heart." Although really neither, it was capable in a given moment of being either or both—something we can only approximate in some metalanguage that might comprehend "the totality of our psychic function" (25). And beyond *hsin* might be found, for example, the *te,* "the unthinkable ingenuity and creative power of man's spontaneous and natural functioning—a power which is blocked when one tries to master it in terms of formal methods and techniques. It is like the centipede's skill in using a hundred legs at once" (27)—or a hundred eyes, perhaps, or a hundred voices. Beyond Watts the "philosopher entertainer," as Roszak calls him (298), barnstorming the Be-In circuit, Watts the Zen-exegete had things to tell Philosophy in the West in ways that even now much of post-structuralist mystagogy itself, in the refusal to contemplate the logic of the supplement contained in *its* own Eastern other, has yet to comprehend.

Webb, Charles. We will never know how many '60s people actually experienced a Charles Webb novel entitled *The Graduate* as opposed to a Mike Nichols film entitled *The Graduate.* We do know that the novel sold a large number of copies. Whatever the readership, the vision one is likely to *see* of one's memory of the text is a film starring Anne Bancroft, Dustin Hoffman, and Katherine Ross or *hear* it as a '60s song by Simon and Garfunkel.

To return to the print-text is to reaffirm if nothing else the pervasiveness of the head-case version of the archetypal '60s youth-narrative. From the standpoint of the private pathologies of life in the land of the Happy Consciousness, here is yet another instance, like those especially of Holden Caulfield and Esther Greenwood, of someone young, intelligent, sensitive, and well-educated—someone who has had, in short, what they used to call "all the advantages"—going crazy in America, wherever that happens to be. From the standpoint of sociocultural diagnostics, as in the works of countless critics of the established culture such as Paul Goodman, Norman O. Brown, or R. D. Laing, madness becomes again that thing constituting the only sane response to an insane world.

As another case study in '60s malaise among upper–middle-class youth, Webb's protagonist, Benjamin Braddock, may claim a certain distinction by having earned his status as borderline sociopath through the utter, quotidian tiresomeness of his angst. He comes by his maladaptation honestly, and he plays it consistently right down the line, keeping within the bounds of a quarrelsome, distracted boorishness. He stays just this side of clinical certifiability but also just that side of empathetic identification. To be specific, Benjamin may be a kind of older Holden Caulfield if Holden Caulfield had turned out to be a grind, an advanced disturbed adolescent now with a high-powered Ivy League degree and the offer of a good graduate fellowship (which he casually blows). As to the relationships with the two women in his life—the bored, cynical, alcoholic Mrs. Robinson and her daughter, the at once mesmerized and repelled but finally compliant Elaine—he is what someone in the '60s would have called a jerk. In the latter case, actually, "creep" would be the better word, perhaps even what our era would call a stalker. When not openly weird and hostile, Benjamin is at best sullen, moody, abrasive; gratuitously rude to anyone who comes into his ambit; and joylessly self-righteous as only a youthful rebel against American affluence, comfort, and complacency can be who has as his main credential the circumstance of having been born to all of it.

To this day, *The Graduate* thus comes back to us as an uncommonly adult '60s youth-classic, in all the senses of that term.[62] For the '60s nostalgist, it is still best perhaps to do a slow fade at the end to the film. Dustin Hoffman crashes Katherine Ross's marriage, going crazy at the altar, wrenching loose the cross and swinging it broadsword-like to rout his foes, the would-be groom, the enraged father, the feckless divine. He spirits Ross from the sanctuary, and then, in a brilliant afterthought (in the movie, though not the book) uses what is left of the cross to bar the door. The two of them rush aboard a city bus and then peer out the back window at the receding scene of black comedy sacrilege; the notes of the song likewise recede in the background: deep, da dee deep, deep da dee deep, deep da dee deep deep. . . .

Here's to you, Mrs. Robinson, Mr. Robinson, Mr. and Mrs. Braddock. Here's to you, everybody. It is the great '60s memory trip, the major motion picture. In the text, the picture is altogether less pretty, something we have not remembered, likely, because even then we wanted well enough to forget. The bus finally starts to move, and the dreadful, familiar dialogue begins again. "Benjamin?" Elaine asks, taking his hand. "What," he answers (191).

Wolfe, Tom. Tom Wolfe's '60s titles read like a set of headlines for the era: *The Kandy-Colored Tangerine-Flake Streamline Baby, The Electric Kool-Aid Acid Test, The Pump House Gang, Radical Chic,* and *Mau-Mauing the Flak Catchers.* As we read them, all the cultural vectors converge in the panoply of indelible '60s images created: Andy Warhol, Baby Jane Holzer, and the New York Pop scene in the East; Kesey and the Pranksters in the West; Surfers; and penthouse-liberals throwing a cocktail party for Black Panthers.

Wolfe's place in '60s cultural memory will be defined by his achievement both as a chronicler and as one of the chief inventors of a whole new applied technology of style. That discourse I will elect to call here The New Writing. Volumes have been written in attempts to assign it names. The New Journalism was the name Wolfe himself gave it. The New Fiction would have applied as readily had not Wolfe reserved that term for what he has called, not admiringly, "neo-fabulation," and others "the literature of exhaustion."[63] Academic discussants have struggled to call examples of such writing nonfiction fictions and fictions of fact. None of these names, however, captures its crucial importance to the '60s, which lay in its attempt as a form of new writing to be a form of altogether *now* writing, a direct stylistic correlative to '60s consciousness at large—an attempt, that is, to reconfigure the very categories of time and reality themselves.

To this degree, exactly as an invention of discourse, the New Writing seemed to echo what R. D. Laing had proposed about the restructuring of our mental lives. "Perception, imagination, fantasy, reverie, dreams, memory," he wrote; these "are simply different *modalities of experience,* no more 'inner' or 'outer' than any other" (6). In a new discourse arising out of some assumed relation with a fact-oriented world that had obviously never existed, Wolfe and others were endowing what had been called journalism with the same openings of phenomenological possibility. The New Journalists were mounting a jazzy, hopped-up, poststructuralist challenge— the latter term being one which Wolfe himself, then or now, would surely resist—much akin to that being addressed by new theoretical criticisms to ideas of language, authority, representation, and the ideological nature of discourse and its claims to truth, value, and meaning. What is an author? the New Writing asked. What is a text? What is a subject? What is an interpretation?

Especially in the hands of word- and sensation-drunk virtuosos like Wolfe, this attempt to capture the style of the times *in* a style of the times often did produce a metadiscourse, a kind of '60s grammatology, a writing calling attention at once to its total rhetoricity and its attempts at total reification, the rendering of the thing itself. To use the '60s argot, the New Writing tried to make us totally "out of it" by getting us totally "into it" at the same time.

From literature and criticism, the project would eventually claim such figures as Norman Mailer, Joan Didion, Truman Capote, William Styron, and Susan Sontag; from commercial journalism, enlistees would include Gay Talese, Terry Southern, John Sack, Joel McGinnis, Gloria Steinem, Gary Wills, Ralph Gleason, Dotson Rader, Michael Herr, and Hunter S. Thompson. In the more proximate precincts of '60s alternative-culture reading and writing, this would also be the heyday of publications such as *The East Village Other,* the *Los Angeles Free Press, Ramparts,* and *Rolling Stone* and of underground New Writers such as Warren Hinckle, Abbie Hoffman, Jerry Rubin, Paul Krassner, and Robin Morgan.

What mesmerized writer and reader alike about the New Writing, then, was its quality of being both utterly relational and endlessly generative: its capacity to absorb consciousness from without and to create new material from within; the ability to become, so to speak, its own textual self-reification. Tom Wolfe's particular achievement in the mode is explained in essentially these terms, for instance, by Todd Gitlin, in the latter's recent tribute to *The Electric Kool-Aid Acid Test,* still surely, from a counterculture perspective, Wolfe's most totally '60s book. It is "unsurpassed as a chronicle," writes Gitlin. More importantly, it also remains unique for "not simply its breathless sense of fun but its capacity to evoke the animal magnitude, and nuttiness, of what the Pranksters were about" (207).

Gitlin is correct. To put this into the context of the present argument, exactly as the world of the Pranksters becomes the text, the text also becomes that world, and everyone, somehow, is there. To open the text is to reenter, in some absolute sense, a happening. The unnamed narrator, a freak named Cool Breeze, "a half-Ottawa girl named Lois Jennings," and a young Mexican astrologer-woman named Black Maria are flying down a San Francisco hill in a pickup truck "blazing silver red and Day-Glo." Cool Breeze has on "some kind of Seven Dwarfs Black Forest gnome's hat covered in feathers and fluorescent colors." Lois Jennings is potting away with a cap pistol at stunned straight civilians, "kheew, kheew, at the erupting marshmallow faces, like Debra Paget in . . . in . . . ." Black Maria is trying to tell the narrator he seems "too . . . *solid* for a Pisces" (3). He infers she means "stolid." The truck has a bumper sticker, eventually to become the title of a book by Vine de Loria, reading "Custer Died for Your Sins." The driver is Stewart Brand, eventually to become Stewart Brand of the Portola Institute and *The Last Whole Earth Catalog.* Today, besides being adorned with a blazing silver disk on his forehead matching that of Lois whose "enamorado" he happens to be, Brand is wearing "a whole necktie made out of Indian beads. No shirt, however, just an Indian bead necktie on bare skin and a white butcher's coat with medals from the King of Sweden on it." (1–2).

We are already on the trip, and we have not yet even gotten on the bus. We go to the warehouse where the court anxiously awaits the arrival of Ken Kesey, Jester-King of the Pranksters. The Chief is about to return, out of jail after being arrested on a dope rap. Among more assorted colorful characters, we find Mountain Girl; Hassler, the freak philosopher who brushes after every meal; and Ken Babbs, an ex–Vietnam War helicopter pilot. We also find "a guy about 40 with a lot of muscles" who keeps "flipping a small sledge hammer up in the air over and over, always managing to catch the handle on the way down with his arms and legs kicking out the whole time and his shoulders rolling and his head bobbing, all in a jerky beat as if somewhere Joe Cuba is playing 'Bang Bang'" (12). When he speaks, it is in a strange monologue, "spinning off memories, metaphors, literary, Oriental, hip allusions, all punctuated by the unlikely expression, 'you understand–'" (14). It is, of course, Neal Cassady, the original Dean Moriarity of *On the Road,* back for a repeat textual performance, in terminal incarnation and parody.

And now, just as the world is formed, the return of the King finally occurs. The Chief is back. From here, the story launches itself into something big enough to contain all the stories. It goes back to Perry Lane in the '50s, Stanford Bohemia, the assembling of the scene. Cassady turns up, then Larry McMurtry, Robert Stone, Jerry Garcia, and Richard Alpert. In the VA Hospital at Menlo Park, Kesey does the volunteer experiments with, as they called them demurely then, "psychomimetic drugs" (36). LSD. After doing more of the whole psycho-ward scene, whether on the outside or the inside becoming increasingly debatable, suddenly Kesey is famous, the world-renowned author of *One Flew Over the Cuckoo's Nest.* Then he publishes *Sometimes a Great Notion.* A great freak-menagerie begins to assemble around him in the Day Glo woods at La Honda. The La Honda group scene becomes the Merry Pranksters. The Pranksters come up with the Bus: a 1939 International Harvester Bus to be specific, a Bus named "Furthur." The Pranksters and the Bus make a Journey to the East, first making the New York scene, then off for a nearby visit with Timothy Leary and his outfit, "The League for Spiritual Discovery" (93). Then back in the West, they experience Fritz Perls and Esalen and reoccupy the old base camp at La Honda. Through Hunter S. Thompson, Kesey meets the Hell's Angels, and at La Honda the Hell's Angels meet the Pranksters. The Pranksters try to meet the Beatles. The Pranksters meet Frank Owsley, Mr. LSD (186). Kesey and the Pranksters come up with the idea of the Acid Test: "And suddenly Kesey sees that they, the Pranksters, already have the expertise and the machinery to create a mindblown state such as the world has never seen, totally wound up, lit up, amplified and . . . controlled—plus the most efficient key ever devised to open the doors in the mind of the world: Owsley's LSD" (205–6). The Acid Tests beget the Great Trips Festival of January 1966 (224). The Trips Festival begets Bill Graham and the Fillmore Auditorium. Meanwhile, Kesey keeps getting busted and finally has to take off to Mexico. The Pranksters persevere, as the Acid Test becomes the Kool-Aid Acid Test, with musical accompaniment by the Grateful Dead. Kesey is on the run. The old faithful attend him. Bob Stone from Perry Lane arrives in a Hertz car to write a profile for *Esquire* on "Kesey in Exile" (286). Kesey returns to California, this time playing Cops and Robbers with the Hell's Angels for security. The Pranksters fall in with Emmett Grogan and The Diggers. The Pranksters fall in with The Pump House Gang, turned-on surfers. Every kid on the Pacific Coast seems to be getting busted and earning membership in "The Probation Generation" (322). Kesey is back, meets with Owsley this time to go "beyond acid," is finally caught, and gets out of the San Mateo Jail and all the charges on a promise worthy of Randall McMurphy himself: to reform LSD users. Kesey organizes the Acid Test Graduation. "And the drums roll and Cassady stiffens and jerks and twitches and the Pranksters hasten forward, Hassler, Babbs, Zonker, The Hermit, Gretch, Paul Foster, Black Maria, Page, Walker, Hagen, Doris Delay, Roy Sherburn, flying up and back in black robes . . . graduate into what on the horizon . . . ." The tribe disperses. Kesey does six months on the work farm for the old La Honda bust. "In February, Neal Cassady's body [is] found beside a railroad track outside the town of San Miguel de Allende, in Mexico" (370). Kesey works on a novel in Oregon, with the Bus "parked beside the Space Heater House."

We have come back more or less where we came in. And what a trip it has been, aboard a vehicle named "Furthur," with Kesey and the Pranksters. It has been one last great pilgrimage in the old American tradition, a pilgrimage, as always, to discover America *and* to invent it. We have had the great ride. We have been on the Bus. We have taken all the tests. We have attended the graduation. We have had a total '60s trip. Thanks to Wolfe, and the style he invented, we have also had *the* total '60s trip. Compatriots in '60s reading and writing would go brilliantly on to stake out new areas of this garish, teeming geography. But Wolfe, the first pranksterking of what he called the New Journalism, remained largely responsible for making the textual explorations possible.

Postscripts and Summations

Sixties reading and writing in America obviously did not end with the '60s. If anything, it became the textual extension of the decade both in consciousness *and* in fact. *The Whole Earth Catalog; Our Bodies, Ourselves;* Annie Dillard's *Pilgrim at Tinker Creek;* Robert Pirsig's *Zen and the Art of Motorcycle Maintenance;* Michael Herr's *Dispatches;* and other exemplary works continued to reveal themselves as fulfillments of a spirit—what a more academic time would have called a zeitgeist—expressing itself in new and often culminating textual moments.

Analyses of '60s consciousness, on the other hand, did not wait for the '60s to end. Indeed, two of the most prominent appeared at the turn of the decade and still speak powerfully to its concerns. The first, Theodore Roszak's *The Making of a Counter-Culture,* remains one of the great achievements of cultural-intellectual synthesis written on the subject. The second, Charles Reich's *The Greening of America,* makes a similar attempt from a posture of empathetic identification but often obscures its insights, which are still considerable, with groovy self-parody.

Curiously, in related areas of social history, one still finds few accounts of the '60s domestic scene with the insight or synthesizing vision found in writing about Vietnam. Expressions of the era have yet to meet with the rock 'n' roll energy of a *Dispatches,* for instance, or the chastened cultural wisdom of a *Fire in the Lake.* Indeed, to date one can point with confidence to a very few major broad-focus texts: Roszak's, Milton Viorst's *Fire in the Streets,* Allen J. Matusow's *The Unraveling of America,* and Morris Dickstein's *The Gates of Eden.*[1] Also noteworthy is Jerome Klinkowitz's *The American 1960s,* a brief, selective study that in its suggestive organization and its focus on important theoretical topics addresses as well as any yet produced basic questions of textuality, authorship, audience, representation, and cultural status.[2] For an active experiment, on the other hand, in poststructuralist pastiche—an eccentric blend of memoir, reportage, reflection, and analysis—one might also consult appropriate portions of Greil Marcus's *Lipstick Traces: A Secret History of the Twentieth Century.*

By their similar configurings of multiple cultural issues and textual possibilities, certain anthologies of the era also give a synthesis of retrospective views. Gerald Howard's vivid collection, entitled simply *The Sixties,* although out of print, remains rich, diverse, and—particularly as far as a certain style of counterculture reading is concerned—deeply representative, with insightful and provocative introductions to various topical sections. *Smiling Through the Apocalypse,* on the other hand, subtitled *Esquire's History of the Sixties,* seems slick, urban, New Journalistic, in retrospect distinctly establishmentarian-hip with really very little of the flavor of the youth-culture. In fact, save for a famous article by Anthony Lukas entitled "The Life and Death of a Hippie"; Michael Herr's groundbreaking Vietnam essay, "Hell Sucks"; and a short apostrophe to LSD from Timothy Leary's *High Priest,* a more likely title for the volume might have been *The '60s According to* Esquire. At the other extreme, however, exists Judith Clavir Albert and Stewart Edward Albert's *The Sixties Papers: Documents of a Rebellious Decade*—for '60s aficionados who want their counterculture information uncut, an absolutely indispensable anthology, teeming with radical texts and documents now unavailable in any other form.

Sixties memoirs are exemplified by at least two recent classics: Todd Gitlin's *The Sixties: Years of Hope, Days of Rage* from the student movement and Abe Peck's *Uncovering the Sixties: The Life and Times of the Underground Press.* Both distinctly anchored in their autobiographical perspectives, they also offer major, even definitive, insights into the meaning of the decade as a cultural phenomenon as well as provocative speculations about its historical importance (both were written in the late '80s). I have already suggested a Vietnam parallel in works of general analysis, and a similar one is also appropriate here. Indeed, what may be called the evolution of the "inside" youth-literature of the '60s resembles rather closely, in equally exacerbated form, the kind of textual debate being produced by the agony of Vietnam that was its geopolitical correlative and, in some bizarre way, even its raison d'etre. To put it simply, both have taken a long time to be written about in their relation to American myth, I would propose, exactly because their relation to each other *and* to American myth struck much too close to home. That is, they themselves, as historical American experiences, depended for their existence on their inextricability from a whole constellation of national mythologies long part and fabric of the American character: the myth of American historical innocence; the myth of American geopolitical invincibility; the myth of the New Eden; the myth of the City on a Hill; and the myth, above all, of eternal American youth. Michael Herr has said of himself and the other correspondents who became literally excitement junkies high on war that "Vietnam is what we had instead of happy childhoods" (244). The same might be said in great measure about a generation of Americans at home high on youth and revolution. Everyone, it turns out, came down at once. And everyone came down with a crash that has taken an equally long time to write about.

Still, a body of textual exploration continues to grow. Various activists have written retrospectively: Abbie Hoffman, Jerry Rubin, David Harris, Tom Hayden, Angela Davis, Gloria Steinem. Of particularly intimate, searing insight is the account of hitting the '60s wall recorded in Mark Vonnegut's harrowed memoir, *The Eden Express*. But one can also find more traditional connections between autobiography and social history in works such as Bob Greene's *Be True to Your School;* Sara Davidson's novelistic memoir, *Loose Change: Three Women of the Sixties;* Geoffrey O'Brien's *Dream Time: Chapters from the Sixties;* and Lawrence Wright's *In the New World.* Further expanses of genre and perspective are taken in by oral histories, retrospective essay collections, and other experiments in biographical and historical reflection: for example, Anthony M. Casale and Philip Lerman's *Where Have All the Flowers Gone? The Fall and Rise of the Woodstock Generation;* Annie Gottlieb's *Do You Believe in Magic?: The Second Coming of the Sixties Generation;* Joan Morrison and Robert K. Morrison's *From Camelot to Kent State: The Sixties Experience in the Words of Those Who Lived It;* and Lauren Kessler's *After All These Years: Sixties Ideals in a Different World.* One essay anthology, Peter Collier and David Horowitz's *Destructive Generation: Second Thoughts About the '60s,* turns out to be a set of revisionary testaments by the authors, former editors of *Ramparts* magazine, in distinctly neoconservative reflection. Another book, edited by Collier and Horowitz, comprises the proceedings of a symposium similarly entitled *Second Thoughts: Former Radicals Look Back at the Sixties.*

In recent years, one need look only as far as the major review media to see a steady increase in the appearance of sundry " '60s" novels attempting to make new sense of the era. Meanwhile, in a rich body of Vietnam writing, some of the best '60s meditations on the moral questions raised generation-wide by the war may be found in the at-home sections of classic Vietnam texts such as Tim O'Brien's *If I Die in a Combat Zone,* Philip Caputo's *A Rumor of War,* and Ron Kovic's *Born on the Fourth of July.*

Predictably, the best popular '60s retrospectives concerning the youth-culture and the general nuttiness of the times make no pretense at heavy analysis. One pure nostalgia trip never likely to be surpassed is Rex Weiner and Deanne Stillman's *Woodstock Census: The Nationwide Survey of the Sixties Generation.* It dabbles in mock-scientific sampling, complete with statistics, tables, graphs, and compilations of questionnaire results. But it is richest on anecdote, a kind of Proustian feast of names, phrases, and remembered events and their associations including lists of Movement Heavies and pages of recollections on what people did the first time they got stoned. There will never be, one suspects, anything else like it. Of wider circulation are also popular histories and pictorial books. One of the most useful for the student of the era remains Paul Sann's breathlessly titled *The Angry Decade: The Sixties.* And of comparable information and interest value now, ironically, are the kinds of middle-class, middlebrow newsweekly volumes that any self-respecting '60s reader would have disdained: Time-Life's 1960–70 volume in the series entitled *This Fabulous Century,* for example, and a more recent *Life* photohistory entitled *Life in the '60s.* Also of appeal and utility, not to mention good humor, are Jane and Michael Stern's *Sixties People* and pertinent portions of their *Encyclopedia of Bad Taste.* One may also consult informative '60s sections of Charles Panati's *Panati's Parade of Fads, Follies, and Manias;* Paul Dickson's *Timelines,* a popular cultural chronology focusing on America since 1945; and the more extensive *Timetables of American History,* edited by Laurence Urdan.

Oddly or not, depending on how one looks at it, among books for a general interest audience, what might be called the counterculture flavor of the times is most vividly supplied in two texts produced for young people, James Haskin and Kathleen Benson's *The 60s Reader* and Jules Archer's *The Incredible Sixties: The Stormy Years that Changed America.* Both are provocative in their organization, complex in their view of issues, and extremely useful in their documentation of particular persons and events.

It has become a commonplace of any serious analysis of the American '60s to suggest that the insistent, even obsessive self-scrutiny to which Americans subjected themselves and their beliefs and values had inevitably to result in a pathological, perhaps fatal narcissism. That, of course, by 1979, was what Christopher Lasch was calling it in *The Culture of Narcissism* as an attempt at new cultural symptomatology: "the fascination with fame and celebrity, the fear of competition, the inability to suspend disbelief, the shallowness and transitory quality of personal relations, the horror of death—originate in the peculiar structure of the American family, which in turn originates in changing modes of production." And family organization has in turn recreated itself as a sinister mirroring of "the organized apparatus of social control" (176). Tom Wolfe likewise, blowing off the heavy social analysis, had already shorthanded the problem to the " 'me' decade."

In much of the writing described above, it has frequently seemed necessary to respond to the question of what happened to the '60s by writing an elegy or an epitaph. In conclusion, I would propose a somewhat more hopeful explanation—at least in terms of functional effect. Americans generally of the post–1945 generation, born to believe in themselves mythologically as the *true* hope of the world, and eventually confronted with a whole mythology of cultural exceptionalism cast in disarray abroad and at home, have rather healthily succeeded simply in arranging priorities so as to tune out the havoc. Indeed, who can*not* say, among most survivors of the '60s—those who took part in cultural upheavals in the streets, those who went to Vietnam, those who did neither, those who did both and more—that going into the '70s with the world coming down all around them *still* did not feel like the worst years of their lives? The Vietnam War, which had effectively slid into futility and irresolution from Tet in 1968 onward, stumbled and murdered on until 1975. The American incursion into Cambodia shortly yielded, in the new era of total Vietnamization, a Laotian fiasco. The North finally made the great invasion of the South. Americans got to witness the great 1975 Xuan Loc-Long Binh-Bien Hoa-Saigon bugout, with a dismal footnote supplied by the *Mayaguez* hijacking, which killed a few more Asians as well as a few more Marines. Laos went over to the Pathet Lao. Cambodia turned into the Killing Fields. At home, the age of assassination, begun with the death of John Kennedy and going on during the decade to claim Medgar Evers, Robert Kennedy, and Martin Luther King Jr., turned to George Wallace, Gerald Ford, and eventually just about anyone in sight. (John Hinckley we later learned apparently stalked Jimmy Carter at some length before electing for Ronald Reagan.) Somewhere out where the '60s ended, everybody seemed to be dying or getting murdered. Weathermen blew themselves up in Manhattan townhouses. Music stars such as Janis Joplin, Jimi Hendrix, and Jim Morrison found starburst deaths. The Manson Family found the La Biancas, Sharon Tate, and the others. Black Panthers went down in raids in cities across the country. The SLA found Patty Hearst and blazing apocalypse in a shootout with an army of police. Meanwhile, "consciousness

consciousness," as Charles Reich had elected to call it, had fallen over the edge of some strange, dreadful fault-line. Hare Krishnas, born-again evangelicals, herbalists, meditationists, enema cultists, and Rajneeshis all sought spiritual masters. Supply met and then quickly outran demand. Werner Erhart (previously an ex-Philadelphia car salesman named John Paul Rosenburg), Fritz Perls, Meher Baba, Baba Ram Dass, the Maharaji Ji, Arthur Janov, Idries Shah, Chogyam Trungpa, and countless other gurus to the stars peddled TM, est, Rolfing, macrobiotics, ashrams, and environmental causes by the truckload. For most people, I would propose, this really had little to do with something as complicated as "narcissism" or even as clear-cut as "me." When everything you believed in one way or another proves of dubious value as an object of belief, you tend to go solo and pick up whatever sustains you along the way. You go back to yourself and start over.

The difficulty of all that—of effectively watching it all come and go at once in the course of a generation and then trying to talk about a '60s "structure" of consciousness as if it were something that really might exist—is reflected in nearly all contemporary chronicles and analyses. The most compelling ones, such as Kunen's *The Strawberry Stateman,* for instance, are deeply anecdotal in the epiphanic style that characterized the era's writing generally. A rather more sober-minded, albeit frequently insightful, contemporary variant is Mark Gerzon's *The Whole World Is Watching: A Young Man Looks at Youth's Dissent.* Very much in the model of "reflections on alienated youth" by elders such as Goodman, Keniston, and others, it is sensible, meditative, and rather solemn. Accurate on many key influences—Camus, Galbraith, Goodman, Riesman, Salinger, McLuhan, Keniston, Erikson, Ellul, Fromm, Whyte, Kozol, Myrdal, Mills, Marcuse, and Bell—it also included somber excurses on song lyric-apothegms from Simon and Garfunkel (in paraphrase because of permissions problems), Scott McKenzie, Janis Ian, the Rolling Stones, Bob Dylan, The American Breed, the Beatles, the Jefferson Airplane, somebody called The Seeds, Country Joe and the Fish, and Spanky and Our Gang.

As to contemporary '60s chronicles from more detached perspectives, the one still most vivid—Tom Wolfe's *The Electric Kool-Aid Acid Test*—does its best work in recreating the manic hubbub and bustle of the Kesey-Prankster operation and their exemplary relation to the inspired craziness of the times. Nicholas von Hoffman's much less well-known, *We Are the People Our Parents Warned Us Against* attempts something similar with the hippies of the Haight, a New Journalism, multimedia collage style of representation. Unlike Wolfe's, however, it founders on the irrepressible solemnity of its empathetic identification. So do the rather piously titled contemporary studies by the social psychologist Kenneth Keniston such as *The Uncommitted: Alienated Youth in American Society; Young Radicals: Notes on Committed Youth;* and *Youth and Dissent: the Rise of a New Opposition* (the latter nevertheless including among its contents an essay with surely one of the most expressive youth-titles of the era: "You have to grow up in Scarsdale to know how bad things really are."). However, one must also credit the genius of Keniston's structural identification of the American cultural production called "youth" as a new life-stage on the scene of history: now wedged powerfully between the traditional stages of adolescence and adulthood, and, seemingly best *and* worst of all, under certain conditions of affluence, educational opportunity, and social fluidity, *infinitely prolongable.*[3] (All of these, though, escape the truly ludicrous solemnity of Lewis Yablonsky's classic *The Hippie Trip,* which notes from the sociologist's perspective how "it was of vital importance for me to *personally experience* some core hippie behavior patterns in order to truly tune-in to what was happening" [xii].)

Thus the perils, then and now, of cosmi-comic solemnity when saying anything about the '60s. In their own cosmi-comic solemnity, they were themselves always but a short hair away from being a parody of themselves, Prospero's Brave New World as some composite technicolor cartoon and migraine headache of the national soul.

Of many '60s voices still speaking, then and now, Joan Didion in this respect gets it right, measures that is the distance that has been crossed. She entitles her late-'60s collection of writings, produced over the span of the decade, *Slouching towards Bethlehem.* In it she measures the '60s in America as some final movement over the abyss of the modern. In contrast, the title of her late-'70s book of writings, produced over the span of *that* decade, turns out to be *The White Album.* Unlike the former, this collection, in the style of the late Beatles, gives us something more cool, more empty, and if anything, more terrifying. Here was no modernist apocalypse nor any movement into some new postmodernist conundrum but simply another day of life in the late Middle Ages. To borrow Didion's wonderful epiphany, we are still just here, somewhere in America, on the morning after the '60s.

Notes

Chapter 1. Mythologizing the '60s

1 As to active political organization, it is also necessary to remember the importance of the early to mid '60s. The date of the Port Huron Statement by the Students for a Democratic Society was 1962, the Free Speech uprising at Berkeley took place in 1964, and by 1965 teach-ins against the war were being regularly conducted on campuses across the country. Nineteen sixty-six saw the founding of the National Organization for Women, which quickly attracted adherents from all segments of the youth-culture. By 1967 the Student Non-Violent Coordinating Committee and the Students for a Democratic Society were working in direct affiliation.

2 And I do mean here to describe such kinds of imaginative commitments as constituting a consciousness of total engagement, a frame of mind that actually could conflate the literary appreciation of humble courage in a Tolkien character with the experiential choice of taking part in a sit-in. If anything, a recurrent feature of '60s thought seemed to be the attempt to reconnect American thinking and acting in just such ways. To be sure, especially on the part of the radical counterculture, one saw enough of the dire consequences arising from any attempt to equate reading revolution with making it. Sacred texts from Frantz Fanon, Mao, Malcolm X, Che, or Marx often resisted movement into cultural circulation in every sense of the term. On the other hand, one cannot help associating the kind of mindset one often found in youthful terrorists with the one that their opposite numbers often awakened to in Vietnam—a kind of cartoon mentality that bombs were not really bombs and bullets were not really bullets. Not surprisingly, the evidence of the connection was linguistic. Phrases such as "Offing the Pigs" and "Zapping the Cong" seemed to flow from the same unreality warp.

3 At the same time, in my next section, I also propose that the particular transaction described, as an experience of language, was deeply entrenched in a long national habit of belief in the power of the word; that it was thus not nearly so spontaneous and self-originating as reckoned but rather a complex function of American thought at large, arising out of the Western experience of print and engrafting upon it in the New World the contrarieties of a distinct historical evolution; and that even in the short space of its '60s unfolding, it proved equally diverse and complex in its constituencies and cultural participations.

4 As noted in my later discussion of Plath, *The Bell Jar* has remained continuously in print and has enjoyed widespread curricular adoption. For the recurrent poetry selections used to represent Plath, one need only consult anthologies in regular college and university use.

5 To document such assertions of "constituency," one may note, for instance, a regular column in *The Chronicle of Higher Education* throughout the late '60s and early '70s entitled "What They're Reading on the Campuses." And, as revealed by the entries, such a quest for the word paid little heed to traditional categories of author, genre, and mode, not to mention literariness or popularity.

6 And often piously adopting, of course, in their housing, their clothes, and their voluntary antimaterialism, something of the political identities of the poor and oppressed so designated in Michael Harrington's original use of the phrase.

7 Here as well, although evidence would be largely anecdotal, one probably cannot underestimate the flowering in the decades after 1945 of an unrivaled science education system offering applied understandings of postmodern discoveries in particle physics and quantum theory. Indeed, one might truly wonder for how many American cultural theorists now in midcareer the first shocks of poststructuralist destabilizations and the first glimpses into radical indeterminacies came initially in a good sophomore chemistry or physics course.

8 As virtually every school child once knew, "East is East, and West is West," or at least so wrote Kipling. One suddenly realizes how Anglo-European a thing that is to say. Americans have never thought that. As far as the idea of the Orient is concerned, East has always been West and vice versa. Hence English and American confusions, especially over regional nomenclature: Middle East, Near East, Far East, and so on. As to literary example in the context of Thoreau or Whitman, see also by comparison, for instance, how "English" are Irving and Poe in their orientalisms of the Arabesque. The proximate historical connections of a "Far Eastern" as opposed to a "Near Eastern" American orientalism are manifold and complex. For a verification of such a myth of Asia as a feature of Western cultural desire deeply associated with the experience of the Americas, consult, for instance, any of the now reliably documented accounts of Renaissance-era New World voyaging and exploration. For the French, English, Dutch, Spanish, Portuguese, and Italian voyagers, the landmass of the Americas was clearly regarded as intermediary to a great western ocean and the riches of Asia. As to the experienced geopolitical history of the United States, from the mid-nineteenth century onward, as a cognate of westward consolidation of the continental territory the Pacific became the major international arena of American expansionism. The annexation of Hawaii and American Samoa was followed by the Spanish-American war, which brought into the American sphere the Philippines and other major island possessions. China, a major destination of trade from the mid-nineteenth century onward, became the site of intense missionary activity. World War II settled for the moment at least the matter of Pacific hegemony. The post-1945 occupation and rebuilding of Japan

has dictated the basic course of Asian economic development to the present. The 1948 loss of China to the Communists similarly dictated the focus of American foreign policy for nearly the next thirty years, with the military intervention in Korea succeeded by the catastrophe of Vietnam. Moreover, at the end of the pipeline in Vietnam, that final collision of East and West as modes for envisioning the world would make every claim to be designated a genuine apocalypse of the national mind. "No bearings and none in sight," says Michael Herr in *Dispatches,* "thinking, *Where the fuck am I?,* fallen into some unnatural East-West interface, a California corridor cut and bought and burned deep into Asia, and no one could remember why" (43).

9 And hence, as noted later and mentioned also in countless individual '60s texts, the intuitional, nonintellective, mystic, deeply "Asian" otherness that still makes American thought seem so functionally Eastern in ways that Anglo-European tradition still struggles to assimilate within the framework of dialectic.

10 Here, moreover, in both cases the crucial conditions of synthesis seem to have been generated by the existence of a certain reading public amidst particular circumstances of textual availability. For the nineteenth-century figures mentioned, one of the great publishing events of the era, following on the Egyptological excitement generated by Champollion's Rosetta Stone and its keying of the hieroglyphics, was the appearance of popular translations of Hindu sacred texts, with particular interest being accorded the *Upanishads* and the *Bhagavad-Gita.* Similarly, in the twentieth century, the Chinese and Japanese studies of Pound and Fenollosa, new translations by Arthur Waley, the prolific output of Suzuki as scholar *and* lay explainer, and the showmanship of Alan Watts in particular, all conspired to make Zen a focal, almost generic staple of '60s Orientalism.

11 Again, in the proximate textual dimension of this study, to give some further notion of the distinctiveness proposed, all this must surely help to account for the appropriations by an American youth-audience of the holymadman Blake, the fantasist-medievalist Tolkien, or the deeply Eastern Hesse as among the very few '60s illuminati of modern English or Continental ancestry. It also goes far to explain why, as the generation of youth inevitably came to formulate its own stratifications of a "high" literary culture, it found its experimentalist idols in magical realists such as the mystical South Americans Borges, Marquez, and Cortazar, or the "non-Western" Europeans such as Nabokov, Grass, and Calvino.

Chapter 2. '60s Readers and '60s Texts

1 Surely Thomas Carlyle must have had the former British colonies of North America in mind as a prime example when he remarked in 1836, "he who

shortened the labor of copyists by the device of movable types was disbanding hired armies, and cashiering most kings and senates, and creating a whole new democratic world" (Boorstin 516). Literacy figures from the colonial period and from the early Republic, while hard to quantify and in some dispute as to what "real" reading and writing actually meant (the ability to read instructions? the capacity to sign one's name? the completion of a certain period of schooling?) are noteworthy for their scope. David Freeman Hawke says that by the end of the seventeenth century between 60 (in Virginia) and 70 (in New England) percent of American males seemed to indicate literacy as an ability to sign their wills (70–71). Of the late eighteenth and early nineteenth century, Jack Larkin asserts, "for a rural people, by the standards of their time, Americans were strikingly literate, surpassing most of the nations of Western Europe" (35). From the late eighteenth century onward, he adds, such general literacy seems to have shown itself in an upsurge in educational and informational reading (53–54). Cathy Davidson notes John Adams's claims to near universal literacy in early nineteenth-century America but also the successive difficulties of historians to validate it. She also makes a useful distinction between "literacy" and "literateness," which she defines as an educational continuity between "rudimentary reading and elementary ciphering, on the one hand, and the sophisticated use of literacy for one's material, intellectual, and political advantage on the other" (59, 61). She then goes on to argue on the basis of contemporary evidence the degree to which women, not afforded an official educational avenue toward literateness in ways comparable to men, often used popular fiction as alternative means of education.

The point of all these studies, dispute over figures and constituencies notwithstanding, would seem to be the visibility of literacy from the outset in the colonies and the early Republic as a cultural concept and a topic of discussion. As a result, for critics and historians looking back on these eras, literacy figures must now surely play a major part in the assessment of political and cultural agendas.

2 And while innocently calling another, of course, *The Autobiography of Alice B. Toklas*.

3 In good Emersonian fashion, he naturally pulls away as quickly in "The Poet," declaring that "all symbols are fluxional" and language mainly "transitive and vehicular."

4 Further, in just these connections, one also notes the frequent wreckage of poststructuralist critiques of language, representation, authority, history, and genealogy against the linguistic and political self-consciousness inscribed in American literary expression from the colonial and classic periods to the present: the built-in textual destabilizations of a literature founded on a supreme, almost obsessive awareness of its own rhetoricity, on its status, that is, as a textual construction quite literally programmed, as it were, to self-deconstruct.

5 And here, of course, we also encounter, as James Twitchell observes, the idea of "image" in the sense widely attributed to Jean Baudrillard. Here indeed is a world of "images" that outnumber the possibilities of representations themselves, one where "we have more signs than referents, more images than meanings that can be attached to them" (51).

6 For those less technologically inclined, an equally suggestive bracketing of the kind of literacy intersection described here has been supplied through the history of writing about literacy education itself. Specifically, it involves the publication of two texts on literacy issues regarded as mid century classics. The first was a book by Rudolf Flesch entitled *Why Johnny Can't Read, And What You Can Do About It.* The publication date was 1956. The second was a famous special issue of *Newsweek* magazine, entitled, after the lead article, "Why Johnny Can't Write." The publication date was 1975. To be sure, Flesch's text had mainly to do with a particular pedagogy of reading in its relation to warnings of a general decline in print skills. The second text, however, clearly made the connection between reading and writing as complementary features of print literacy, and made much of a current decline in reading as crucial to a decline in writing. Further, it put the finger directly on the culprit: television. And the diagnosis, with the addition perhaps of a corresponding influx of other nonprint media now also competing intensely for the attention of youth, must surely still stand. We truly have lived through the utter displacement into obsolescence of print reading *and* writing as the basis of human communication in the space of a single generation between the years 1957 and 1975—a period that we have also taken to calling, approximately, the '60s.

7 At the upper end of educational scale especially, where we will be most concerned, the figures were astonishing. Milton Viorst notes, for instance, that a 1960 total of three-and-a-half million college students had by 1965 jumped to five-and-a-half million. This accounted for half of all late adolescent white Americans and a quarter of young adults between 21 and 24. To summarize, there had developed overnight an unprecedented "ratio of *students* in a society" (164).

Paul Johnson similarly describes the era as "the most explosive decade in the entire history of educational expansion" (641). Building its power with the post–World War II G.I. Bill, its post-Korea reinstitution, and the 1958 National Defense Education Act, which "doubled the Federal education budget," the "central government" became "the financial dynamic of education." He goes on:

The number of state teachers grew from 1 million in 1950 to 2.3 million in 1970, as spending per person rose over 100 per cent. The growth of higher education was the most marked because it was now contended that it should be universally available. "The important question," an official report argued, "need not be 'Who deserves to be admitted?' but 'Whom can the society, in conscience and self-interest, exclude?'" since nobody could be "justly" denied a university education unless "his deficiencies are so severe" that even the "most flexible and dedicated institution could not help him" (641–42).

Similar growth, Johnson concedes, may have been international. But "the American experience was most striking because of the statistics involved": "Between 1960 and 1975, the number of American colleges and universities rose from 2,040 to 3,055. During the 'golden years' of expansion, new ones were opening at the rate of one a week. Students rose from 3.6 million in 1960 to 9.4 million in 1975, the bulk of the increase (4 million) coming in the public sector. Including non-degree students, they passed the 11 million mark in 1975, at an annual cost of $45 billion" (642).

8 The particular analysis of such consequences, to be sure, will be a matter for another generation of futurists to describe. Here, nonetheless, some early notes are worth recording on how many of the direst predictions of '60s theorists of mass consciousness and present-day theorists of mass communications have proved congruent in ways that neither surely could have imagined. As Donald Lazere writes in an essay extending from current media speculations through the work of major literacy theorists, in addition to increased "egocentrism and sociocentrism," "among the further cognitive deficiencies found by researchers in the language of mass media and its reception by audiences are an absence of the analytic and synthetic modes of reasoning necessary to relate the personal and the impersonal, concrete and abstract, cause and effect, or past, present, and future (compare the 'present orientation' of the culture of poverty and of oral societies), as well as to view issues in sufficient complexity to resist stereotyping, either/or thinking, and demagogic emotional appeal." He continues: "In the present American political context these cognitive deficiencies comprise yet another factor contributing to conformity, authoritarianism, and passivity" (291–92). This, of course, would not have been news to the '60s and to thinkers such as Herbert Marcuse, for instance, who stressed the dangers of one-dimensional communication as an incitement to one-dimensional thinking, i.e. the regime of the totally functional or operational. The current problem is that, where alternative modes of consciousness capable of contending with traditional linguistic reason might have arisen as forms of critique, there is now simply semiotic bewilderment. "Perhaps the most profoundly conservative force in all of the cognitive patterns discussed here," Lazere writes, "is their potential for inhibiting people from being able to imagine any social order different from the established one. The present reality is concrete and immediate, alternatives abstract and distant; ability to understand an alternative is further obstructed by lack of the sustained attention span necessary for analytic reasoning, the capacity to imagine beyond the actual to the hypothetical (which semantically entails reasoning from the

literal to the figurative to the symbolic), and a sense of irony, necessary to question the social conditioning that endorses the status quo" (295–96).

9 Todd Gitlin, for instance, convincingly traces out the origins of the Student Movement alliance with various constituencies of the Old Left. On the other hand, he notes that, even so, "youth culture might have remained just that— the transitional subculture of the young, a rite of passage on the route to normal adulthood—had it not been for the revolt of black youth" (83).

10 On the first point, histories of the event remark on the cross section of '60s youth who made the pilgrimage. For a recent account, see Joel Makower's *Woodstock: The Oral History*. As to the influence of the movie and the album, it remains an eye-opening experience today to note the capacity of people in their thirties and forties to recite in a kind of Homeric catalog the major groups and performers present. With these points in mind, it is clear Rex Weiner and Deanne Stillman chose wisely in entitling their historical and demographic survey of '60s popular youth-culture *Woodstock Census*.

11 Further, in its insistence on a nomenclature heavy with adjectives such as "student," "youth," "people's," and the like, such linguistic behavior often seemed to invoke the totalitarian logic of the self-reifying verbal formula so often visible in government and advertising—in usages such as NATO, for instance, or "your" congressman and "your" Buick dealer.

12 In a newly added preface to *The Sixties: Years of Hope, Days of Rage,* Todd Gitlin offers an analogous listing of achievements and after effects under such categories as "Social Equality," "Wide-Open 'Life-Styles,' " "The Limitation of National Violence and the Care of the Earth," and "Democratic Activity."

13 More than occasionally, of course, it also reached a kind of Millerite idiocy in its promises to levitate the Pentagon or to lace the main water supply for New York City with LSD. Nonetheless, there seems no doubt that the youth-generation of the '60s and '70s saw itself as empowered across a whole range of thought and action by what one might call its totems and icons, the vast intertextuality of its sacred objects: hair, love beads, peace signs, placards, outlandish costumes, song lyrics, slogans, and eventually even the roster of legendary events of folk history (concerts such as Monterey Pop, Altamont, Woodstock and political dramas such as the March on the Pentagon, The Siege of Chicago, the Trial of the Chicago Seven, and the Moratorium).

14 Indeed, this will continue to be my main proposition about mythologizing the '60s, especially as it relates to a particular *category* of cultural remembering called '60s reading and writing: that the decade will remain singular as one of the last in which a main dimension of memory is still bibliographic. Such a spirit, one must admit, is increasingly hard to recapture. One can still find it in many '60s texts themselves, however, as well as in pronouncements such as Kurt Vonnegut's classic essay of the era, "Why They Read Hesse."

15 For a variety of examples, see, for instance, Raymond M. Olderman's *Beyond*

the Waste Land: A Study of the American Novel in the Nineteen-Sixties; Ihab Hassan's *Contemporary American Literature: 1945–72;* Josephine Hendin's *Vulnerable People: A View of American Fiction since 1945;* Tony Tanner's *City of Words: American Fiction 1950–1970;* Frederick Karl's *American Fictions 1940/1980: A Comprehensive History and Critical Evaluation;* and Malcolm Bradbury's *The Modern American Novel.*

Even a more self-avowedly ecumenical study such as Larry McCaffery's *Postmodern Fiction* offers discussions of youth-writers such as Brautigan, Castaneda, Pirsig, Pynchon, Vonnegut, and Wolfe as only six among its twenty-seven chapters. It also includes a few figures of related interest, such as the science-fictionist Ursula K. LeGuin and the cult-autobiographer Frederick Exley, and '70s favorites such as Joan Didion, John Irving, Tom McGuane, and Tom Robbins. But the bulk of the text is still reserved for the more officially literary attractions of John Barth, Donald Barthelme, Thomas Berger, Robert Coover, E. L. Doctorow, Stanley Elkin, John Fowles, William Gaddis, Gabriel Garcia Marquez, John Gardner, William Gass, Jerzy Kozinski, Toni Morrison, Ishmael Reed, and Robert Stone.

16 Dispiritingly, the only works one finds here even resembling '60s reading and writing turn out to be Richard Bach's *Jonathan Livingston Seagull* in 34th place and Rod McKuen's *Listen to the Warm* at 48th.

17 More detailed annual summaries in *Publishers Weekly,* broken down by publisher and market, add little to any argument for general mass-market popularity of '60s texts. At most, certain familiar titles prove notable within a particular set of years. Salinger's *The Catcher in the Rye,* Heller's *Catch-22,* and Golding's *The Lord of the Flies,* for instance, prove to be important mass-market paperbacks during the first half of the decade. Other texts mentioned on paperback and trade lists include Salinger's *Nine Stories* and *Franny and Zooey,* Albert Camus's *The Stranger,* James Baldwin's *Nobody Knows My Name* and *Another Country,* William Whyte's *The Organization Man,* David Riesman's *The Lonely Crowd,* C. Wright Mills's *The Power Elite,* Betty Friedan's *The Feminine Mystique,* and Michael Harrington's *The Other America* (*PW,* January 21, 1963; January 20, 1964; January 18, 1965).

In contrast, dominating the lists from mid decade onward were J. R. R. Tolkien's *The Hobbit* and *The Lord of the Rings.* Appearing prominently in addition was Hermann Hesse's *Siddhartha.* Also notable were some new curricular favorites: Marshall McLuhan's *Understanding Media,* for instance, and Joanne Greenburg's *I Never Promised You a Rose Garden,* both noted as syllabus items in many college psychology courses. A steady rise of interest in black history and culture brought continuing prominence to Eldridge Cleaver and Malcolm X. Science fiction bestsellers included Robert A. Heinlein, Frank Herbert, and Ursula K. LeGuin. For two years running, 1968–69, Dutton reported their bestseller to be the *I Ching* (*PW,* January 17, 1966; January 30, 1967; January 29, 1968; February 9, 1970).

Only in the succeeding decade did '60s reading and writing live up to any myth of mass-market popularity. And by now it was clear that the myth was the creation so to speak of its own market dynamic. Large sales were achieved, for instance, by heavily promoted, uniform paperback editions of Tolkien, Hesse, and Vonnegut. On the strength of the movie, *Catch-22* sold 1.5 million new paperbacks. Perhaps most revealing of the convergence of myth and market, however, was an unlikely academic hit from Doubleday selling a quarter of a million copies in its first year. By Theodore Roszak, it was entitled *The Making of a Counter-Culture* (*PW,* February 8, 1971).

18 Somewhat shocking long-term confirmation was provided by *The Chronicle of Higher Education* in the form of a survey (February 22, 1971) of popular campus reading over the preceding five years. At the top of the list was Kahlil Gibran's *The Prophet,* a choice many might have deemed somewhat retrograde but in any event still plausible. Second was the real surprise: Rod McKuen's *Listen to the Warm.* Beyond that, the data seemed only to compound the confusion. "The only other works among the top five at more than three campuses," the survey noted in its concluding paragraph, "were *The Family of Man,* photographs [selected] by Edward Steichen, and *The Lord of the Rings,* a trilogy by J. R. R. Tolkien" (4).

The valedictory continued to seem warranted, moreover, by ongoing developments. In a survey from October of the same year, as part of a regular *Chronicle* feature entitled "What They're Reading on the Campuses," *The Last Whole Earth Catalog* stood promisingly high on the list among best-sellers reported. Also appearing were Charles Reich's *The Greening of America,* Germaine Greer's *The Female Eunuch,* and Dee Brown's *Bury My Heart at Wounded Knee.* On the other hand, equally popular texts included Alvin Toffler's *Future Shock, The Pentagon Papers,* Mike Royko's *Boss,* Charles Silberman's *Crisis in the Classroom, The Sensuous Woman* by "J," and R. F. Delderfield's *God is an Englishman.*

19 Here, in contrast to *Publishers Weekly* figures, the standard guide would remain the volume in the Bowker series entitled *Eighty Years of Best Sellers, 1895–1975,* published in 1977.

20 Corroboration here is supplied by an ingenious variety of samplings of student reading preferences conducted firsthand by one Cal Tech English instructor, Charles Newton, in the early '70s. Dismayed by his students' apathy toward the modernist canon, he tried initially to survey their own out-of-class reading. "'Asimov,'" he remembered them as saying. "'Arthur Clarke, Heinlein, Tolkien'—and a few dozen others" (Newton 337). Next, however, he asked them to survey the dorm and apartment bookshelves of their cohorts. Again, the vast majority of names were familiar: Heinlein, Asimov, Hesse, Tolkien; Clarke, Kafka, Vonnegut, Sartre, Camus. Then came lists of sales leaders in student-oriented bookstores: Brautigan, Clarke, Gibran, Golding, Heinlein, Hesse, Kesey, and Vonnegut. And finally, after a semester in search of a new

curriculum, came new student paper topics in place of the usual Conrad, Hemingway, and Eliot: Vonnegut, Herbert, Asimov, Gibran, Tolkien, Hesse, Heinlein.

Four times Newton had asked a version of a single question about the relation of reading to the spiritual propensities of his students. And four times he had gotten a version of the '60s bookshelf. Just as important, he also seemed to arrive at some personal conclusions consonant with the rhetorical model of the '60s text proposed here on a broader scale. The alternative curriculum his students kept going back to, he discovered, possessed a curiously composite rhetorical appeal. Its texts were simultaneously "literary like" without being literary and current without being ephemeral. Accordingly, they responded in a consistently authentic way to the students' own spiritual attempts to navigate between modernist conceit and trendy cliché. Given their preferences, these readers invariably opted for texts "written as if *man mattered*" (344).

Chapter 3. '60s Texts and '60s Writers

1 Although hardly scientific, one other informal measure of '60s status should be mentioned as proving oddly infallible to the researcher in this respect. Entirely appropriate to the times, it involves the number of libraries from which a text has been stolen.

2 To borrow a description applied to talk show guests, these were figures who were well-known for being well-known. They included some who wrote not at all; some who had things they had written collected; some who wrote single best-sellers or popular classics; and others who wrote a very great deal but were not really much read save perhaps in scholarly texts or in offbrand, fugitive paperbounds now reclaimable from the bookshelves of veterans. Some *just* talked, or sang, or performed, or were quoted, or in some cases managed somehow to *be* themselves long enough to become textual icons in an assumed rhetoric or discourse of the era. Timothy Leary would be a good example of the personified text—so good, in fact, as to be accorded an individual listing below.

3 One could fill pages listing individual textual artifacts of relatively the same status. Various "holy" texts, for example, were in some cases rediscovered and in others newly created: the *I Ching, The Tibetan Book of the Dead,* the *Kamasutra, The Autobiography of a Yogi,* the works of Gurdjieff, Ouspenska, Blavatsky, key texts of Sufi Mysticism, and new translations of the *Upanishads* and the *Vedas.*

Included here also would be a whole galaxy of nontraditional publications categorized under the general heading of journalism, and variously called so within an array of prefixes: "pop" journalism, "rock" journalism, "underground" journalism, "counterculture" journalism, "alternative" journalism, "gonzo" journalism. There was the commercial counterculture press apparatus: *Ms., Rolling Stone, Ramparts, Dissent, Evergreen Magazine, The Village Voice, Scanlan's Monthly,* and *Screw.* There was the thriving underground press network—the *San Francisco Oracle,* the *Berkeley Barb, The Realist,* the Liberation News Service, *New Left Notes,* the *Los Angeles Free Press, The East Village Other* (described by Abe Peck as "the first underground paper to be more Groucho Marx than Karl" [33]), the *Berkeley Tribe,* and the *New York Rat;* there were underground comics (or comix, according to one's preference) featuring R. Crumb's Mr. Natural, Fritz the Cat, Whiteman, Angelfood McSpade, or Gilbert Shelton's The Fabulous Furry Freak Brothers.

Also in this textual arena were a host of freestanding statements, declarations, or manifestos: The SDS Port Huron Statement, Casey Hayden and Mary King's *Sex and Caste,* Valerie Solanis's S.C.U.M. Manifesto, and Annie Koedt's *The Myth of the Vaginal Orgasm.*

Then there was the music scene: events, happenings, classic performances, lyrics, public pronouncements, and texts sometimes engendered by just the simple aura of presence in a name: concerts (Monterey Pop, Woodstock, Altamont); performers (Joan Baez, Janis Joplin, Jimi Hendrix, Peter, Paul, and Mary, Arlo Guthrie, Crosby, Stills, Nash, and Young, Simon and Garfunkel, Bob Dylan, Chubby Checker, Dusty Springfield, and Donovan); and groups (The Beatles, The Rolling Stones, The Doors, The Mamas and the Papas, The Who, The Jefferson Airplane [later Starship], Buffalo Springfield, Creedence Clearwater Revival, Big Brother and the Holding Company, Led Zeppelin, The Kinks, The Animals, The Box Tops, Country Joe and the Fish, Sly and the Family Stone, The Grateful Dead, Moby Grape, The Electric Prunes, Canned Heat, Cream, The Moody Blues, Steppenwolf, Ohio Express, The Lemon Pipers, The Strawberry Alarm Clock, Quicksilver Messenger Service, The Blues Magoos, The Turtles, Santana, and Iron Butterfly).

Finally, working themselves into the textual stew were all the period acronyms—NSA, SDS, LSD, CORE, SNCC, SLA, FBI, CIA, NAACP, ROTC, TM, PCP, est, JFK, LBJ, VVW, NOW, WITCH, and SCUM.

4 Here, as with all the gurus, perfect masters, and other holy ones of the era, the mind dulls with remembered trade names and hip technologies: Esalen, Rolfing, Primal Scream Therapy, TM, est. Purported extensions of the '60s spirit, their common property proved to be a brisk totalitarianism that mirrored rather exactly the conservative backswing of the established culture. See, for instance, Michael Rossman, "Ram Dass, Kali Yuga," in *New Age Blues* (30–37); or Jerome Klinkowitz in *The American 1960s,* describing "the dictatorial fascination exercised by such guru-leaders as Werner Erhard, Arthur Janov, and Richard Alpert/Ram Dass who quiet personal fears of the abyss by offering a tried and true master's way" (18).

5 A 1978 issue in turn yields credit to "The Hanuman Foundation." Of inter-

est here, it also notes sales of the first through twenty-sixth printings at 710,400 copies. A twenty-seventh, in 1984, announces itself with Benjamin-Franklinesque precision as numbering fifteen thousand.

6 Successful spinoffs ensued as well, most notably a movie starring Natalie Wood. Print sequels included *Sex and the Office* (1964), *The Single Girl's Cookbook* (1969), and a lavishly promoted reissue of the original (1970) presumably capitalizing on the new visibility of the women's movement at the turn of the decade. Nor does it now seem coincidence at all that a contemporary, Betty Friedan, in *The Feminine Mystique* (1963), would choose a title sounding like a *Cosmo* cover blurb to launch her own deeply revisionary project. Still, in academic discussions of women's writing Brown's role is usually accorded but a brief, perplexed notation or, as in a recent history of the women's movement, *Born for Liberty,* is simply ignored.

7 So would it also be recognized as the project of Robert Pirsig in *Zen and the Art of Motorcycle Maintenance,* where the author, by applying the spirit of Zen toward the breakdown of a traditional western dialectics of "Classic" and "Romantic" thought, relocates consciousness at its pre-Socratic origins. As will be seen in the case of Brown's counterpart Marcuse, the intellectual synthesis would be similar but achieved—albeit with Marcuse's attempts to downplay the background of Marxist assumption derived from his connections with the Frankfurt School of Theodore Adorno, Walter Benjamin, and others—in the opposing direction.

8 Brown's use of the term "alienated consciousness" here exactly echoes Marx's in the *Economic Political Manuscripts of 1844,* where he talks first about "alienated" labor.

9 We also know now that the title was actually suggested by a colleague on the basis of the work's opening vignette and confirmed by an editor's discovery of an epigraph from Keats—"The sedge is withered from the lake,/and no birds sang."

10 The date frequently assigned to mark the inception of an American critical theory movement is 1966. In this year appeared a special issue of *Yale French Studies* entitled "Structuralism." There also occurred a groundbreaking conference at Johns Hopkins, "The Languages of Criticism and the Sciences of Man." Attendees included Roland Barthes and Jacques Derrida.

11 On the other hand, as with male fantasists of the era such as Kesey or Mailer, Castaneda also earned the antagonism of women. Don Juan's descriptions of his "worlds" were deeply gendered. Of special interest were his distinctions between masculine and feminine versions of the diablero figure, carefully styled the *diablero* and *diablera* according to Spanish usage and heavily differentiated as to power and function (182, 186).

12 Indeed, official controversy would arise as late as the mid '80s over whether Castaneda had falsified "research" and whether "fact" from the outset had been mainly "fiction." On the other hand, as Walter Goldschmidt wrote in his

foreword to the paperback *Don Juan,* one should expect in Castaneda "both ethnography and allegory" (9). To seek one *or* the other, he seemed to suggest, would be largely to miss the point.

13 To some degree, this could be said generally of youth-oracles of the era. Surely visual images and speech acts comprise most people's memories, for instance, of Timothy Leary, Abbie Hoffman, or Jerry Rubin as opposed to the texts of *The Psychedelic Experience, Steal This Book,* or *Do It!* The reason for this, of course, was the increasing dominance in communications of nonprint media.

14 A first paperback appearance was in the intellectual-literary Delta Books series. The smaller, mass-market Dell version quickly followed.

15 So the literary criminal-saint Genet had traveled here to exchange wisdom with the Black Panthers, whose ideology he was said to admire. And until Alexander Solzhenitzyn proved uncomfortably rightist in his antitotalitarian parables, *Ten Days in the Life of Ivan Denisovich, Cancer Ward,* and *The First Circle* had also enjoyed wide '60s readerships.

16 See the multiple references to Fanon, for instance, in the authoritative counter-culture memoirs of both Gitlin and Peck.

17 Simone de Beauvoir's *The Second Sex* had been published in English in 1961. It was well known, but its reading audience was limited to the academic and intellectual communities.

18 I am grateful to Signe Wegener for the phrase "constructing the icon" that so nicely captures the genius of Friedan's rhetorical achievement. On the other hand, even a glance at current women's magazines attests to the endlessness of the project. In 1992, the thirtieth anniversary of the appearance of the earliest portions of Friedan's text in *Mademoiselle, Ladies' Home Journal,* and *McCall's,* the covers of the same magazines advertised titles including, "Your Man Can Have Multiple Orgasms," "The Beauty Decision That Can Change Your Life," "Why Perfect Mothers Make Lousy Lovers," and "The Swimsuit No Man Can Forget."

19 According to the authors of *Woodstock Census,* Gibran was rivaled only by Vonnegut as a popular literary figure. Both were favored by drug users. Gibran was also "preferred by nearly twice as many women (44%) as men (25%)" (74).

20 One remembers, for instance, the debut of Benjamin Franklin's Poor Richard or of the paper trail laid by Irving for the *History of New York.* As to the art of poetry promotions in particular, the forebear to be invoked is surely Walt Whitman. One may recall the unorthodox printing and production methods of the 1855 edition of *Leaves of Grass,* its unusual size and format, the charges of obscenity that greeted it, Whitman's composition of appreciative reviews for newspaper circulation, and his reprinting of Emerson's private praise for the 1855 volume as an 1856 broadside: "I greet you at the beginning of a great career."

21 I am grateful to Jennifer Horne for acquainting me with this publication history. The scandal Ferlinghetti-Ginsberg partisans hoped to create, of course,

would recall that of some years earlier involving another reviled masterpiece, Joyce's *Ulysses*. Whether or not the literary parallel succeeded, the case surely carried much weight in precedental value. There is no question that it enabled the publication and distribution within the decade of two other challenged works, D. H. Lawrence's *Lady Chatterley's Lover* and Henry Miller's *Tropic of Cancer*.

22 He did so only in 1974, however, a full seven years after Sylvia Plath and, with queer irony, Ferlinghetti had gotten there first. Further, he continues to be represented in all anthologies largely by early poems: *Howl*, "A Supermarket in California," and the antiwar polemic "Sunflower Sutra."

23 In retrospect, critics have rightly challenged particular features of his argument, such as Goodman's male-oriented view of alienated youth on the basis of gender patterns of socialization themselves radically in need of change—especially the requirement of "making something of oneself" in the world. Also, Goodman has been accused of romanticizing the Beat style and the image of the juvenile delinquent as new culture-hero. Yet one must still admire his diagnosis of the general social malaise of the era and his ability to communicate a sense of the urgency of present response required.

24 Richard Ohmann's classic essay "The Shaping of a Canon: U.S. Fiction, 1960–75" identifies "the sickness narrative" as the period's major genre. I think it is important to note the emphasis on mental illness in a figure either personally youthful—late-adolescent through college-age and young adult—or identified with the values of youth.

25 In the essay described in note 24, Ohmann finds the text comparable in this respect to Joseph Heller's *Catch-22* and Henry Roth's *Call It Sleep*. It seems a strained conjunction. Heller's text was certainly made visible through academic celebrity and the media attention given to the Mike Nichols film. Roth's text, on the other hand, never approached the sales figures of the other two. More important to the discussion at hand is Ohmann's failure to mention Green's book in his overview of the "illness narrative" as '60s genre, while addressing in addition to those above such analogues as *Portnoy's Complaint, Franny and Zooey, Breakfast of Champions, The Crying of Lot 49*, or *Something Happened*.

26 Although Sylvia Plath's Esther Greenwood surely belongs among such figures, it is hard to know how widely circulated *The Bell Jar* may have been between its 1963 British publication, shortly before Plath's death, and the mid-to-late-'60s surge of interest in her poetry. As noted elsewhere, we do know for certain that U.S. paperback publication of the novel did not occur until 1971.

27 Other writers who attracted significant '60s followings included Frank Herbert, C. S. Lewis, Arthur C. Clarke, Isaac Asimov, Ursula K. LeGuin, and Philip Jose Farmer. It is also important to remember that Kurt Vonnegut, until the mid '60s, was regarded more as a science fiction writer than

a contemporary social satirist. As to actual sales, only Clarke's *2001: A Space Odyssey*—itself, as is often forgotten, a "novelization" of the screenplay for the classic movie (which in turn derived from a Clarke short story entitled "The Sentinel")—approached the Heinlein text as a popular favorite.

28 For anyone familiar with the military, the irony here is especially pronounced. There exists, in print, for the use of all services, just such a code. It is called, without an eyeblink of irony, *The Uniform Code of Military Justice.*

29 Herr used the phrasing in the completed book. He also went on to write the Conradian voiceover narration for Francis Ford Coppola's *Apocalypse Now,* one of the great early films about the war, and he later collaborated on the screenplay for Stanley Kubrick's *Full Metal Jacket.*

30 A good capsule history of the '60s book business among youth as to matters of textual production, promotion, marketing, and distribution could, in fact, be written on the basis of Hesse titles alone. The work of a career extending over decades from the period of World War I, in German and English alone they appeared in a hodgepodge of European, English, and American editions. German originals arrived here often by multiple English translations. (As to other venues, by 1968 *The Journey to the East* had made it, ironically, into Vietnamese.) Then, mainly in the '50s and early '60s, the competition began among American publishers, some avant-garde and literary, such as Noonday and New Directions, others more seriously academic, such as Frederick Ungar. Eventually, the Hesse business attracted the big American houses. Harper & Row published a 1965 edition of *Demian.* Holt, Rinehart and Winston got in with a 1964 *Steppenwolf* and stayed for a 1969 *The Glass Bead Game* (also titled *Magister Ludi*). But the main battle had been joined by two other powers. In 1968, Farrar, Straus & Giroux issued *Beneath the Wheel, Journey to the East,* and *Narcissus and Goldmund.* Shortly, however, Bantam countered with a cheap, uniform paperbound series of varied titles extending into the early '70s: including earlier favorites such as *Demian* and *Siddhartha* and additions such as another *Beneath the Wheel, Magister Ludi* (as noted above, the alternative title of *The Glass Bead Game*), and *Rosshalde.*

31 With Hesse here and elsewhere, as with comparable figures such as Tolkien or Vonnegut, to invoke a single name, title, or phrase is often to trace a pop-culture shadow across the era. *Steppenwolf* became the name of a well-known rock band. *Siddhartha,* of course, was recognized to be the name of the Buddha himself. The name of the devil-god Abraxas in *Demian* was appropriated for a classic album by the group Santana.

32 Or, as will be seen in the case of Dr. Benjamin Spock, a generational copy of yourself in ever new and improved forms.

33 On the other hand, if one looked closely enough at the title page, under the spurious attribution of "Pirate Editions" one could detect the imprint of Grove Press.

34 The other that comes immediately to mind is J. D. Salinger's *The Catcher*

in the Rye. Although set in the '50s but not published until 1963 in England and 1971 in the U.S., Sylvia Plath's *The Bell Jar* would, in theme and spirit, suggest a third.

35 Also in this role, to note yet another literary extension, he becomes the model of the burnt-out guru, Dieter, in Robert Stone's *Dog Soldiers,* one of the most searing depictions of a drug-ridden post-'60s and post–Vietnam America.

36 Mainly autobiographical narrative and essay, these works would include Kesey's *Garage Sale, Demon Box,* and *The Further Inquiry.* A new novel, *Sailor Song,* appeared in mid 1992.

37 In addition to the manic performances of figures such as Abbie Hoffman and Jerry Rubin in *Revolution for the Hell of It* or *Do It!* (see entries for these authors), the only other attempt by a contemporary to address the youth-scene was Mark Gerzon's soberly analytic and discursive 1969 volume, *The Whole World Is Watching: A Young Man Looks at Youth's Dissent.* As for inside documentary, one had to settle for two rather melodramatic 1968 offerings, Nicholas von Hoffman's *We Are the People Our Parents Warned Us Against* and Lewis Yablonsky's *The Hippie Trip.*

38 Albeit not directly relevant to the present discussion, technically interesting is the relationship of Laing's speculations to the contemporary work of Michel Foucault, particularly in his classic *Madness and Civilization,* where he like-wise posited on one hand a madness once visionary, magical, perhaps even holy—a discourse of the other—and on the other a pathology, increasingly consigned in post-Enlightenment culture by an authoritarian, imperial Rea-son fearing the power of its upheaving, chaotic, subversive otherness to the silences and imprisonments of the culture of the institution. This was clearly the direction of Laing's thought as well.

39 Indeed, exemplary of Laing's "place" among such a visionary lot is the cover design of the paperbound *Politics of Experience* by which he was most likely known to late '60s readers: a mystic inner eye on a field of black space is surrounded by a circular collage of images ranging from mystic Oriental to Renaissance and pop, something like a crossing, one gets the feeling, between a Mandala and the cover of a late-'60s Beatles album.

40 This may constitute Leary's permanent claim to textual celebrity, according to the one measure (see note 1) that proves infallible with any real icon of '60s reading and writing. Along with *Do It!* and *Steal This Book* and per-haps a very few others—*One Flew Over the Cuckoo's Nest, Soul on Ice, The Whole Earth Catalog,* and *Radical Feminism*—it is invariably listed in libraries as "missing."

41 The title of Kurt Vonnegut's well-known essay, "Why They Read Hesse," captures exactly my point about such communal reading sensibilities on the part of the youth-culture and explains why both Vonnegut and Hesse achieved the kind of scriptural status denied to Mailer. It is clear that the proper name invoked refers *not* to an author but to a body of text.

42 Such also, one might add, would be the fate of Mailer's truly brilliant topical novel of the era, *Why Are We in Vietnam?,* amidst the increasingly vast body of literary response to the experience of the war. Like *The Armies of the Night,* it continues to stand as a structural tour de force—an astonishing authorial performance *and* a definitive pronouncement on the subject. Particularly ingenious is the fictional narrative's "voice of America" conceit, devised through the doubled discourses of D.J., scion of a gun-nut Texas magnate, and deejay, a crippled genius in Brooklyn. Here, Mailer truly tried to ask the decade's big question through a novel that is a broadcast, a mass-media assault coming through on all channels at once. Only on the last page of the novel is the war itself finally, quite stunningly, mentioned. "We're off to see the Wizard," shout D.J. and his hunting buddy, Rusty. "Vietnam, hot damn." The genius of the structure, on the other hand, had to be measured also by the final ideological irrelevance to a '60s youth-audience of the rhetorical product.

Furthermore, this sense of Mailer's rhetorical irrelevance to the generation of youth would also be confirmed by the drift of his public personality. He had been noted for years as being susceptible to unfortunate confusions of himself with characters in his writing. During the late '60s and early '70s especially, such manifestations of this including his increasing truculence in the gender wars and his quixotic political adventures contributed to his nearly total alienation from the youth-constituency of '60s reading and writing. Why they read Hesse, Vonnegut, and Castaneda turned out to be exactly why they lost textual interest in Mailer. The audience wanted the existential personality as defined by the texts and not the reverse.

43 Moreover, in ways unforeseen during the late '50s to mid '60s when such major texts appeared, such an irrational response would eventually be reinforced at the turn of a new decade when Marcuse would gain brief media notoriety as Angela Davis's research advisor and intellectual mentor.

44 In a current phrasing, this would come close to the idea of hegemonics, the study of the way in which all dominant cultures—both ostensibly "free," "egalitarian," or "democratic" or otherwise—enforce transcendental master-narratives as forms of social control.

45 At the same time, for a reader familiar with de Beauvoir's *The Second Sex,* one could see distinct structural similarities. Book 1 of de Beauvoir's text, "Facts and Myths," contained sections on Destiny, History, and Myths. Book 2 on "Women's Life Today" continued with sections entitled "Formative Years," "Situation," "Justifications," and "Toward Liberation." There was then a concluding section on "Woman as Myth" addressing specifically "The Myth of Woman in Five Authors"—Motherlandt, Lawrence, Claudel, Breton, and Stendhal.

46 In books and essays on innumerable topics, he was a brilliant analyst. On the technologies of nuclear proliferation, for instance, he wrote, "the immediate cause of World War III is the preparation of it" (59).

47 This philosophical moment also comes close, one finds, to a *scientific* position that we would now call Heisenbergian, uniting an old philosophical problem of subject and object in a new quantum arrangement of relationship, a complete reciprocity, yet tending in any observational moment to total destabilization.

48 Plath actually had such a sponsor, Olive Higgins Prouty, author of *Stella Dallas*.

49 In retrospect, one suspects that Pynchon's subsequent masterwork of cosmic techno-paranoia, *Gravity's Rainbow,* put the demographic problem in reverse. Issued simultaneously in hardcover and paperback, it achieved substantial sales. Its expanse and tremendous technical difficulty, on the other hand, consigned it from the outset to the status of recondite pursuit.

50 Credit for the over-thirty version of the line, much more widely quoted, goes to Jack Weinberg during the Berkeley Free Speech Movement.

51 In retrospect, it should probably not surprise anyone that the '60s Rubin had his own version of "Turn on, tune in, and drop out." According to Allen Matusow, the Rubin-gospel went "Tune In, Drop Out—Take Over" (276).

52 Sadly, it would also make a last, dreadful iconic appearance in the entertainment news as the '60s and '70s most fully started coming down. The assassin of John Lennon, a youthful worshipper of the eccentric, increasingly reclusive celebrity, when he was led away by police was found to have been carrying a copy.

53 On reviewing any complete text, one is astonished at how relentlessly "technical" a book it really is. In the 1946 edition, indeed, only the first few of the 507 pages of text—"A Letter to the Mother and Father" and, under the first topical heading, "Preparing for the Baby," a three-paragraph pep talk entitled "Trust Yourself"—might be considered within the purview of philosophy or moral psychology. The book then plunges directly in the same section into "Things You'll Need" and "Help and Medical Care" and speeds on to "The Right Start," "Breast Feeding," "Bottle Feeding," "Adding Vitamins and Water," "Daily Care," and the plethora of advice, instruction, and practical detail that made it perhaps the most widely used technical manual in human history. The "baby book" become the Baby Bible as a source of quite infallible practical knowledge. To be sure, even at this stage, Spock's discussion is inevitably forced to contemplate what might be called developmental issues of growth, social attitude, and acculturation. Yet even here one notes how slight a portion of the text such considerations actually occupy. Infant issues of development are essentially covered in a section with the quite businesslike heading, "Managing Young Children." Those associated with ages three to six, six to eleven, and puberty receive roughly ten pages each. A chapter entitled "Problems of Feeding and Development" concerns itself with largely technical nutritional and medical issues as do subsequent long sections on "Illness," "First Aid," and "Special Problems."

Further, in the 1957, 1968, and 1986 editions, the preponderance of practical information does not significantly vary. There is some increased interest in developmental, social, moral, and cultural issues, but this is much outweighed by response to changes in technology.

54 On the other hand, it should be noted, impossible expectation was a two-way street. Parents may have expected much of the young in terms of the latter's new potentialities. The young in turn looked back in tremendous admiration to the generation of World War II and the new era of human possibility it seemed to have introduced to the world.

55 At the same time, 1993 has produced two competing biographies of the aging gonzo superstar, each claiming to capture most fully what one calls "the strange and savage life of Hunter S. Thompson."

56 Conscientious mentors would also make the historical link, of course, between "transcendental" and "transcendentalist," linking Thoreau to Emerson or to his kindred proto-hippie, Whitman.

57 Thoreau's injunction was explicit: "I would not have any one adopt *my* mode of living on any account; for, beside that before he has fairly learned it I may have found out another for myself, I desire that there may be as many different persons in the world as possible; but I would have each one be very careful to find out and pursue *his own* way, and not his father's or his mother's or his neighbor's instead" (53).

58 In the real dimension of experience, he likewise remained significantly uncorrupted: he died in relative youth chronologically, uncompromised, celibate— in something still close to prepubescent innocence.

59 Published in three volumes separately entitled *The Fellowship of the Ring, The Two Towers,* and *The Return of the King,* the work has ordinarily been referred to as a trilogy. Tolkien, on the other hand, as frequently cited in the critical literature, always considered it a single text.

60 As that story went, the obscure, fanciful, earnest scholar, himself a 1916 veteran of the western front, had started out to allegorize a world of war newly on the eve of global conflict and somehow wrote out that desperate, apocalyptic conflict through the tales unfolding themselves into his corporate master-text. A publication account, on the other hand, tends to bear out the larger thesis proposed here of "production." *The Hobbit,* for instance, first saw publication in England in 1937 and a year later in America. Although Tolkien discounted the importance of the darkening portents of world conflagration of his own era, surely the work, to the extent it was read at the time, was taken to allegorize that very thing. Similarly, although Tolkien saw *The Lord of the Rings* as a continuous text, installments in the "trilogy"—albeit again in toto a seeming allegory in many ways of what had turned out to be the actual catastrophe of the times and apparently written between 1937 and 1949 (Carpenter 266) during the darkest of those times—appeared after the war in serial sequence, with *The Fellowship of the Ring* appearing in 1954, *The Two Towers* in 1955,

and *The Return of the King* in 1956. (In England, the first two were released in 1954 and the last in 1955 [Carpenter 266] presumably, it is most often claimed, because one massive, continuous text might make for poor sales.) Until the turn of the decade, all of the books enjoyed a cultish admiration but remained the province mainly of aficionados, the eccentric pursuit of an odd coterie, numbering among them not surprisingly an older C. S. Lewis crowd and also academic medievalists who knew Tolkien as a scholar who wrote fantasy as an arcane avocation. Shortly, however, in the early '60s, the word began to spread. Just before mid decade, Ace Books came out with an unauthorized American paperback edition. This was followed quickly by a Tolkien-approved Ballantine version. The cult was expanded into a craze. Eventually, the covers of successive printings themselves became copyright billboards and bookkeeping tally sheets, announcing themselves as fully "authorized," listing dates of old editions surpassed, retotaling numbers of new copies sold (in the same vein as the signs once used by McDonald's). In 1977, the much heralded collection of early writings, *The Silmarillion*—begun in 1917 during the author's post-western front convalescence as "The Book of Lost Tales" (Carpenter 265) and edited by his medievalist son Christopher—was offered as a "prequel" setting much of the established work in an even more detailed context. As late as the centenary of the author's birth, there had been no letup. News stories and advertisements noted the appearance of a new, illustrated edition of *The Lord of the Rings* at last in the single-tome format preferred by Tolkien himself. Another Sunday supplement survey notes the "trilogy" as fifth on the list of those mentioned by readers as most influential in their lives, just behind The Bible, *Atlas Shrugged, The Road Less Traveled,* and *To Kill a Mockingbird* and just ahead of *Gone With the Wind, How to Win Friends and Influence People,* and *The Book of Mormon.*

61 The '80s and the '90s, one is pleased to say, have witnessed the return of Kurt Vonnegut (he dropped the *Jr.* in 1976). He has once again gained popular and academic attention as Kurt Vonnegut, the author of *Galapagos* (1985), *Bluebeard* (1987), and *Hocus Pocus* (1990). The last, especially, returns to many of his classic themes and narrative ingenuities. The text spills out a domestic inventory of new American fraudulences and absurdities while returning us forcefully in particular to the cultural memory of Vietnam. A recent autobiographical collection is entitled *Fates Worse Than Death* (1991).

62 In its dreadful candor about its youth-protagonist, as disturbing as he is disturbed, it is perhaps most reminiscent of an analogous cult book of the era, Frederick Exley's *A Fan's Notes.*

63 The latter widely circulated phrase comes from John Barth, who would also claim for self-conscious fiction new possibilities as a "literature of replenishment." Wolfe, on the other hand, has made no such peace, celebrating the publication of his own teeming novel of manners, *The Bonfire of the Vanities,*

with a manifesto on behalf of social realism, "Stalking the Billion-Footed Beast," published in the November 1989 *Harper's*.

Chapter 4. Postscripts and Summations

1 Viorst's, it should be noted, most closely reconciles chronicle and analysis, giving the work more documentary than critical focus. On the other hand, for the real brilliance of the more purely analytic sophistication offered in moments by Roszak and Dickstein, their studies may remain more persuasive as intellectual fiction than as actual cultural critique. How many '60s people really made the kinds of syntheses that Roszak elegantly constructs? How many people felt the passion of Blakean epiphany summoned up by Dickstein's "Eyes of Fire"?

2 As impromptu glosses on much of what I have attempted here, Klinkowitz's eight chapter headings alone give some sense of the richness of his extremely brief study: "Kennedy and Nixon: Images as Fictions"; "McMurphy and Yossarian as Politicians"; "Frank O'Hara and Richard Brautigan: Personal Poetry"; "Kurt Vonnegut and Donald Barthelme: The American Image"; "James Kunen, Dotson Rader, and Hunter S. Thompson: The Art of Protest"; "Vietnam"; "Bob Dylan and Neil Young: The Song of Self"; "The Sixties Aesthetic."

3 This, one must admit, seems, if anything, more persuasive a concept today than ever—not so much about current "youth," perhaps, as about '60s "youth" still unwilling to grow up in many of the ways it resisted two and three decades ago. To borrow Charles Reich's coinage, for many '60s people "Consciousness III" proves handsomely resistant to age.

Bibliography

Abbott, Keith. *Downstream from* Trout Fishing in America. Santa Barbara, Calif.: Capra Press, 1989.

Albert, Judith Clavir, and Steward Edward Albert. *The Sixties Papers: Documents of a Rebellious Decade.* New York: Praeger, 1984.

Aldredge, John W. *"Catch-22* Twenty-Five Years Later." *Michigan Quarterly Review* 26, 2 (Spring 1987): 379–86.

Alpert, Richard [Baba Ram Dass]. "Anxiety in Academic Measurement Situations: Its Measurement and Relation to Aptitude." Ph.D. diss., Stanford University, 1957.

———. *Be Here Now, Remember.* New York: Crown, 1971.

———. *The Only Dance There Is.* Garden City, N.Y.: Anchor, 1974.

Alpert, Richard [Baba Ram Dass], and Sidney Cohen. *LSD.* New York: New American Library, 1966.

Anonymous. *Go Ask Alice.* Englewood Cliffs, N.J.: Prentice-Hall, 1971; New York: Avon, 1972.

Archer, Jules. *The Incredible Sixties: The Stormy Years that Changed America.* New York: Harcourt Brace Jovanovich, 1986.

Atwan, Robert, Barry Ortman, and William Vesterman, eds. *American Media: Industries and Issues.* New York: Random House, 1978.

Baldwin, James. *The Fire Next Time.* New York: Dial Press, 1963.

Blake, William. *Complete Writings.* Ed. Geoffrey Keynes. London: Oxford University Press, 1966.

Benét, Stephen Vincent. *Ballads and Poems, 1915–1930.* New York: Doubleday, Doran & Co., 1931.

Bonn, Thomas L. *Undercover: An Illustrated History of Mass Market Paperbacks.* New York: Penguin, 1982.

Boorstin, Daniel. *The Discoverers.* New York: Random House, 1983.

Boston Women's Health Book Collective. *Our Bodies, Ourselves.* New York: Simon and Schuster, 1973; Revised and Expanded, 1975.

———. *Ourselves and Our Children.* New York: Random House, 1978.

Bradbury, Malcolm. *The Modern American Novel.* New York: Oxford University Press, 1983.

Brautigan, Richard. *Trout Fishing in America.* San Francisco: Four Seasons Foundation, 1967; New York: Delta, c1967.

Brooks, Paul, ed. *The House of Life: Rachel Carson at Work.* Boston: Houghton Mifflin, 1972.

Brown, Claude. *Manchild in the Promised Land.* New York: Macmillan, 1965.

Brown, Dee. *Bury My Heart at Wounded Knee.* New York: Bantam, 1970.

Brown, Helen Gurley. *Sex and the Single Girl.* New York: Bernard Geis Associates, 1962.

Brown, Norman O. *Life Against Death: The Psychoanalytical Meaning of History*.
    Middletown, Conn.: Wesleyan University Press, 1959; New York:
    Vintage, 1959.
Brustein, Norman. Rev. of *Catch-22*. *New Republic* (November 13, 1961). 11.
Carpenter, Humphry. *Tolkien: A Biography*. Boston: Houghton-Mifflin, 1977.
Carson, Rachel. *Silent Spring*. Boston: Houghton Mifflin, 1962.
Casale, Anthony M., and Philip Lerman, eds. *Where Have All the Flowers Gone?*
    The Fall and Rise of the Woodstock Generation. Kansas City, Mo.: Andrews and
    McMeel, 1989.
Castaneda, Carlos. *The Teachings of Don Juan: A Yaqui Way of Knowledge*.
    Berkeley: University of California Press, 1968; New York: Ballantine
    Books, 1969.
Clareson, Thomas D. *Understanding Contemporary Science Fiction*. Columbia:
    University of South Carolina Press, 1990.
Clarke, Arthur C. *Childhood's End*. New York: Ballantine Books, 1953.
Cleaver, Eldridge. *Soul on Ice*. New York: McGraw Hill, 1967; New York:
    Dell, 1968.
Collier, Peter, and David Horowitz. *Destructive Generation: Second Thoughts*
    about the '60s. New York: Summit Books, 1989.
———, eds. *Second Thoughts: Former Radicals Look Back at the Sixties*. New
    York: Madison Books, 1989.
Cook, Bruce. *The Beat Generation*. New York: Scribner's, 1971.
Davidson, Cathy N. *Revolution and the Word*. New York: Oxford University
    Press, 1986.
Davidson, Sara. *Loose Change: Three Women of the Sixties*. Garden City, N.Y.:
    Doubleday, 1977.
Davis, Kenneth C. *Two-Bit Culture: The Paperbacking of America*. Boston:
    Houghton Mifflin, 1984.
de Beauvoir, Simone. *The Second Sex*. New York: Knopf, 1957.
de Loria, Vine. *Custer Died for Your Sins*. New York: Macmillan, 1969.
Dickson, Paul. *Timelines*. New York: Addison-Wesley, 1990.
Dickstein, Morris. *The Gates of Eden: American Culture in the Sixties*. New York:
    Basic Books, 1977.
Didion, Joan. *Play It As It Lays*. New York: Farrar, Straus & Giroux, 1970.
———. *Slouching towards Bethlehem*. New York: Touchstone, 1979.
———. *The White Album*. New York: Pocket Books, 1979.
Dillard, Annie. *Pilgrim at Tinker Creek*. New York: Harper's Magazine
    Press, 1974.
Eddins, Dwight. *The Gnostic Pynchon*. Bloomington: Indiana University
    Press, 1990.
Emerson, Ralph Waldo. *Selections from Ralph Waldo Emerson*. Ed. Stephen E.
    Whicher. Cambridge, Mass.: Riverside Press, 1957.
Evans, Sara M. *Born for Liberty*. New York: Free Press, 1989.

Exley, Frederick. *A Fan's Notes.* New York: Harper & Row, 1968.

Fanon, Frantz. *The Wretched of the Earth.* Preface by Jean Paul Sartre; trans. Constance Farrington. New York: Grove Press, 1966.

Fariña, Richard. *Been Down So Long It Looks Like Up to Me.* New York: Random House, 1965; New York: Dell, 1966.

Ferlinghetti, Lawrence. *A Coney Island of the Mind.* New York: New Directions, 1958.

Fetterley, Judith. *The Resisting Reader.* Bloomington: Indiana University Press, 1978.

Fiedler, Leslie. Afterword to *The Innocents Abroad,* by Mark Twain. New York: New American Library, 1966.

———. "The New Mutants" in *The Oxford Reader.* Ed. Frank Kermode and Richard Poirier. New York: Oxford University Press, 1971.

Fitzgerald, Frances. *Fire in the Lake: The Vietnamese and the Americans in Vietnam.* New York: Random House, 1972.

Flesch, Rudolf. *Why Johnny Can't Read, And What You Can Do About It.* New York: Harper & Brothers, 1956.

Foucault, Michel. *The Order of Things.* New York: Vintage, 1973.

Friedan, Betty. *The Feminine Mystique.* New York: Norton, 1963; New York: Dell, 1974.

Friedman, Melvin J. "To 'Make it New': The American Novel Since 1945." *Wilson Quarterly* (Winter 1978): 133–42.

Furlong, Monica. *Genuine Fake: A Biography of Alan Watts.* London: Heineman, 1986.

Gerzon, Mark. *The Whole World Is Watching: A Young Man Looks at Youth's Dissent.* New York: Viking, 1969.

Gibran, Kahlil. *The Prophet.* New York: Knopf, 1923.

Giddings, Robert, ed. *J. R. R. Tolkien: This Far Land.* Towata, N.J.: Barnes & Noble, 1984.

Ginsberg, Allen. *Howl and Other Poems.* San Francisco: City Lights Press, 1956.

Gitlin, Todd. *The Sixties: Years of Hope, Days of Rage.* New York: Bantam Books, 1987; rev. ed., 1993.

Golding, William. *The Lord of the Flies.* New York: Capricorn Books, 1959; New York: Coward, McCann, 1962; New York: Perigee, c1954.

Goodman, Paul. *Growing Up Absurd: Problems of Youth in the Organized System.* New York: Random House, 1960.

Gottlieb, Annie. *Do You Believe in Magic?: The Second Coming of the Sixties Generation.* New York: Times Books, 1987.

Green, Hannah [Joanne Greenburg]. *I Never Promised You a Rose Garden.* New York: Holt, Rinehart and Winston, 1964.

Greene, Bob. *Be True to Your School.* New York: Atheneum, 1987.

Greer, Germaine. *The Female Eunuch.* New York: McGraw-Hill, 1971; New York: Bantam Books, 1972.

Hackett, Alice Payne, and James Henry Burke. *Eighty Years of Best Sellers, 1895–1975.* New York: Bowker, 1977.

Harrington, Michael. *The Other America: Poverty in the United States.* New York: Macmillan, 1964.

Haskins, James, and Kathleen Benson. *The 60s Reader.* New York: Viking Kestrel, 1988.

Hassan, Ihab. *Radical Innocence: Studies in the American Contemporary Novel.* Princeton, N.J.: Princeton University Press, 1961.

Hawke, David Freeman. *Everyday Life in Early America.* New York: Harper & Row, 1988.

Hawkins, Harriett. *Classics and Trash: Traditions and Taboos in High Literature and Popular Modern Genres.* New York: Harvester/Wheatsheaf, 1990.

Hayes, Harold, ed. *Smiling Through the Apocalypse: Esquire's History of the Sixties.* New York: Crown Publishers, 1987.

Heinlein, Robert A. *Stranger in a Strange Land.* New York: Putnam, 1961; New York: Berkley Books, 1981.

Heller, Joseph. *Catch-22.* New York: Simon and Schuster, 1961; New York: Dell, 1962.

Hendin, Josephine. *Vulnerable People: A View of American Fiction since 1945.* New York: Oxford University Press, 1978.

Herr, Michael. *Dispatches.* New York: Knopf, 1977.

——— . "Hell Sucks." *Esquire* 70 (August 1968): 66–69+.

——— . "High on War." *Esquire* 87 (January 1977): 82–88+.

——— . "Khesanh." *Esquire* 72 (September 1969): 118–23+.

——— . "War Correspondent: A Re-Appraisal." *Esquire* 73 (April 1970): 95–101.

Hesse, Hermann. *Siddhartha.* New York: New Directions, 1957.

——— . *Steppenwolf.* New York: F. Ungar, 1957.

Hirsch, E. D. *Cultural Literacy.* Boston: Houghton Mifflin, 1987.

Hoffman, Abbie. *Revolution for the Hell of It.* New York: Dial Press, 1968.

——— . *Steal This Book.* New York: Pirate Editions, 1971.

Howard, Gerald, ed. *The Sixties: The Art, Attitudes, and Media of Our Most Explosive Decade.* New York: Pocket Books, 1982.

Johnson, Paul. *Modern Times.* New York: Harper & Row, 1983.

Joseph, Peter, ed. *Good Times: An Oral History of America in the Nineteen Sixties.* New York: William Morrow, 1974.

Karl, Frederick R. *American Fictions 1940/1980: A Comprehensive History and Critical Evaluation.* New York: Harper & Row, 1983.

Kazin, Alfred. *Bright Book of Life.* Boston: Little, Brown, 1973.

Kearns, Godfrey A. "United States of America." In *Literature of Europe and America in the 1960s.* Ed. Spencer Pearce and Don Piper. Manchester: Manchester University Press, 1988.

Keniston, Kenneth. *The Uncommitted: Alienated Youth in American Society.* New York: Harcourt Brace, 1965.

———. *Young Radicals: Notes on Committed Youth.* New York: Harcourt Brace and World, 1968.

———. *Youth and Dissent: the Rise of a New Opposition.* New York: Harcourt, Brace, Jovanovich, 1971.

Kerouac, Jack. *On the Road.* New York: Viking, 1957; New York: Signet, 1958.

Kesey, Ken. *One Flew Over the Cuckoo's Nest.* New York: Viking, 1962; New York: Signet, 1962.

———. *Sometimes a Great Notion.* New York: Viking, 1964.

Kessler, Lauren. *After All These Years: Sixties Ideals in a Different World.* New York: Thunder's Mouth Press, 1990.

King, Martin Luther, Jr. "Letter from the Birmingham Jail." *Why We Can't Wait.* New York: Harper and Row, 1963.

Klinkowitz, Jerome. *The American 1960s.* Ames: Iowa State University Press, 1980.

———. *Structuring the Void.* Durham, N.C.: Duke University Press, 1992.

Knowles, John. *A Separate Peace.* New York: Dell, 1961.

Koedt, Anne, ed. *Radical Feminism.* New York: Quadrangle, 1973.

Kostelanetz, Richard. *The End of Intelligent Writing: Literary Politics in America.* New York: Sheed and Ward, 1973.

Kuhn, Thomas S. *The Structure of Scientific Resolutions.* Chicago: University of Chicago Press, 1970.

Kunen, James Simon. *The Strawberry Statement: Notes of a College Revolutionary.* New York: Random House, 1969.

Laing, R. D. *The Divided Self.* New York: Pantheon, 1969.

———. *The Politics of Experience.* New York: Pantheon, 1967; New York: Ballantine Books, 1967.

Larkin, Jack. *The Reshaping of Everyday Life, 1790–1840.* New York: Harper & Row, 1988.

Lasch, Christopher. *The Culture of Narcissism: American Life in an Age of Diminishing Expectations.* New York: Norton, 1978.

Lazere, Donald. "Literature and Mass Media: The Political Implications." In *Reading in America.* Ed. Cathy N. Davidson. Baltimore: Johns Hopkins University Press, 1989.

Leary, Timothy. *High Priest.* New York: College Notes and Texts, 1968.

———. *Jail Notes.* New York: Douglas BookCorp, 1968.

———. *The Politics of Ecstasy.* New York: Putnam, 1968.

Leary, Timothy, Ralph Metzner, and Richard Alpert. *The Psychedelic Experience: A Manual Based on the Tibetan Book of the Dead.* New Hyde Park, N.Y.: University Books, 1964.

Leary, Timothy. Introduction to *LSD,* by David Solomon and Timothy Leary. New York: Putnam, 1966.

Leitch, Vincent B. *American Literary Criticism from the 30s to the 80s*. New York: Columbia University Press, 1986.

Mailer, Norman. *Advertisements for Myself*. New York: G. P. Putnam, 1959.

———. *The Armies of the Night*. New York: New American Library, 1968.

———. *Cannibals and Christians*. New York: Dial Press, 1966.

———. *Why Are We in Vietnam?* New York: Putnam, 1967.

Makower, Joel. *Woodstock: The Oral History*. New York: Doubleday, 1989.

Malcolm X, with Alex Haley. *The Autobiography of Malcolm X*. New York: Grove Press, 1965.

Maloff, Saul. "Waiting for the Voice to Crack." *New Republic* (May 8 1971): 33–35.

Manchester, William. *A World Lit Only by Fire*. Boston: Little, Brown, 1992.

Marcus, Greil. *Lipstick Traces: A Secret History of the Twentieth Century*. Cambridge: Harvard University Press, 1989.

Marcuse, Herbert. *Eros and Civilization: A Philosophical Inquiry Into Freud*. Boston: Beacon Press, 1956.

———. *One-Dimensional Man*. Boston: Beacon Press, 1964.

Matusow, Allen J. *The Unravelling of America*. New York: Harper & Row, 1984.

McCaffery, Larry, ed. *Postmodern Fiction*. New York: Greenwood Press, 1986.

McLuhan, Marshall. *Understanding Media*. New York: Signet, 1964.

Miller, Douglas T., and Marion Nowak. *The Fifties: The Way We Really Were*. Garden City, N.Y.: Doubleday, 1977.

Miller, James. *"Democracy is in the Streets": From Port Huron to the Siege of Chicago*. New York: Simon & Schuster, 1987.

Millett, Kate. *Sexual Politics*. Garden City, N.Y.: Doubleday, 1970.

Mills, C. Wright. *The Causes of World War III*. New York: Oxford University Press, 1958.

———. *The Power Elite*. New York: Oxford University Press, 1956.

———. *White Collar*. New York: Oxford University Press, 1951; New York: Oxford/Galaxy, 1956.

Morgan, Robin, ed. *Sisterhood Is Powerful*. New York: Random House, 1970; New York: Vintage Books, 1970.

Morrison, Joan, and Robert K. Morrison. *From Camelot to Kent State: The Sixties Experience in the Words of Those Who Lived It*. New York: Times Books, 1987.

Mott, Frank Luther. *Golden Multitudes: The Story of Best Sellers in the United States*. New York: Macmillan, 1947.

Newton, Charles. "Underground Man, Go Home." *College English* 37 (December 1975): 337–44.

O'Brien, Geoffrey. *Dream Time: Chapters from the Sixties*. New York: Viking, 1988.

Ohmann, Richard. "The Shaping of a Canon: U.S. Fiction, 1960–75." In *Canons*. Ed. Robert von Hallberg. Chicago: University of Chicago Press, 1984, 377–401.

Olderman, Raymond M. *Beyond the Waste Land: A Study of the American Novel in the Nineteen-Sixties*. New Haven, Conn.: Yale University Press, 1972.

O'Neil, Doris C. *Life: The 60s*. Boston: Little, Brown, 1989.

Panati, Charles. *Panati's Parade of Fads, Follies, and Manias*. New York: Harper Collins, 1991.

Peck, Abe. *Uncovering the Sixties: The Life and Times of the Underground Press*. New York: Pantheon, 1985.

Pirsig, Robert. *Zen and the Art of Motorcycle Maintenance*. New York: William Morrow, 1974.

Plath, Sylvia. *Ariel*. London: Faber & Faber, 1965; New York: Harper & Row, 1966.

———. *The Bell Jar*. London: Heinemann, 1963; New York: Harper & Row, 1971; New York: Bantam, 1972.

Portola Institute. *The Last Whole Earth Catalog*. Menlo Park, Calif.: Random House, 1971.

Postman, Neil. *Amusing Ourselves to Death*. New York: Penguin, 1986.

Pynchon, Thomas. *The Crying of Lot 49*. Philadelphia: Lippincott, 1966; New York: Harper & Row, 1986.

———. *Gravity's Rainbow*. New York: Viking, 1973.

Reich, Charles. *The Greening of America*. New York: Random House, 1970; New York: Bantam, 1971.

Rossman, Michael. *New Age Blues*. New York: E. P. Dutton, 1979.

Roszak, Theodore. *The Making of a Counter-Culture*. Garden City, N.Y.: Doubleday, 1969.

Rubin, Jerry. *Do It!: Scenarios of the Revolution*. New York: Simon & Schuster, 1970.

Rubin, Joan Shelley. *The Making of Middlebrow Culture*. Chapel Hill: University of North Carolina Press, 1992.

Said, Edward. *Orientalism*. New York: Pantheon, 1978.

Salinger, J. D. *The Catcher in the Rye*. Boston: Little, Brown, 1951; New York: Signet, 1953; New York: Bantam, 1964.

———. *Franny and Zooey*. Boston: Little, Brown, 1961.

———. *Nine Stories*. Boston: Little, Brown, 1953; New York: Bantam, 1954.

———. *Raise High the Roof-Beam, Carpenters; and Seymour: An Introduction*. Boston: Little, Brown, 1963.

Sann, Paul. *The Angry Decade: The Sixties*. New York: Crown Publishers, 1979.

Seales, Baird, Martin Last, Beth Meacham, and Michael Franklin. *A Reader's Guide to Science Fiction*. New York: Facts on File, 1980.

Sheils, Merrill. "Why Johnny Can't Write." *Newsweek* 86 (December 8, 1975): 58–62, 65.

Shi, David E. *The Simple Life: Plain Living and High Thinking in American Culture*. New York: Oxford University Press, 1985.

————, ed. *In Search of the Simple Life.* Salt Lake City, Utah: Peregrine Smith Books, 1986.

Skinner, B. F. *Walden Two.* New York: Macmillan, 1962.

Slater, Philip. *The Pursuit of Loneliness.* Boston: Beacon Press, 1970.

Smith, Larry. "Lawrence Ferlinghetti," in *The Beats: Literary Bohemians in Postwar America.* Ed. Ann Charters. New York: Gale Research, 1982.

Solatoroff, Theodore. *The Red Hot Vacuum and Other Pieces of Writing on the Sixties.* New York: Atheneum, 1970.

Spock, Benjamin. *The Common Sense Book of Baby and Child Care.* New York: Duell, Sloan and Pearce, 1946; revised, *Baby and Child Care.* New York: Hawthorn, 1968; revised, *Dr. Spock's Baby and Child Care.* New York: Pocket Books, 1989.

Stein, Gertrude. *Lectures in America.* New York: Random House, 1935.

Steiner, George. "Books in an Age of Post-Literacy." *Publishers Weekly* 227 (May 24, 1985): 44–48.

Stern, Jane, and Michael Stern. *The Encyclopedia of Bad Taste.* New York: Harper Collins, 1990.

————. *Sixties People.* New York: Knopf, 1990.

Tanner, Tony. *City of Words: American Fiction 1950–1970.* New York: Harper & Row, 1971.

Thompson, Hunter S. *Fear and Loathing in Las Vegas.* New York: Random House, 1971; New York: Warner, 1971.

————. *Fear and Loathing on the Campaign Trail.* San Francisco: Straight Arrow Books, 1973; New York: Popular Library, 1973.

————. *The Great Shark Hunt.* New York: Fawcett, 1979.

————. *Hell's Angels.* New York: Random House, 1967; New York: Ballantine, 1967.

Thoreau, Henry David. *Walden.* New York: Norton, 1968.

————. *Walden and Civil Disobedience.* New York: Signet, 1960.

Tolkien, J. R. R. *The Fellowship of the Ring.* Boston: Houghton Mifflin, 1965; New York: Ballantine, 1965.

————. *The Hobbit.* Boston: Houghton Mifflin, 1966; New York: Ballantine, 1966.

————. *The Return of the King.* Boston: Houghton Mifflin, 1965; New York: Ballantine, 1965.

————. *The Two Towers.* Boston: Houghton Mifflin, 1965; New York: Ballantine, 1965.

Trudeau, G. B. *The Doonesbury Chronicles.* New York: Holt, Rinehart and Winston, 1975.

Twitchell, James B. *Carnival Culture: The Trashing of Taste in America.* New York: Columbia University Press, 1992.

Urdan, Laurence, ed. *The Timetables of American History.* New York: Simon & Schuster, 1981.

Viorst, Milton. *Fire in the Streets: America in the 1960s*. New York: Simon & Schuster, 1979.

von Hoffman, Nicholas. *We Are the People Our Parents Warned Us Against*. Chicago: Quadrangle Books, 1968.

Vonnegut, Kurt, Jr. *Cat's Cradle*. New York: Holt, Rinehart and Winston, 1964.

————. *Slaughterhouse Five*. New York: Delacorte Press/Seymour Lawrence, 1969.

————. *Wampeters, Foma & Granfalloons*. New York: Delacorte Press/Seymour Lawrence, 1974.

Vonnegut, Mark. *The Eden Express*. New York: Praeger, 1975.

Watts, Alan W. *The Joyous Cosmology: Adventures in the Chemistry of Consciousness*. Foreword by Timothy Leary and Richard Alpert. New York: Pantheon Books, 1962.

————. *The Spirit of Zen*. New York: Grove Press, 1960, c1958.

————. *The Way of Zen*. New York: Pantheon, 1957.

Webb, Charles. *The Graduate*. New York: New American Library, 1963.

Weiner, Rex, and Deanne Stillman. *Woodstock Census: The Nationwide Survey of the Sixties Generation*. New York: Fawcett Columbine, 1979.

Whitman, Walt. *Leaves of Grass*. New York: Norton, 1968.

Wolfe, Tom. *The Electric Kool-Aid Acid Test*. New York: Bantam, 1968; New York: Farrar Straus and Giroux, 1968.

————. "Stalking the Billion-Footed Beast." *Harper's* 279 (November 1989): 45–56.

————, ed. *The New Journalism*. New York: Harper & Row, 1973.

Wright, Lawrence. *In the New World*. New York: Vintage, 1989.

Yablonsky, Lewis. *The Hippie Trip*. New York: Pegasus, 1968.

Index

Abbey, Edward, 10
Abbott, Keith, 44
Abrams, Meyer, 42
Ace Books, 232 (n. 60)
Adams, Henry, 15
Albert, Judith Clavir, and Stewart
    Edward Albert, eds., *The Sixties
    Papers,* 207
Aldredge, John W., 5
Alger, Horatio, 184
Ali, Muhammad, 118, 136
Alpert, Richard [Baba Ram Dass], 10,
    11, 23, 34–36, 129; *Be Here Now,
    Remember,* 8, 35–36; *LSD,* 34; *The
    Psychedelic Experience,* 34, 131;
    "The Politics of Consciousness
    Expansion," 131; preface to *The
    Joyous Cosmology,* 131, 198
Altamont, 219 (n. 13)
American Academy and Institutes of
    Arts and Letters, 26
Anonymous, *Go Ask Alice,* 28, 36–38,
    87, 88
Archer, Jules, *The Incredible Sixties,* 209
Arkin, Alan, 5
Arnold, Matthew, 134
Atkinson, Ti-Grace, 93
Axelrod, Beverly, 61

Bach, Richard, *Jonathan Livingston
    Seagull,* 220 (n. 16)
Baez, Joan, 188
Baez, Mimi, 68
Bakhtin, Mikhail, 156
Baldwin, James, 26, 38–40, 46, 136;
    The Fire Next Time, 39; *Giovanni's
    Room,* 39; *Another Country,* 220
    (n. 17); *Nobody Knows My Name,*
    220 (n. 17)

Ballantine Books, 232 (n. 60)
Bancroft, Anne, 200
Bantam Books, 121, 227 (n. 30)
Baraka, Amiri, 40
Barlow, Joel, 46
Barth, John, 27, 196, 232 (n. 63); *The
    End of the Road,* 70; *The Floating
    Opera,* 70; *The Sot-Weed Factor,* 70
Barth, Karl, 196
Barthes, Roland, 135, 196
Bartram, William, 10
Baudrillard, Jean, 217 (n. 5)
Beatles, 195, 212
Beats, 10, 33, 40, 45, 69, 71, 72, 78, 84,
    113
Bell, Daniel, 134; *The End of Ideology,*
    148
Bellow, Saul, 27, 176
Benét, Stephen Vincent, "American
    Names," 48
Benjamin, Walter, 140, 144
Benson, Kathleen, 133
Berkeley *Barb,* 145
Berkeley Free Speech Movement, 213
    (n. 1), 230 (n. 50)
Berkley Books, 95
Black Panthers, 225 (n. 15)
Blake, William, 23, 33, 40–42, 81, 129,
    215 (n. 11); *The Marriage of Heaven
    and Hell,* 40, 76; "Auguries of
    Innocence," 41; *Jerusalem,* 41
Bloom, Harold, 42
Book-of-the-Month Club, 55
Borges, Jorge Luis, 31
Boston Women's Health Book
    Collective: *Our Bodies, Ourselves,* 4,
    29, 42–44, 75, 146, 153, 206;
    Ourselves and Our Children, 43;
    Ourselves, Growing Older, 43

Bowker, *Eighty Years of Best Sellers,
1895–1975,* 221 (n. 19)

Brand, Stewart, 203

Brautigan, Richard, 10, 21, 28, 44–46,
97, 103; *Trout Fishing in America,*
45–46

Brown, Claude, *Manchild in the
Promised Land,* 46–47, 117–18

Brown, Dee, *Bury My Heart at
Wounded Knee,* 47–50, 221 (n. 18)

Brown, H. Rap, 23, 40, 60, 118, 136

Brown, Helen Gurley, 50–51; *Sex and
the Single Girl,* 11, 50–51

Brown, Norman O., 10, 23, 34, 51–55,
63, 88, 107, 128, 135, 140, 142, 170,
178–79, 200; *Love's Body,* 52, 55;
Life Against Death, 52–55, 84, 141,
148

Brustein, Norman, 4

Burroughs, John, 10

Burroughs, William, 127, 149

Bush, George, 12

Cambodia, 210

Camus, Albert, *L'Etranger,* 20, 220
(n. 17)

Capote, Truman, 112

Caputo, Philip, *A Rumor of War,* 209

Carlyle, Thomas, 215–16 (n. 1)

Carmichael, Stokely, 23, 60, 118, 136

Carnegie, Dale, 184

Carroll, Lewis, *Alice in Wonderland,* 37

Carson, Rachel, 55–58; *Silent Spring,*
34, 55–58; *The Edge of the Sea,* 55;
The Sea Around Us, 55

Carter, Jimmy, 210

Casale, Anthony M., and Philip
Lerman, eds., *Where Have All the
Flowers Gone?,* 208

Cassady, Neal, 111, 204

Castaneda, Carlos, 8, 10, 11, 20, 47,
58–60, 81–82, 97, 103, 191, 229
(n. 42); *Journey to Ixtlan,* 58; *A*

Separate Reality, 58; *The Teachings
of Don Juan,* 58–59

Cather, Willa, 15

Cheever, John, 176

Chicago Democratic Convention
(1968), 2, 22, 29, 219 (n. 13)

Chicago Seven, 2, 219 (n. 13)

Chronicle of Higher Education, The,
20, 214 (n. 5), 221 (n. 18)

City Lights Books, 78

City Lights Bookshop, 71

Civil Rights Act (1964), 1

Clareson, Thomas D., 97

Clarke, Arthur C., *2001: A Space
Odyssey,* 28, 227 (n. 27)

Cleaver, Eldridge, 25, 40, 46, 60–63,
133, 220 (n. 17); *Soul on Ice,* 3, 8, 28,
47, 60–63, 118

Clinton, Bill, 12

Coffin, William Sloane, 169

Cohen, Sidney, *LSD,* 34

Coles, Robert, *The Children of Poverty,*
46

Collier, Peter, and David Horowitz:
Destructive Generation, 208; *Second
Thoughts,* 208

Columbia University, 124

Conner, Bull, 119

Conrad, Joseph, 82; *Heart of Darkness,*
83, 102

Cosmopolitan, 51, 224 (n. 6)

Davidson, Cathy, 216 (n. 1)

Davidson, Sara, *Loose Change,* 208

Davis, Angela, 93, 208, 229 (n. 43)

Davis, Ossie, 139–40

Davis, Rennie, 2, 188

Days of Rage, 22

de Beauvoir, Simone, 23; *The Second
Sex,* 145, 150, 225 (n. 17), 229 (n. 45)

de Crèvecoeur, St. John, 10

Dell, 60, 121, 195, 225 (n. 14)

Dellinger, David, 2

de Loria, Vine, *Custer Died for Your Sins,* 47, 48, 203

Delta Books, 225 (n. 14)

Dessauer, John, 19

Dial Press, 108

Dickinson, Emily, 10, 156

Dickson, Paul, *Timelines,* 209

Dickstein, Morris, *The Gates of Eden,* 34, 42, 52, 141, 171, 206

Didion, Joan, 150; *Play It As It Lays,* 64; *Slouching towards Bethlehem,* 212; *The White Album,* 212

Dillard, Annie, 10, 63–65; *Pilgrim at Tinker Creek,* 29, 63–65, 206

Donleavy, J. P., *The Ginger Man,* 70

Doubleday, 221 (n. 17)

Douglass, Frederick, 10, 15, 138

Durden, Charles, *No Bugles, No Drums,* 101

Dutton, 220 (n. 17)

Dylan, Bob, 188; *Tarantula,* 30

Eastlake, William, *The Bamboo Bed,* 101

East Village Other, 132

Eddins, Dwight, 169

Edwards, Jonathan, 9, 15

Eliot, T. S., 10, 42, 82; *The Waste Land,* 63, 80, 116

Ellison, Ralph, 15, 46; *Invisible Man,* 61

Emerson, Ralph Waldo, 9, 10, 78, 120–21, 225 (n. 20), 231 (n. 56); *Nature,* 15, 16; "The Poet," 216 (n. 3)

Equal Rights Amendment, 75

Erhard, Werner, 35

Esquire, 11, 102–3, 207

Esterhas, Joe, 185

Evers, Medgar, 210

Exley, Frederick, *A Fan's Notes,* 30, 87, 232 (n. 62)

Fanon, Frantz, 65–67, 213 (n. 2); *The Wretched of the Earth,* 34, 65–67, 148

Fariña, Richard, 67–71, 97, 114; *Been Down So Long It Looks Like Up to Me,* 67–71, 87

Farrar, Straus & Giroux, 227 (n. 30)

Faulkner, William, 15

Ferlinghetti, Lawrence, 71–73, 78–79, 225 (n. 21), 226 (n. 22); *A Coney Island of the Mind,* 71–73

Fetterley, Judith, 150

Fiedler, Leslie, 17, 23; *Waiting for the End,* 12; *What Was Literature?,* 12; "The New Mutants," 178–79

Fitzgerald, Frances, *Fire in the Lake,* 30, 206

Flesch, Rudolf, *Why Johnny Can't Read, And What You Can Do About It,* 217 (n. 6)

Fonda, Jane, 188

Ford, Gerald, 210

Foucault, Michel, 31, 88, 135, 174; *Madness and Civilization,* 115, 228 (n. 38)

Frankfurt School, 140, 224 (n. 7)

Franklin, Benjamin, 10, 15, 138, 184, 225 (n. 20)

Frederick Ungar, 227 (n. 30)

Freedom Rides, 1

Freud, Sigmund, 10, 23, 52, 53, 63, 82, 84, 140, 141, 142, 171

Friedan, Betty, 23, 27, 73–75, 150; *The Feminine Mystique,* 28, 47, 73–75, 85, 145, 150, 220 (n. 17), 224 (n. 6)

Froines, John, 2

Frye, Northrop, 42

Fuller, Margaret, 150

Furlong, Monica, 199

Galbraith, John Kenneth, *The Affluent Society,* 148

Gandhi, Mohandas, 61, 118, 119, 188, 189

Gates, Henry Louis, Jr., 38, 40

Geismar, Maxwell, 60

Genet, Jean, 225 (n. 15)

Gerzon, Mark, *The Whole World Is Watching,* 211, 228 (n. 37)

Gibran, Kahlil, 75–78; *The Prophet,* 75–78, 88, 221 (n. 18)

Ginsberg, Allen, 10, 23, 25, 26, 33, 40, 45, 72, 78–82, 111, 131, 132, 181, 198; *Howl and Other Poems,* 71, 78–81; "HOWL," 79–81; *Collected Poems, 1947–84,* 81; *Kaddish,* 81; *Planet News,* 81; "A Supermarket in California," 226 (n. 22); "Sunflower Sutra," 226 (n. 22)

Gitlin, Todd, 1, 134, 219 (n. 9); *The Sixties,* 11, 203, 207, 219 (n. 12), 225 (n. 16)

Golding, William, 82–84; *The Lord of the Flies,* 28, 82–84, 121, 220 (n. 17)

Goldschmidt, Walter, 224–25 (n. 12)

Goodman, Paul, 10, 23, 34, 51, 63, 84–87, 88, 135, 140, 170, 200, 211; *Growing Up Absurd,* 52, 84–87, 121, 141, 148

Gottlieb, Annie, *Do You Believe in Magic?,* 208

Grateful Dead, 186

Greenburg, Joanne [Hannah Green], *I Never Promised You a Rose Garden,* 28, 36–37, 87–91, 150, 220 (n. 17)

Greene, Bob, *Be True to Your School,* 208

Greer, Germaine, 91–95; *The Female Eunuch,* 4, 75, 91–95, 221 (n. 18)

Grove Press, 65, 66, 227 (n. 33)

Guernica, 186

Guevara, Che, 65, 213 (n. 2)

Gulliver's Travels, 83

Haley, Alex: *Roots,* 136; *The Autobiography of Malcolm X* (with Malcolm X), 136, 139

Harper & Row, 227 (n. 30)

Harrington, Michael, 23; *The Other America,* 46, 148, 214 (n. 6), 220 (n. 17)

Harris, David, 208

Haskins, James, and Kathleen Benson, 133; *The 6os Reader,* 209

Hawke, David Freeman, 216 (n. 1)

Hawthorne, Nathaniel, 10, 15

Hayden, Casey, "Sex and Caste," 145

Hayden, Tom, 188, 208

Hearst, Patty, 188, 210

Hegel, Friedrich, 157

Heinlein, Robert A., 95–97, 191, 220 (n. 17); *Stranger in a Strange Land,* 28, 95–97, 193

Heller, Joseph, 23, 26, 27, 45, 97–101, 107, 114, 123; *Catch-22,* 3, 4–5, 11, 20, 27, 28, 69, 75, 88, 97–101, 161, 162, 178, 220–21 (n. 17), 226 (n. 25); *Something Happened,* 148

Hemingway, Ernest, 45; *The Sun Also Rises,* 45; *In Our Time,* 122

Hendrix, Jimi, 210

Herbert, Frank, 191, 220 (n. 17); *Dune,* 28, 193

Herr, Michael, 101–3, 185; *Dispatches,* 101–3, 206, 208, 215 (n. 8); "Hell Sucks," 207; *Apocalypse Now,* 227 (n. 29); *Full Metal Jacket,* 227 (n. 29)

Hesse, Hermann, 11, 23, 25, 33, 44, 58, 59, 88, 97, 103–6, 129, 134, 191, 215 (n. 11), 229 (n. 42); *Steppenwolf,* 6, 36, 103, 104, 105–6; *Siddhartha,* 28, 103, 104, 220–21 (n. 17); *Demian,* 30, 103, 104; *Journey to the East,* 103, 104; *Magister Ludi,* 104; *Narcissus and Goldmund,* 104; *Krisis,* 105

Hinckley, John, 210

Hinduism, 10, 40, 190, 215 (n. 10)

Hirsch, E. D., 32

Hitler, Adolf, 61

Hoffman, Abbie, 2, 23, 61, 85, 106–10, 208, 225 (n. 13); *Revolution for the Hell of It,* 11, 106, 107–9, 228

(n. 37); *Steal This Book,* 106–7, 109–10, 225 (n. 13)
Hoffman, Dustin, 200, 201
Hoffman, Julius, 2
Holt, Rinehart and Winston, 227 (n. 30)
Horne, Jennifer, 225 (n. 21)
Howard, Gerald, *The Sixties,* 12, 207
Hughes, Ted, 4, 158
Hurston, Zora Neale, 15
Hutchinson, Anne, 10
Huxley, Aldous, 10, 128, 129; *The Doors of Perception,* 40

I Ching, 220 (n. 17)
Illych, Ivan, 174
Irving, Washington, 15, 214 (n. 8); *A History of New York,* 225 (n. 20)

Jackson, George, *Soledad Brother,* 61
Jackson State University, 2
Jakobsen, Roman, 156
James, Henry, 15, 121
Janov, Arthur, 35
Jefferson, Thomas, 10, 15–16
Jefferson Airplane, 19; "White Rabbit," 37
Johns Hopkins Conference, "The Languages of Criticism and the Sciences of Man," 224 (n. 10)
Johnson, Lyndon B., 1, 2
Johnson, Paul, 6, 217–18 (n. 7)
Joplin, Janis, 25, 210
Joseph, Peter, ed., *Good Times,* 12
Joyce, James, *Ulysses,* 225–26 (n. 21)

Kafka, Franz, *The Trial,* 61
Kazin, Alfred, 4–5, 99, 101
Keats, John, 224 (n. 9)
Keniston, Kenneth, 23, 211, 212; *The Uncommitted,* 212; *Young Radicals,* 212; *Youth and Dissent,* 212

Kennedy, John F., 1, 16–17, 21, 122, 210; *Profiles in Courage,* 117
Kennedy, Robert F., 2, 29, 210
Kent State University, 2, 22
Kerner Commission Report, 2
Kerouac, Jack, 10, 16–17, 23, 25, 33, 40, 45, 46, 69, 72, 97, 110–13, 114; *On the Road,* 61, 87, 110–13, 127, 137, 150, 160, 178, 204
Kesey, Ken, 23, 27, 69, 97, 107, 113–17, 128, 131, 188, 204–5, 224 (n. 11); *One Flew Over the Cuckoo's Nest,* 3, 27, 61, 87, 88, 114–17, 137, 205; *Sometimes a Great Notion,* 30, 114, 117
Kessler, Lauren, *After All These Years,* 208
King, Martin Luther, Jr., 2, 10, 29, 38, 60, 61, 117–21, 136, 188, 189, 210; *Stride Toward Freedom,* 118; *Why We Can't Wait,* 118; "Letter from the Birmingham Jail," 118–21
King, Mary, "Sex and Caste," 145
Kinsey reports, 50
Kipling, Rudyard, 214 (n. 8)
Klinkowitz, Jerome, *The American 1960s,* 206–7, 223 (n. 4)
Knopf, Alfred A., 76
Knowles, John, 121–24; *A Separate Peace,* 121–24
Koedt, Anne, ed., *Radical Feminism,* 44, 75, 88, 145, 153
Koestler, Arthur, *Darkness at Noon,* 61
Kovic, Ron, *Born on the Fourth of July,* 209
Kozol, Jonathan, *Death at an Early Age,* 46
Kunen, James S., 124–27; *The Strawberry Statement,* 124–27, 211

Ladies' Home Journal, 225 (n. 18)
Laing, R. D., 10, 23, 34, 51, 52, 53, 81, 88, 107, 127–31, 135, 170, 174, 181,

Laing, R. D. (*continued*)
199, 200, 202; *The Politics of Experience,* 91, 116, 127, 128–31, 148; *The Divided Self,* 127, 128, 148
Larkin, Jack, 216 (n. 1)
Lasch, Christopher, *The Culture of Narcissism,* 209–10
"Laugh-In," 167
Lawrence, D. H., *Lady Chatterley's Lover,* 226 (n. 21)
Lazere, Donald, 218–19 (n. 8)
Leary, Timothy, 10, 23, 34, 58, 61, 85, 115, 128, 129, 131–33, 188, 198, 222 (n. 2), 225 (n. 13); *The Psychedelic Experience,* 34, 131, 225 (n. 13); *Jail Notes,* 131; *LSD,* 131; "The Politics of Consciousness Expansion," 131; *The Politics of Ecstasy,* 131; *Psychedelic Prayers after the Tao te ching,* 131; *The Psychedelic Reader,* 131; preface to *The Joyous Cosmology,* 131, 198; *High Priest,* 131, 207; *Start Your Own Religion,* 132
Lee, Harper, *To Kill a Mockingbird,* 159
Lee, Spike, 136
LeGuin, Ursula K., 220 (n. 17)
L'Enfant, Pierre, 15
Lennon, John, 133, 230 (n. 52)
Leopold, Aldo, 10
Lessing, Doris, 150
Levi-Strauss, Claude, 82
Lewis, C. S., 232 (n. 60)
Liddy, G. Gordon, 133
Life in the '60s, 209
Lowell, Robert, 162
Lukas, Anthony, "The Life and Death of a Hippie," 207

Macmillan, 121
Mademoiselle, 225 (n. 18)
Maharaj Ji, 11, 34

Maharishi Mahesh Yogi, 11, 34
Mailer, Norman, 4, 26, 34, 46, 84, 132, 133–35, 224 (n. 10); *Why Are We In Vietnam?,* 101, 229 (n. 42); "The White Negro," 133, 135, 137; *The Armies of the Night,* 133–35
Makower, Joel, *Woodstock: The Oral History,* 219 (n. 10)
Malcolm X, 25, 40, 46, 136–40, 213 (n. 2), 220 (n. 17); *The Autobiography of Malcolm X,* 3, 11, 28, 60, 117, 136–40
Manson Family, 210
Mao Tse-Tung, 65, 213 (n. 2)
March on the Pentagon, 22, 219 (n. 13)
March on Washington for Jobs and Freedom, 1
Marcus, Greil, *Lipstick Traces,* 207
Marcuse, Herbert, 5, 10, 23, 34, 51, 52, 53, 63, 88, 140–45, 170, 181, 218 (n. 8), 224 (n. 7); *Eros and Civilization,* 11, 52, 84, 140, 141–42, 148; *One-Dimensional Man,* 52, 84, 115, 140, 142–45, 148
Marx, Karl, 10, 23, 52, 53, 63, 84, 140, 141, 142, 171, 213 (n. 2), 224 (n. 7); *The Economic and Political Manuscripts of 1844,* 224 (n. 8)
Mather, Cotton, 184
Matusow, Allen, 52, 230 (n. 51); *The Unraveling of America,* 206
Mayaguez incident, 210
McCaffery, Larry, *Postmodern Fiction,* 220 (n. 15)
McCall's, 225 (n. 18)
McCarthy, Mary, 150
McGraw-Hill, 60
McKuen, Rod, *Listen to the Warm,* 220 (n. 16), 221 (n. 18)
McLuhan, Marshall, 18, 23, 172; *The Gutenberg Galaxy,* 18; *Understanding Media,* 18, 220 (n. 17)
Melville, Herman, 6, 10, 15, 154, 156;

Moby-Dick, 5, 45, 50; *Billy Budd,* 116

Meredith, James, 120

Metzner, Ralph: *The Psychedelic Experience,* 34, 131, *The Psychedelic Reader,* 131

Mexican War, 189

Miller, Henry, 26; *Tropic of Cancer,* 226 (n. 21)

Miller, James, *"Democracy is in the Streets,"* 11

Millett, Kate, 145–48; *Sexual Politics,* 4, 75, 93, 146–48, 150

Mills, C. Wright, 10, 23, 34, 148–49, 170; *White Collar,* 84, 148; *The Power Elite,* 148–49, 220 (n. 17)

Milne, A. A., 68

Monterrey Pop, 219 (n. 13)

Moody Blues, 124

Moon, William Least Heat, *Blue Highways,* 156

Moratorium (1969), 22, 219 (n. 13)

Morgan, Robin, ed., *Sisterhood Is Powerful,* 4, 8, 44, 75, 88, 145, 150–53; "Good-Bye To All That," 145

Morrison, Jim, 40, 210

Morrison, Joan, and Robert K. Morrison, *From Camelot to Kent State,* 208

Morrison, Toni, 40

Ms., 146, 150

Muhammad, Elijah, 136

Muir, John, 10

Nabokov, Vladimir, 27

National Book Award, 26, 55, 81, 133

National Organization for Women, 75, 213 (n. 1)

New Criticism, 42

New Directions, 71, 227 (n. 30)

New Frontier, 17, 21

New Journalism, 102, 185, 202, 205, 207

Newsweek, 75; "Why Johnny Can't Write," 217 (n. 6)

Newton, Charles, 221–22 (n. 20)

Newton, Huey, 40, 118

New Yorker, 55

New York *Rat,* 145

New York Times Book Review, 47

New York Women's League, *Notes from the First Year,* 145; *Notes from the Second Year,* 145

Nichols, Mike, 5, 200, 226 (n. 25)

Nietzsche, Friedrich, 105

Nin, Anaïs, 150

Nixon, Richard, 2, 24

Noonday, 227 (n. 30)

Norton Anthology of American Literature, 81, 159

O'Brien, Geoffrey, *Dream Time,* 208

O'Brien, Tim, *If I Die in a Combat Zone,* 209

Odyssey, The, 68

Ohmann, Richard, 27; "The Shaping of a Canon: U.S. Fiction, 1960–75," 226 (nn. 24, 25)

Paine, Thomas, 10

Panati, Charles, *Panati's Parade of Fads, Follies, and Manias,* 209

Parks, Rosa, 120

Pathet Lao, 210

Peck, Abe, 223 (n. 3); *Uncovering the Sixties,* 207, 225 (n. 16)

Pirsig, Robert, 10, 153–58, 174, 199; *Zen and the Art of Motorcycle Maintenance,* 3, 4, 5, 29, 45, 153–58, 206, 224 (n. 7)

Plath, Sylvia, 23, 25, 26, 28, 150, 158–63, 226 (n. 22); *The Bell Jar,* 3, 4, 37, 73, 87, 114, 150, 158, 159–62, 178, 200, 213 (n. 4), 226 (n. 26), 228

Plath, Sylvia (*continued*)
(n. 34); *Ariel,* 4, 150, 159; *Colossus,* 4,
158; "Daddy," 4, 159; "Lady
Lazarus," 4, 159; "Ariel," 159, 163
Pocket Books, 60
Poe, Edgar Allan, 10, 15, 214 (n. 8);
Eureka, 15
Poirier, Richard, 134
Poor People's March on Washington,
2, 29
Port Huron Statement, 11, 213 (n. 1)
Portola Institute, *The Last Whole
Earth Catalog,* 5, 29, 43, 109,
163–66, 203, 206, 221 (n. 18)
Postman, Neil, 14; *Amusing Ourselves
to Death,* 18
Pound, Ezra, 10, 81
Prouty, Alice Higgins, 230 (n. 48)
Psychedelic Review, 131
Publishers Weekly, 20, 220 (n. 17), 221
(n. 19)
Pulitzer Prize, 26, 133
Putnam, 131
Pynchon, Thomas, 26, 28, 45, 68, 70,
97, 114, 134, 138, 166–69; *The
Crying of Lot 49,* 20, 71, 166–69;
Gravity's Rainbow, 27, 230 (n. 49); *V,*
166; *Vineland,* 169

Ramparts, 60, 208
Ray, James Earl, 118
Reader's Digest, 55, 57
Reagan, Ronald, 210
Reed, Ishmael, 40
Reich, Charles, 169–72, 233 (n. 3); *The
Greening of America,* 11, 28, 52, 85,
169–72, 206, 210, 221 (n. 18)
Riesman, Daniel, *The Lonely Crowd,*
148, 220 (n. 17)
Robbins, Tom, *Another Roadside
Attraction,* 30
Robinson Crusoe, 83

Ross, Katherine, 200, 201
Rossman, Michael, *New Age Blues,* 223
(n. 4)
Roszak, Theodore, 10; *The Making of
a Counter-Culture,* 34, 42, 171, 199,
200, 206, 221 (n. 17)
Roth, Henry, *Call It Sleep,* 226 (n. 25)
Roth, Philip, *Portnoy's Complaint,* 121
Rubáiyát of Omar Khayyám, 76
Rubin, Jerry, 2, 23, 85, 172–75, 188,
208, 225 (n. 13); *Do It!,* 8, 107, 108,
172–75, 225 (n. 13), 228 (n. 37)

Sack, John, *M,* 101
Salinger, J. D., 10, 23, 25, 27, 82, 176–
79; *The Catcher in the Rye,* 4, 27, 28,
75, 87, 88, 111, 114, 150, 159, 160,
176–79, 200, 201, 220 (n. 17), 227–28
(n. 34); *Nine Stories,* 176, 220 (n. 17);
Franny and Zooey, 220 (n. 17)
San Francisco Be-In, 81, 198
San Francisco Chronicle, 79
San Francisco Renaissance, 78
Sann, Paul, *The Angry Decade,* 209
Santana, 227 (n. 31)
Sartre, Jean-Paul, 66; *No Exit,* 162
Savio, Mario, 23
Schulz, Charles, 58
Seale, Bobby, 40, 60, 118
Seneca Falls Declaration, 150
Shelley, Percy, 81
Shi, David, 10
Simon and Garfunkel, 200, 201
Simon and Schuster, 60
Six Gallery Reading, 78
Skinner, B. F., 179–82; *Walden Two,*
179–82
Smiling Through the Apocalypse, 11,
207
Snyder, Gary, 10, 45, 198
Solanis, Valerie, 93; "S.C.U.M.
Manifesto," 11, 145

Solatoroff, Theodore, 85

Solomon, David, *LSD,* 131

Solzhenitzyn, Alexander, 225 (n. 15)

Southern, Terry, 185

Spock, Benjamin M., 169, 182–85, 188, 227 (n. 32); *The Common Sense Book of Baby and Child Care,* 29, 182–85

Stalin, Joseph, 185

Steadman, Ralph, 186

Stein, Gertrude, 10, 15, 150; "The Gradual Making of the Making of Americans," 15; *The Making of Americans,* 15, 184; *The Autobiography of Alice B. Toklas,* 216 (n. 2)

Steinem, Gloria, 23, 150, 208

Steiner, George, 18

Steppenwolf, 227 (n. 31)

Stern, Jane, and Michael Stern: *Encyclopedia of Bad Taste,* 209; *Sixties People,* 209

Stevens, Wallace, 10; *Notes Toward a Supreme Fiction,* 15

Stone, Robert, *Dog Soldiers,* 228 (n. 35)

Student Non-Violent Coordinating Committee, 145, 213 (n. 1)

Students for a Democratic Society, 23, 145, 213 (n. 1)

Suzuki, D. T., 10, 198, 215 (n. 10)

Taoism, 41

Taylor, Edward, 9

This Fabulous Century, 209

Thompson, Hunter S., 185–88; *Fear and Loathing in Las Vegas,* 185, 186–87; *Fear and Loathing on the Campaign Trail,* 185, 187–88; *Hell's Angels,* 185–86

Thoreau, Henry, 10, 15, 23, 25, 33, 63, 118, 119, 154, 156, 188–90, 213 (n. 8); *Walden,* 3, 5, 9, 16, 45, 63, 64–

65, 143, 179–80, 189–90; "Civil Disobedience," 61, 188; *A Week on the Concord and Merrimack Rivers,* 190; *Cape Cod,* 190; *Journals,* 190

Time, 57

Tolkien, J. R. R., 11, 21, 23, 28, 33, 44, 58, 59, 88, 97, 103, 191–95, 213 (n. 2), 215 (n. 11), 220–21 (n. 17), 227 (n. 31); *The Hobbit,* 191–95, 220 (n. 17), 231 (n. 60); *The Lord of the Rings,* 191–95, 220 (n. 17), 231–32 (n. 60); *The Silmarillion,* 232 (n. 60)

Trudeau, Gary, *Doonesbury Chronicles,* 169

Twain, Mark, 15, 195; *Huckleberry Finn,* 45, 137, 159

Twitchell, James, 217 (n. 5)

Uniform Code of Military Justice, 227 (n. 28)

University of California Press, 58

Updike, John, 176

Urdan, Laurence, ed., *Timetables of American History,* 209

Vietnam Conflict, 1, 5, 20, 23, 24, 66, 81, 101–3, 122, 134–35, 188–89, 195, 197–98, 206, 207, 208–9, 210, 213 (n. 2), 215 (n. 8), 229 (n. 42), 232 (n. 61); Tet Offensive, 1, 28, 102, 210; Cambodian invasion, 2, 22, 210; My Lai massacre, 28; Geneva Accords, 189; Gulf of Tonkin incident, 189; American evacuation, 210; Laotian invasion, 210

Viorst, Milton, 217 (n. 7); *Fire in the Streets,* 11, 206

von Hoffman, Nicholas, *We Are the People Our Parents Warned Us Against,* 211–12, 228 (n. 37)

Vonnegut, Kurt, 8, 10, 11, 15, 21, 23, 26, 27, 28, 29, 44, 45, 58, 59, 82, 123,

Vonnegut, Kurt (*continued*)
131, 134, 138, 154, 155, 169, 181, 191,
195–98, 220 (n. 17), 225 (n. 19), 226–
27 (n. 27), 227 (n. 31), 229 (n. 42);
Slaughterhouse Five, 3, 28, 88, 96,
101, 178, 195, 196–98; *God Bless
You, Mr. Rosewater*, 88, 195, 196;
"Why They Read Hesse," 103, 104,
228 (n. 41), 291 (n. 14); *Player Piano*,
148, 195; *Deadeye Dick*, 195;
Jailbird, 195; *Mother Night*, 195;
Palm Sunday, 195; *Sirens of Titan*,
195; *Slapstick*, 195; *Wampeters,
Foma, and Granfalloons*, 195;
Welcome to the Monkey-House, 195;
Breakfast of Champions, 195, 196;
Cat's Cradle, 195, 196; *Hocus Pocus*,
196, 232 (n. 61); *Bluebeard*, 232
(n. 61); *Fates Worse Than Death*, 232
(n. 61); *Galapagos*, 232 (n. 61)
Vonnegut, Mark, *The Eden Express*,
208

Walker, Alice, 40
Wallace, George, 210
Warhol, Andy, 145
Washington, Denzel, 136
Watts, Alan, 10, 23, 34, 51, 128, 198–
200, 215 (n. 10); *The Joyous
Cosmology*, 129, 131, 198;
Psychotherapy East and West, 198;
The Spirit of Zen, 198; *This is It*,
198; *The Way of Zen*, 198, 199–200
Weathermen, 210
Webb, Charles, *The Graduate*, 87, 178,
200–201
Wegener, Signe, 225 (n. 18)
Weil, Gunther M., *The Psychedelic
Reader*, 131
Weinberg, Jack, 230 (n. 50)
Weiner, Lee, 2

Weiner, Rex, and Deanne Stillman,
Woodstock Census, 209, 219 (n. 10),
225 (n. 19)
Whitman, Walt, 9, 10, 45, 68, 78, 81,
154, 156, 213 (n. 8), 231 (n. 56);
"Song of Myself," 15, 16; *Leaves of
Grass*, 225 (n. 20)
Whyte, William, Jr., 170; *The
Organization Man*, 84, 148, 220
(n. 17)
Williams, Robin, 1, 2, 26
Williams, Roger, 10
Williams, William Carlos, 10, 79, 81;
"This is Just to Say," 46
Wills, Garry, 14
Winthrop, John, 12, 15
Wolfe, Tom, 27, 185, 201–5, 210; *The
Electric Kool-Aid Acid Test*, 3, 114,
201, 211; *The Kandy-Colored
Tangerine-Flake Streamline Baby*,
201; *Mau-Mauing the Flak Catchers*,
201; *The Pump House Gang*, 201;
Radical Chic, 201; *The Bonfire of the
Vanities*, 232–33 (n. 63); "In Search
of the Billion-Footed Beast," 233
(n. 63)
Wollstonecraft, Mary, 150
Woodstock, 22, 219 (n. 13)
Woolf, Virginia, 150
Woolman, John, 9, 119
Wright, Lawrence, *In the New World*,
208
Wright, Richard, 46

Yablonsky, Lewis, *The Hippie Trip*,
212, 228 (n. 37)
Yale French Studies, "Structuralism,"
224 (n. 10)

Zen, 10, 41, 45, 155, 156, 157, 198–200,
215 (n. 10), 224 (n. 7)